COUNTY DURHAM AVIATION STORIES

Graeme Rendall

Reiver Country Books

Also by the same author:

To the Ends of the Earth: A Snapshot of Aviation in North-Eastern Siberia, Summer 1992

RAF Morpeth: A Forgotten Airfield in Northumberland

UFOs Before Roswell: European Foo-Fighters, 1940-1945

Northumberland Aviation Stories Volumes 1-3

Dawn of the Flying Saucers: Aerial UFO Encounters & Official Investigations, 1946-1949

Flying Saucer Fever: Aerial UFO Encounters, 1950-1952

From Airfields to Aerials: The History of Anthorn Airfield

Intercept & Identify: Aerial UFO Encounters, 1953-1954 (forthcoming)

This book is published in conjunction with Reiver Country Books. "On demand" is a unique service allowing books to be made available to the general public via retail sale, using a combination of on-demand manufacturing and Internet marketing.

Copyright © 2023 Graeme Rendall

All rights reserved. No part of this publication may be reproduced or transmitted in any form or by any means, electronic or mechanical, including photocopying, recording, or by any information storage and retrieval system, without permission in writing from Reiver Country Books. Reviewers may quote brief passages.

reivercountrybooks@gmail.com

CONTENTS

Introduction	Page 5
First Casualty: The Boldon Balloon	Page 9
Farman Fatality	Page 15
The Southwick Catastrophe	Page 19
Would-Be Ace Down at Bishop Auckland	Page 33
Rough Landing at Annfield Plain	Page 37
Fairey Fatality	Page 43
Tragedy at Seaton Carew	Page 47
Crash at Carrville	Page 51
An Exercise in Disaster: Part One	Page 55
A Family Tragedy	Page 61
The Moth and the Slurry Pit	Page 67
Disaster at Dawdon	Page 71
Urpeth Forge Calamity	Page 75
The King's Jockey	Page 79
Lost at Sea	Page 87
Gardening on the Beach	Page 89
The Red Cross Incident	Page 95
Black Thursday Over County Durham	Page 101
Nightmare on Suffolk Street	Page 117
No.43 Squadron at Usworth, Autumn 1940	Page 123
The Middle End Moor Blenheim	Page 131
Hudson Down Off Hartlepool	Page 135
Hurricane Horror	Page 137
Masters Mid-Air Collision	Page 141
The Roddymoor Crash: A Sacrificial Act?	Page 145
Snowy Owls at Middleton St. George	Page 151
Wellington Down at St. John's Chapel	Page 167
The Bunker Hill Wellington	Page 173
Stirling Break-Up Over Shildon	Page 177
The Mickle Fell Stirling	Page 183
The Tudhoe V-1	Page 191
A Deadly Mock Attack	Page 199
Mosquito Crash at Old Thornley	Page 203
Airshow Horror at Teesside Airport	Page 207
A Shower of Meteors	Page 211
Meteor Mid-Air Near Stanhope	Page 225
Mid-Air Collision Off Hartlepool	Page 227
It Came in Through the Roof	Page 233
Seconds From Disaster	Page 235
Turbi Turmoil	Page 255
The Fallen Musketeer	Page 259
An Exercise in Disaster: Part Two	Page 261
Tragedy at Kip Hill	Page 269
Back to School with a Bump	Page 277

Not on the Map	Page 283
The Stainmore Tornado	Page 291
One Leg Only	Page 295
The Barnard Castle Aviation Memorials	Page 297
Acknowledgements and Sources	Page 301
About the Author	Page 303
Also by the Author	Page 303

INTRODUCTION

> **Royal Electric Theatre,**
> WHITBY-STREET (OPPOSITE GENERAL POST OFFICE).
> ..... MR. ROBERT EVERTON.
>
> **TO-NIGHT!   TO-NIGHT!!   TO-NIGHT!!!**
>
> "To-morrow is the FOOL'S holiday, the WISE lived yesterday, the SENSIBLE live to-day." (Read this again, it's good.)
>
> LAST NIGHT of the RECORD BREAKER,
>
> **THE ROYAL FLYING CORPS LANDING WITH THEIR**
>
> **AEROPLANES AT SEATON CAREW.**
>
> "UNERASABLE FROM THE SCROLL OF FAME."
> PEANS OF PRAISE FROM PUBLIC, PRESS, & PICTURE PROPRIETORS.
>
> TO-NIGHT'S YOUR LAST CHANCE.
> So Hustle, or you'll B left right enough.

20th May 1914 – less than three months before the outbreak of the First World War – even film of aeroplanes landing at an aerodrome in County Durham was exciting news for the public. People went to see such footage, which was billed as being "unerasable from the scroll of fame".

Once I had completed the third volume of Northumberland Aviation Stories, I thought it might be interesting to research some of the crashes and other incidents that took place south of the Tyne. At that time (2021), little did I know that I would end up living in Stanhope, County Durham, not far from the sites of three aircraft crashes, and close to where two Gloster Meteor jets collided in mid-air in the early 1950s.

For the purposes of this book, "County Durham" includes land that was lost when the county of Tyne and Wear was created in 1974, therefore the likes of South Shields and Sunderland feature here. In addition, a few parts of upland North Yorkshire were handed over to Durham, and so the Mickle Fell incident is included too, despite the site being (historically) in another county. Some crash sites are said to fall within County Durham, but this is not the case - the incident involving a Bőlkow Monsun light aircraft back in 1975 is one such case that springs to mind.

**SEATON CAREW AERODROME,
Near West Hartlepool.**

Messrs. WALTON & PHŒNIX

AUCTIONEERS,

Instructed by the owners, will offer for SALE BY PUBLIC AUCTION, on WEDNESDAY, OCTOBER 13th, at 2 p.m., at the AERODROME GROUND, Seaton Carew, one Complete Aeroplane and a large quantity of Aeroplane Spare Parts, including the following:

1 Complete D.H.6 CURTISS AEROPLANE, fully licensed and registered for passenger flying; Spare Engines, Wheels with Palmer Cord Tyres (700 x 100), and Inner Tubes, Radiators, Propellers, Carburettors, Valves, Electric Switches, Control Cable, Shock Absorbers, and numerous other Aeroplane Spare Accessories, 2 Bell Tents, 2 Deck Chairs, etc., etc.

A large quantity of the above are new and unused.

The Aerodrome is about 1 mile from Seaton Carew Station and ¼ mile from Tram Terminus, Seaton Carew, and about 3 miles from Transporter Bridge.

Further particulars and full list can be had on application to the Auctioneers:
21, Scarborough-st., West Hartlepool.
Tel. 187.

A notice advertising the auction of an Airco DH.6 aircraft, spares and tents at the aerodrome at Seaton Carew, County Durham, on 13th October 1920.

After detailed examination, some crash locations turn out to be just over the border with another county. The Monsun crashed about a mile or so across in Northumberland, between Allenheads and the Killhope Mining Museum in County Durham. If a fourth volume of *Northumberland Aviation Stories* ever appears, it will be featured in that work!

County Durham Aviation Stories contains chapters dealing with crashes involving balloons, gliders, helicopters and powered aircraft, plus details of air combat and bombing raids over the region in the Second World War. It is not meant to be a comprehensive account of Durham's aviation history. Some well-known events (such as the visit of "Air Force One" to Teesside Airport in November 2003) have been omitted – but may appear in a future volume! This has allowed the inclusion of other, long-forgotten incidents.

County Durham saw Zeppelin raids in the First World War, RAF fighters attacking *Luftwaffe* bombers in the Second, various types being based at Middleton St George before it was transferred to civilian ownership and became Teesside International Airport, the expansion of the latter, and the growth of recreational aviation across the county. Aerodromes sprang up in Durham during the First World War, with Hylton and Seaton Carew being the most famous of these. The former languished after the end of the war but was resurrected as RAF Usworth in 1930. Squadrons based there were pitted against Hitler's bombers and maritime patrol aircraft during the first years of the Second World War, subsequently becoming a busy training station. Like RAF Middleton St. George, Usworth would end up in private hands, being operated as Sunderland Airport prior to its closure in 1983, in order to make way for the construction of the Nissan Car Factory.

Much of County Durham is made up of hills, fells and moorland, which presented problems for pilots flying in bad weather or poor visibility prior to the introduction of radio aids, radar and high-tech navigation systems. Aircraft crashes on high ground were not unusual, especially during the Second World War when numerous training flights were conducted across the Pennines, often at night and involving inexperienced aircrew. Lost and sometimes disorientated, one solution to their predicament was to try and descend below cloud cover to work out their position using landmarks on the ground. It often led to them flying into the side of a hill, with fatal results. Even after the war, when navigation systems and aids improved, accidents still occurred, and the growth of recreational flying by civilian pilots threw new problems into the mix. They were caught out by mechanical failure and bad weather, just as much as their military forebearers were – and the RAF continued to lose aircraft and aircrew in the post-war years. It is inconceivable that the loss rate among those training to fly Gloster Meteors at Middleton St. George in the early 1950s would be tolerated today. Jets would be lost in successive decades, including an infamous incident when a crewless Vulcan bomber crashed near Wingate in 1971, but the loss rate wasn't anything like the heady days of old.

Each of those stories was either a tragedy or the potential for a major incident. In the case of the Vulcan crash, it was only a miracle that no-one at the scene was injured or killed. Hundreds could have died if the huge bomber had crashed just seconds earlier or later. The Vulcan story is possibly the best-known of all the tales told here. Others may never have appeared beyond brief reporting at the time or a page on a website dealing with high ground aircraft crashes. Their stories need to be told before they are forgotten.

This book does not just cover historic aircraft – Bede G-BOPD was involved in a landing accident at Fishburn in July 2022, which is described in the final chapter. It is pictured here in happier times at the Druridge Bay Fly-in, Northumberland, on 6th July 2013. (Author)

Some of the chapters in this book are brief by design or are limited in size due to little historical details remaining. Others benefit from much longer explanations. Although listed in chronological order, this history of aviation incidents in County Durham does not need to be read from cover to cover. Dipping in to read a chapter or two at random will work just as well.

I welcome comments and memories regarding the incidents listed in this book – if you remember anything about them, have relatives who were involved or have visited the crash sites yourselves, I would love to hear from you. I can be contacted at the email address listed below.

Graeme Rendall
Stanhope, County Durham
March 2023

reivercountybooks@gmail.com

FIRST CASUALTY: THE BOLDON BALLOON

NEWCASTLE—SERIOUS ACCIDENT TO AN AERONAUT.—On Monday evening last, Captain Hall ascended in his balloon, and while in sight of the thousands of spectators below, performed a number of acrobatic feats on a trapeze suspended from the car. It was the captain's intention to descend at Boldon, between Newcastle and Sunderland, but through some accident, when 30 feet from the ground, the grappling irons failed to hold, and the daring aeronaut was precipitated to the earth. He was taken up in a state of insensibility, and conveyed to the house of Mr Hugh Lee Pattison, near at hand. The balloon again arose, and when last seen, was floating in a south-easterly direction, towards the German Ocean.

The Teesdale Mercury newspaper carried the above story in their 17th August 1859 edition. Captain Hall died as a result of his injuries.

Arguably the first aviation fatality to occur in County Durham took place on 17th August 1859 when Captain Hall, the pilot of an early gas balloon known as "The Florence Nightingale" fell from his charge, sustaining serious injury in the process. He later died as a result of his injuries.

Born at Countessthorpe, Leicestershire, William Henry Hall was 39 years of age and lived in Attercliffe, near Sheffield. He had gained a bit of a reputation for "acrobatic antics" which he carried out from a small trapeze suspended below his balloon's basket (referred to a "car" in the newspaper reporting). His aerial exploits attracted the attention of huge numbers of residents, crowds gathering to watch him and his balloon.

William Hall, although granting himself the title "Captain", did not appear to have ever earned that rank, and certainly not in Her Majesty's Navy. This omission did not seem to be diminish his popularity, however, and Hall's balloon antics provided newspapers with columns of exceedingly detailed copy, with his performance in Newcastle-upon-Tyne being no exception, as the *Newcastle Guardian and Tyne Mercury* reported at length in its 20th August issue:

"There was a grand gala in this town on Monday, on the occasion of Mr. Hall, a well-known aeronaut in the town and neighbourhood of Sheffield (having made his debut there about two years ago), making an ascent in his 'Florence Nightingale' balloon from the Cricket Ground, Northumberland Street. Mr. Hall, who styles himself 'Captain' in the 'R.N.', had announced that he should be glad of the company of a lady and gentleman in his aerial voyage, as there was room for two in his car in addition to himself and lady. It was expected that the editor of the Daily Chronicle would have been one of the voyageurs, but he was deterred by the statement of Mrs. Hall that the captain's feats aloft rendered his companionship dangerous.

Other persons were ambitious of soaring high above their fellows; and among these were a confectioner and bricklayer, who had to be drawn by force of arms from the neighbourhood of the car. The captain's price for allowing any one to risk his neck is a £5 note. No one appeared with cash in hand – the editor's proffered return was a 'leader', which the aeronaut did not appear to sufficiently value; but we hear that a gentleman who occupies a leading position in the Town Council of Newcastle would not have been indisposed to take a seat in the car and pay the smart money, had he been fully acquainted with the opportunity and its terms. As it was, the captain sailed alone.

The occasion drew together an immense concourse of people, who began to throng the ground soon after three o'clock in the afternoon; but the great influx of visitors occurred between half-past five and half-past six o'clock, at the latter time there being probably from two to three thousand persons on the ground, among whom were the members of several of the leading families in the district.

Those who were on the ground in the earlier part of the afternoon had the advantage of seeing the balloon inflated, a work which was performed with much care, the Gas Company having laid a heavy main from the artery leading up Northumberland Street to the Cricket Ground. The balloon was a fine specimen of its class, made of oilskin, and covered with caoutchouc varnish. It was not a monster in size, being 33 yards in circumference, but well-made, 'and in every way (as the charter-parties for sea voyages have it) fitted for the voyage.'

The captain seemed well up in his business, and he is, we have reason to believe, one of the most skilful of aerial voyageurs. He paid great attention to the machine as the process of inflation went on, and was in every way ready for the ascent half-an-hour before the appointed time, 6.45. He then appeared in an inner ring (admission to which was purchased by an extra shilling), in acrobatic costume, a slight disappointment to some parties who had expected to find a captain in Her Majesty's navy attired in true blue uniform. The adopted costume was, however, seeing the tricks the aeronaut subsequently performed, the best adapted to his purposes.

When the hour for ascending had arrived, Captain Hall despatched a pilot balloon, which ascended and rode off in a north-easterly direction. The heavens were now clear, the threatened aspect overhead having brightened into a warm and genial sunshine. The atmosphere was light, and there was a gentle breeze blowing in the direction named.

After once more inspecting the cording which encased the balloon, the captain entered the car to the great interest of the spectators. Numbers of these 'squatted' in the ring, forming a circle around the balloon, the dozen or two men who held down the balloon, at the word of command, gradually drew themselves together, around the car, and as they did so, let go their hold of the net work, and held on by the car only. 'All right', said the captain, but thinking himself of future wants, he turned to his lady with 'hey madam, I've only a sovereign in my pocket, that won't do.' A supply of the needful having been tendered, and a small dog, previously his companion in the clouds, having also taken his place, the captain gave the word, and the balloon, released from the grasp of many brawny arms, ascended in gallant style, amid the applause of the spectators.

The aeronaut stood up in the car and waved the union Jack, and triumphant banner of St. George, and the people clapped their hands, cheered and waved handkerchiefs. Whilst gazing upon the frail vehicle, as it mounted higher and yet higher, not a few of the spectators were horrified to see the captain seize a couple of ropes, which dangled from beneath the car and sustained at their extremity a piece of wood a few inches in thickness, slide down like a cat, turn a somerset [sic] on this piece of wood, and (most frightful of all) suspend himself head downwards by the feet. The only hold he had at this time upon the stick was that which he maintained by his feet. After performing for a few seconds after this terrible fashion, the captain by sheer muscular strength, drew his body up, and having obtained again his gravity, clambered into the car to the no small delight of the spectators."

"Captain" Hall therefore seemed to be as much a circus showman as he was a ballooning pioneer. The newspaper report continued with details of his flight:

"The balloon now sailed steadily onward and upward. In a few minutes, distance considerably diminished its size to the eye of the spectator, and it seemed to glide on in ethereal space as well as the aeronaut could desire. In the space of ten minutes or a quarter of an hour it suddenly descended and disappeared. It was then supposed that the aeronaut had alighted in the neighbourhood between Boldon and Marsden. But in a few moments, it reappeared, and shot up with amazing velocity, and to an immense altitude. Those who had so provided themselves, brought their telescopes to bear, but in vain were all attempts to spy out the captain made. The

balloon, moreover, oscillated in its career as though it had lost its ballast, but on it went until its appearance in the heavens was no bigger than a man's hand, and ultimately the shades of night shut it entirely from view."

Nobody seemed able to confirm whether William Hall was still standing in the balloon's car. The truth was that a terrible accident had occurred near Felling, as the newspaper report went onto state:

"From the time when the balloon reappeared in the heavens, doubts were expressed that the aeronaut was not in the car; and about nine o'clock the doubt became a certainty, news having reached the town of an accident having befallen Mr. Hall near to the Felling.

The balloon was seen to descend by a farmer and his son who were employed in an adjoining field to that in which the machine alighted. There was but little wind up at that time, but it appears that the grappling iron failed to keep its hold, and that the balloon dragged a few yards along the ground, causing some of the ballast to be upset, thus lessening the weight to be sustained. At that moment, the daring voyageur seems to have been getting out of the car, when the balloon rose with sudden velocity, caught his feet in the ropes and whirled him unexpectedly into the air. For a moment he was seen hanging with his head downwards, in the next the rope was disentangled, and he fell into the clover-field beneath, a distance estimated at about 120 feet.

The persons near him immediately ran to his assistance. To their surprise, he was not dead, but spoke in an incoherent manner, complaining that he was nearly suffocated by gas. Immediately afterwards, however, he was found to be insensible, and was carried into 'Scot's House', the residence of Mr. H. L. Pattinson, who hastened to the spit and personally rendered all the aid he could give. Mr. Grant, a surgeon residing in the vicinity, was promptly in attendance, whilst a cabman who had gone in pursuit returned to inform Mrs. Hall of the catastrophe. Exaggerated reports of the occurrence prevailed, and it having been stated that no surgeon had been employed, Mr. Smith, of the Victoria Rooms, under whose management the fete came off, forthwith drove out, accompanied by a medical gentleman, and arrived soon after eleven o'clock. Captain Hall was then in a profound sleep.

Upon careful examination it was discovered that no bones were broken, though the right shoulder and side of the neck were severely contused, and the patient complained of a sense of cramp in the muscles there. When first brought in he was suffering from collapse and shock, but shortly afterwards revived, and asked for his wife. A slight delirium supervened, after which he sank into a deep sleep, without any serious symptoms. The utmost care and attention were bestowed upon him by the gentleman into whose house he had been taken.

Mrs. Hall, shortly after her arrival, was recognised by her husband. The patient remained, however, during the greater part of the night in a state of insensibility, but about three o'clock on Tuesday morning he recovered his consciousness, and during that day talked a good deal regarding the accident and the engagements he has thereby been prevented from fulfilling. He was removed in a spring-cart to the Newcastle Infirmary on Tuesday, whither he was accompanied by his wife. Throughout the day, he remained in pretty much the same condition as when he arrived in the town. Owing to the injuries sustained by the spine, the lower part of his body continued in a state of complete paralysis that seemed to auger ill for his recovery. In the latter part of the evening, however, he seemed livelier than he had been during the day, while his symptoms, if anything, were a shade more promising than at any time since the occurrence of the accident."

Further information regarding the incident – apparently direct from the dying balloonist's lips - had come to light before the newspaper went to press, and this was included on another page of the same edition:

"Since writing that account, we have heard the following as Captain Hall's version of the accident. Having crossed the Tyne and deeming the Felling neighbourhood favourable for making a descent, he opened the valve and let off a large quantity of gas. The result was that the balloon came down much more rapidly than the aeronaut had anticipated.

He states that it descended with great force, and with such violence as to throw both him and the ballast out of the car. On this occurring, the valve closed, and the balloon having become suddenly released from the heavy burden of ballast and voyager, rose again almost instantly, dragging up with it the captain, whose right leg had become entangled in the netting.

Finding himself in this unenviable situation, Captain Hall strove with all his might to reach the car, but his efforts were unavailing, and the cording having given way, he was precipitated to the earth. He makes no mention of the grappling irons having given way; and therefore, it is highly probable that the rapid descent of the balloon prevented these from being thrown out."

Despite the optimism recorded at the end of the Newcastle newspaper's reporting, Hall's condition would worsen. Media reports of the time seemed to carry lurid and grisly details of accidents, injuries and deaths. *The Buckinghamshire Advertiser and Free Press* was no exception, as its 20th August 1859 edition confirmed:

"The accident to Captain Hall, in falling from his balloon Florence Nightingale as he was descending on Monday night near Baldon [sic], is more serious that was at first thought. His spine is seriously injured, and there are remote hopes of his recovery. From the nature of the injuries, he appears to have fallen head foremost to the ground from the balloon, his head and shoulder coming first in contact with the earth, the body and extremities being bent over so as to break the back."

The Newcastle Chronicle carried details of Captain Hall's condition after he had fallen to the ground:

"On Wednesday night, Captain Hall, who had been worse during the day, had been cupped on the neck, and pronounced himself much relieved. Subsequently he was able to converse. The paralysis of the arms and legs continued, though some slight movement, it is said, has been made by the former. Owing to the nature of the accident, the mass of nervous matter known as the 'spinal marrow' has been compressed, so as to cut off from the limbs all power of the will in the brain to communicate motion to them. The case is almost hopeless, but in a medical point of view exceedingly interesting.

Of the balloon, nothing whatever had been heard, the reports about its discovery at Whitby, Hull, etc. having proved erroneous. It is probable that it would retain its floating power two or three days at least and would travel probably SE by E at the rate of about five miles an hour. It may therefore be expected to be heard off [sic] by vessels plying from the mouth of the Elbe or from Hamburg correspondents. This supposition is founded upon the assumption that the wind remained in the same direction. A very general hope has been expressed that the faithful little dog who remained in the car to guard his master's clothes and purse may safely arrive on terra firma; dog-wise persons consider that the poor creature could exist possibly for eighty hours without either water or food."

However, the plucky balloonist finally succumbed to the injuries sustained in the accident. *The Westmorland Gazette* published news of Captain Hall's demise in their 27th August 1859 edition, the information taken from the *Manchester Guardian*:

"We regret to state that Captain Hall, the well-known aeronaut, who fell from his balloon at Newcastle-on-Tyne, on Monday last, died yesterday, Friday, in the Infirmary of that town, from the injuries which he had sustained. The case had been pronounced almost hopeless from a very short time after the accident, and it was stated on Thursday night that death appeared to be slowly taking place from gradual suffocation. Captain Hall's mother and another relation, who had been sent for from Leicester, saw him on Thursday, and he conversed rationally with them, expressing his conviction that no hope of recovery remained. Mrs. Hall has been with her husband ever since the accident. It is stated that she will now be left utterly destitute; and that the lost balloon was being paid for by instalments. A subscription on her behalf has been already commenced."

And what of the balloon itself? Did it fly across the North Sea (known back then as the German Ocean)? The *Morpeth Herald's* 20th August 1859 issue gave what details were known at the time:

"The balloon appeared at North Shields about seven o'clock and passed over the high part of the town and the Tyne at a low level; it then floated up amongst a mass of clouds. It twice emerged from them and presented a beautiful sight. It was lost sight of about 8 o'clock. It passed over Sunderland at 20 minutes to 8 o'clock and went to sea almost direct east. It was an object of great interest and was watched by large crowds of people till out of sight."

Neither the balloon nor the unfortunate dog was ever seen again.

FARMAN FATALITY

A photograph of Madame Franck at the controls of a Farman biplane, presumably taken in around 1910.

One of the earliest French female aviators was Rosalind Mathilde Franck, who was born in 1866. She learned to fly in 1910 at the age of 44 after having flown as a passenger with Michael Effimoff in February that year. During that flight, she was scalded with hot water from a burst pipe leading to the aircraft engine's radiator, but this didn't dampen her enthusiasm for aviation. A second flight occurred later the same year with Henry Farman, her husband also going up to allow the French pioneer to set a record for carrying two passengers. Her first public flight was not without difficulty:

"One day that I shall long remember was that of my first public flight. Naturally the apparatus had been delayed on the road. I only got it at the last moment, when it was just time to mount. And yet my troubles were only beginning. The crowd could not understand that the wind was blowing a gale and that the aerodrome was relatively no bigger than a pocket handkerchief, that it was surrounded with houses and cut in two by a railway, and that it was dangerous to venture out in such circumstances.

To cut a long story short, in the evening, the wind having gone down a bit, I consented to come out in order to escape the cries and howls of the public and the threats of the managers. I flew at will and made my way towards the sea, where there were at least no more obstacles or chimneys. But a fog came on and thickened so that I lost my way. I sought a meadow and in spite of the fright of the horses grazing in it, came to earth without mishap. I heard outcries and the sound of motor horns and I saw the managers coming with faces of dismay at my long absence. They expected to find me lying under my machine! I had to listen to the outbursts of the directors of the show. They threatened to cancel my contract if I did not fly exclusively within their pocket handkerchief enclosure. They knew nothing of the risks, but the accident which nearly killed me revealed these to them."

> TO-DAY,
> # Boldon Races,
> SATURDAY, JULY 30th.
> Great Sporting Match between J. Longstaff's Well Read and J. Lowe's Mary Gloucester, for £50; mile, owners up; catch weights.
> SATURDAY AND MONDAY AT BOLDON.
> RACING AND AVIATION MEETING.
> FIRST OF ITS KIND IN THIS COUNTRY.
>
> MESSRS THORNTON AND STONE have pleasure in announcing that in addition to their usual Racing Programme, they have secured the services of that Expert French Lady Aviator
> MDLLE. FRANCK,
> of Rue Bernie, Paris, the First Lady Aviator to appear in England,
> who will at a salary of £500 (weather permitting) GIVE EXHIBITIONS OF FLYING WITH AND WITHOUT PASSENGERS AT BOLDON RACES SATURDAY, JULY 30th, and BANK HOLIDAY MONDAY, AUGUST 1st, 1910.
> £200 will be given for Racing, etc., making in Prize Money £700.

Newspapers carried advertisements for Madame Franck (titled Mademoiselle here) and her aviation exploits. This one was carried by the Sunderland Daily Echo in its 30th July 1910.

Mathilde Franck learned to fly with the assistance of staff at the Farman Brothers' manufacturing plant, located near Paris. She performed a record-breaking non-stop 14-mile-long flight on 20th July 1910 and was set to fly across the English Channel, but bad weather foiled her attempt. Franck's exploits were featured in newspapers across the world, including County Durham. Seeing the reports, the manager of Sunderland's Empire Theatre invited the intrepid aviatrix to carry out a series of demonstration flights in connection with the Boldon Races in July 1910. These race meetings were held every Easter, Whitsun and August Bank holidays.

Madame Franck performed two flights at Boldon Flats, located near Cleadon Village. The first, using a Farman Biplane which was owned by Mr. G. W. Parkinson, occurred on 30th July, when she flew for a mile and a half, this feat being the first significant distance covered by a female aviator in Britain at that time.

An early Farman Biplane, similar to the machine that Madame Franck was flying on the day of the crash at Boldon Flats in August 1910.

The second flight – which also proved to be her last – took place two days later. On take-off, Mathilde Franck flew into a flagstaff and the impact caused the Farman to hit the ground. A 15-year-old boy, Thomas Wood, one of the spectators at the event, was struck and killed by the aircraft's engine as the wrecked airframe hit the ground. The pilot suffered a broken leg in the accident, which brought her flying career to an end. Somewhat surprisingly, Franck had never obtained a flying licence. The accident was one of, if not the first one involving a Farman Biplane in Britain. News of the incident was reported across Britain, the following story published in *The Banffshire Advertiser* being representative:

"There was a distressing ending to a series of aviation feats at Boldon racecourse, near Sunderland, on Monday night, resulting in the death of a

boy, serious injuries to the French aviatrix Madame Franck, and slight injuries to persons in the crowd.

The chief attraction of the race meeting was the appearance of Madame Franck, who was billed as a Parisian airwoman. She made a successful start in bright and almost windless weather, and as she glided about and turned on her flying machine, a Farman biplane, the huge crowd of many thousands cheered her enthusiastically. She kept unusually low to the ground, many of the spectators thinking she did this to prevent the thousands outside the ring from seeing too much of the performance.

After circling eastwards and westwards alternately, she finally took a longer detour in the direction of the sea. In returning she seemed too low to escape a row of houses which skirt the field, but she avoided these.

Unfortunately, however, she struck a flagstaff in the garden of the corner house of Mr. Coulthard, of the race-course cottages. It was decorated with bunting, and the whole thing was torn down with the biplane, its manipulator coming down on the top of it. In the descent, a boy seated on a race-course hoarding was killed instantaneously. Part of the biplane wing rested on the hoarding, and broke Madame Franck's fall. It was this that killed the lad but saved her life. She did not escape injury however, her left leg being fractured in two places, and her throat being badly cut by the flying machine wires. Many persons in the crowd were injured, but not seriously, cuts about the face, head and legs being the principal results of the accident.

The name of the boy proved to be Thomas Wood, aged 15, of the Library, Boldon Colliery. Madame Franck was removed to Sunderland Infirmary, where at a late hour she was reported to be progressing favourably. Doctors Cort, Armstrong, Wharton and others quickly arrived on the scene after the police had rendered first aid to the injured in the house of Mr. Hepple, of the cottages, in whose garden the wrecked flying machine lay.

Madame Franck is the wife of an English journalist working in Paris. Many of the women in the crowd fainted when the accident occurred and were promptly attended to. There were to have been further flights on Tuesday, but the unfortunate accident curtailed the programme of the meeting."

According to the Newcastle *Evening Chronicle* of 27th October 1910, the bones in Madame Franck's fractured leg had yet to unite, so it was stated she would have to remain in hospital for at least a further two months. In August 1911, the *Jarrow Express* reported that she did not return home to Paris until the end of 1910.

Located not far from East Boldon Metro Station, Boldon Flats is now home to the Tileshed Nature Reserve. The heritage trail features several interpretation boards. One of these gives a brief description of Mathilde Franck's tragic flight. The site that she flew from is unremarkable, just one of many farmers' fields where cows now graze. The board is the only reminder of an early female pioneer and the tragedy that occurred there back in August 1910.

THE SOUTHWICK CATASTROPHE

A Royal Aircraft Factory BE.2c training aircraft. Machines identical to this were used by No.36 (Home Defence) Squadron over North-East England in the early years of the First World War. Although two-seater aircraft, some were operated as single seaters by the removal of one of the seats. One of them crashed at Southwick, near Sunderland, in May 1917. (Copyright expired)

As its name implied, No.36 (Home Defence) Squadron was responsible for defending a section of the East Coast of England against Zeppelin attacks. The unit was formed at Cramlington, located north of Newcastle, with its primary task being to defend the shipyards and other industries along the River Tyne and the River Wear at Sunderland. Once the threat of German airships ceased in late 1917, the unit devoted itself to training pilots.

On the early evening of 24th May 1917, Lieutenant Philip Thompson, who was a member of No.36 Squadron's "A" Flight, based at Hylton Aerodrome near Sunderland, took off in a BE.2c aircraft which had a newly fitted Lewis machine-gun. His intention was to test fire it over the sea in advance of that evening's Zeppelin patrol flight.

A public meeting on food saving had been organised for residents at Southwick Green, with a start time of 2030 hours. Thompson flew over the assembled crowd but did not see a flagstaff as he made a run at low level. The BE.2c struck this obstacle, the top of the structure severely damaging one of the aircraft's wings. The pilot was unable to prevent his machine crashing into the Co-Operative Society building situated on the corner of Stoney Lane. Five civilians were killed, and eight others injured, although Lieutenant Thompson survived. The *Sunderland Daily Echo's* 25th May 1917 edition carried the following story which told of the tragic incident and its immediate aftermath:

"A shocking catastrophe involving the deaths of five persons and injury to eight others occurred on the Green at Southwick shortly before nine o'clock last night. The accident arose through an airman crashing into the Southwick branch of the Sunderland Co-Operative Society's premises with his biplane and then falling onto a crowd of people that had gathered to listen to addresses on the question of food economy.

Two of the five persons were killed outright, one of them a little boy, having a portion of his head cut off, and the other three died a few hours later. Ten injured were conveyed to the Royal Infirmary, and there three of them succumbed to their injuries, and the surviving seven still remain in that institution. It is, however, anticipated that they will soon be able to return to their homes. Another of the injured persons, Mrs. Brannigan, was treated at the Monkwearmouth Hospital. There were thus in all 13 victims, the complete list and particulars concerning them being as follows:

Killed:
Elizabeth Curry (49), Southwick, wife of George Curry, a patternmaker.
Injured on head, etc.
Robert Spargo (11), son of Robert Spargo, a labourer living at Southwick.
Severe injuries to the head, part of which was taken off.
John Connolly (29), of Southwick, married, plater at Messrs. Priestman's.
Injuries to head. Died at 10:30 pm.
George Davison (47), of Southwick, insurance agent.
Injuries to face, head and fractured ribs. Died at 11:30 pm.

Injured:
Ellen Rowell (14), Southwick.
Shock and concussion.
Thomas Corner (21), Southwick, miner at Hylton Colliery.
Shoulder injured.
Robert Peary (54), Southwick, labourer at Messrs. Priestman's.
Injuries to back and face.
Isabella Unwin (58), Southwick, wife of a joiner at Messrs. Priestman's.
Injuries to arm.
Annie Cullerton (17), Southwick, employee Swan and Hunter's, Southwick.
Injuries to arm and face.
William Hodgson (13), Monkwearmouth, son of a soldier.
Concussion.
Bernard Smith (10), Southwick, son of a riveter at Messrs. Doxford's.
Lacerated leg.
Elizabeth Brannigan (76), Southwick.
Injury to hands and shock.

It appears that the promoters of the Food Economy Meeting at the west end of The Green had arranged for a series of flights during the time the meeting was in progress. The meeting began shortly after eight o'clock, and while the Chairman was making the opening speech an airman made his appearance from a westerly direction. His coming was hailed with loud applause by a crowd that quickly assumed quite large proportions and must have numbered several thousands."

Born on 30th March 1898, Philip Thompson came from Kensington, London. Both a skilled carpenter and a good long-distance runner, he left school in April 1916 to join the Royal Flying Corps and after four month spent serving in France, was then recalled to England to take part in defensive night patrols at a time when night raids on London were increasing. However, he was assigned to No.36 (Home Defence) Squadron at Hylton so did not participate in the sorties against German bombers operating over the capital. This photograph was taken on 14th July 1916.

"The airman travelled a short distance beyond the crowd, and then turned and flew about the vicinity to the great delight of the people. The intending speakers who were seated on a form on the rolley [a mining trolley] also appeared to enjoy the flights. Indeed, he quite captivated the crowd, both the Chairman and the Rev. Father Smith (who was the first speaker) were unable to proceed with their addresses, having to stop every now and then owing to the attention of the crowd being riveted on the machine each time it hove in sight.

In the course of these periodical visits the airman came down quite low, and it was during one of these dives that the catastrophe occurred. It may be stated that the meeting was being held at the west end of The Green, just at the top of Stoney Lane. At the top of the Lane, and facing The Green, is the Southwick branch of the Sunderland Co-Operative Society's premises, which are very high. In the centre of The Green is a flagstaff some 40 or 50 feet in height, and when the meeting began the Union Jack was taken down and put on the waggon.

The airman, in what proved to be the last flight, came straight up The Green, with the intention evidently of flying just over the crowd. As he came along, with all eyes upon him, one of the planes struck the flagstaff. The machine, however, still came along, and passed just over the heads of the people and those on the waggon. All ducked as speedily as possible, and the machine continuing its course crashed into the Co-Operative building and dropped on the portion of the crowd behind the rolley.

So suddenly had the whole thing occurred that it took some seconds for people to grasp that something serious had happened. Fortunately there were a number of soldiers and special constables on the scene, and while some made a cordon around the debris others at once set to work to get the people out from underneath. The airman was got out to P.C. Atkinson and others, and was found to be uninjured, though naturally very much upset. He was taken into a house close by, where every attention was accorded him. The search quickly revealed the fact that a little bare-footed boy had been killed outright, and his head taken practically off by some portion of the machine. A middle-aged woman had also been instantly killed by a blow on the head. Both bodies were reverently covered up until they could be removed to their homes. Some fifteen or a score of men and women were also badly hurt.

Drs. Brears, Thompson and Carruthers rendered all possible aid to the sufferers. Meanwhile, ambulances had been telephoned for, and soon Red Cross and police ambulance vans were on the scene, and in these the injured persons were conveyed to hospitals or houses close by. The injured having been attended to, the damaged biplane was removed to headquarters. Two of the large windows in the shop were completely broken, and a portion of the machine rested in the shop window. Several people were hurt through the falling glass when the panes were broken.

The news of the disaster quickly spread, and soon many thousands were wending their way up from the town to The Green, the cars being also packed. It was well onto midnight ere the throughfare resumed its normal appearance, and long before that time arrived, the only indication of anything having occurred was the boarding up of the windows of the stores. It was noticed this morning that the top of the flagstaff, a model of a ship, was missing, it evidently having been knocked off by the airman in the course of his flight.

The Borough and County Coroners have been officially notified of the deaths, and the inquests will be held in due course. It is probably that they will be formally opened, so that certificates for burial be granted, and then adjourned for a week."

The former Co-Operative Society building at the top of Stoney Lane in Southwick is now a Lifestyle Express mini supermarket. The Green, where Lieutenant Thompson crashed in 1917, lies behind the photographer. The pilot's BE.2c aircraft lay in the shop window on the ground floor after coming to rest. (Author)

The coroner remarked that it had been regrettable that so many had lost their lives in the manner that they had:

"They had gone to a meeting on The Green at Southwick, and while there an airman, from some cause or other, which would have to be dealt with by the jury later, descended so low as to strike some obstruction, with the result that it was driven out of control among the crowd. Several were injured and up to now five had died."

The *Sunderland Daily Echo* carried details of the two inquests which were held on 31st May 1917. One concerned the deaths at the scene of the crash and the other regarding those who had subsequently died at the Royal Sunderland Infirmary.

The first enquiry, which examined the deaths of Elizabeth Curry and Robert Spargo, was held in the Boardroom of the Southwick Urban District Council building. In attendance was Lieutenant Thompson, the pilot, accompanied by several members of the Royal Flying Corps, plus his representative, Mr. W. H. Bell, who also appeared on behalf of the Southwick Food Economy Campaign Committee. Dr. Brears, a senior police officer from the Jarrow Division and two clergymen were also present. Reverend Father Smith, from St. Hilda's Presbytery at Southwick was the first witness called. He provided the following details:

"He stated that about 8:45 pm last Thursday he was present at a food economy meeting at the top of Stoney Lane and was one of the speakers. They had a rolley for a platform. Just at that time, an aeroplane came in sight, travelling from east to west, and at a fairly good height. The machine was travelling in the direction of The Green, and the airman apparently had the engine shut off, although he could not definitely say. It was also his impression that when the airman reached about the centre of The Green, the engine was started again and the machine commenced to rise. Almost immediately he saw it strike the top of the flagstaff, which was at the end of the upper portion of The Green.

The impact broke the propeller, and so stopped the engine. One of the wings appeared to be broken and seemed to lift up, while the other came along curved. Ultimately, the machine crashed to the ground about a yard or two behind the rolley, and pulled up at the Co-Operative Stores premises, breaking the drapery department window. As soon as possible, he [Rev. Father Smith] jumped off the rolley, and the first thing he saw was the body of the boy Spargo, and near the Stores he saw the body of Mrs. Curry. There were a number of police and ambulance men about, and the injured people were conveyed to the surgeries of Drs. Brears and Carruthers."

Mr. Bell from the Food Committee was questioned about whether the pilot had been requested to fly over the crowd or not. Various rumours had been circulating since the incident and the coroner wanted to find out the truth about exactly what had happened in terms of arrangements. Mr. Bell had indeed contacted the pilot three days before the crash and had asked him whether there would be any flying that evening. He had also requested that there not be any flying before a certain time, so that the crowd would not be drawn away from the meeting. According to Mr. Bell, Lieutenant Thompson *"did not make any promise. I suppose if I may put it, he acted like a gentleman, and he did not directly refuse. He said the flying would depend upon the night and circumstances."* Despite the pilot not making promises that he would attend, a rumour started that an aeroplane would be present when the meeting was being held.

Another witness giving evidence at the enquiry was Sergeant Flynn, a member of Durham County Constabulary. He had also been present at the meeting in Southwick and reckoned the attendance figure was around 300:

"The aviator passed twice over the meeting before the accident occurred, but he was on those occasions not directly over it, but a little to the right. At the time he was flying fairly low.

Returning about a quarter to nine, the aviator planed down to a low altitude. He then endeavoured to rise in order to clear the top of the flagstaff but struck it. This damaged his propeller, and the machine struck the store and came down among the people. Going to the spot, witness found Mrs. Curry and the boy Spargo lying dead, and he removed their bodies to the mortuary. The airman walked away from the machine after the accident and went into a house in the vicinity. He appeared to be no worse for the accident except that he might be suffering from shock, and he was able to walk unassisted."

A blue plaque affixed to the side of the building overlooking Southwick Green gives details of the incident in May 1917. (Author)

Sergeant Flynn then provided the weather vane which had been located at the top of the flagstaff struck by Lt. Thompson. It had been found lying on the roof of a house 37 yards from the flagstaff itself. The height of the latter was measured at 50 feet and the distance from it to where the aircraft had fell was 114 yards. The policeman believed that the pilot had perfect control of his machine until it struck the obstacle. Next to give evidence to the inquest was the pilot, Lieutenant Thompson, whose testimony suggested he knew nothing about the meeting at Southwick in advance of his flight:

"Philip Thompson, the aviator, stated he was a lieutenant in the Royal Flying Corps, and was 19 years of age in March last. He joined the Corps on April 22nd, 1916, and on July 14th following qualified as a pilot. From July 18th until Nov. 24th, 1916, he was in France and during that time acted as a pilot. He had done 180 hours flying, which was equal to 12,600 miles, without any previous accident.

On Thursday last, at 8:25 pm, he left the aerodrome on a machine to carry out a test of a newly fitted gun. The machine was a single seater. Passing over Southwick, he saw a crowd on The Green and came down to see what was happening. He passed over The Green twice, flying upward and towards the open country a few hundred yards distant. Then he proceeded towards the sea, skirting the town and flying at a height of about 1,500 feet.

Having successfully carried out the gun test, he circled over Sunderland at a height varying between 1,300 feet and 2,300 feet. In returning towards the aerodrome, he again passed over Southwick and planed down towards the fields, passing over The Green. The sun was shining in his eyes rather brightly and it was fairly windy."

Lieutenant Thompson was asked whether he had come down lower than usual. The pilot agreed, stating that he "did not intend to be below the level of the houses." He admitted he had not noticed the flagstaff beforehand, as he had flown to the right of The Green on his previous passes:

"I never saw the flagstaff until I hit it."

The pilot stated that he had no knowledge of the meeting at Southwick and had never been asked to fly over it or was such a thing suggested to him. He also mentioned that he believed he would have easily cleared the nearby buildings if he hadn't struck the flagstaff, as he was doing around 105 mph at the time. Someone in the Royal Flying Corps had in fact been asked about not flying aircraft over the Southwick area before 2000 hours that evening. According to the Station Commander at Hylton Aerodrome, Captain Joseph Griffiths, a request along these very lines had been made:

"Rev. Father Smith called upon him and stated that they were having a food demonstration at Southwick and suggested that if there was to be any flying it should not take place before eight o'clock. Witness made no promise to fly over the meeting and did not mention the matter to the aviator.

On the day of the accident, he was returning by car from Southwick, accompanied by Lt. O'Neill, about 8:35. He saw Thompson flying over Sunderland at a height of about 1,500 or 2,300 feet. On reaching Southwick, witness had to pass through a large crowd that had congregated on The Green. Just before reaching the end of The Green, he heard a crash, and on looking round saw that the biplane had a 'side spin', a technical term for it going sideways.

The left wing of the plane was severed and was held onto the body by the bracing wires. The machine then crashed down, and he was not sure whether or not it first struck the Stores before dropping down onto the people. Witness was unable to get near owing to the crowd. Lt. Thompson was a careful and a very good pilot, having had considerable experience, including four months in France."

Captain Philip Thompson, Royal Flying Corps, pictured after his promotion to that rank, possibly in early 1918 before his death in March of that year.

Other witnesses stated that the BE.2c aircraft was in good shape. It had been flown as far as Easington on the same day by the same pilot. Both the airframe and the engine were described as in "perfect order". The wreck was taken to Hylton for examination. There, it was noted that the machine's Royal Aircraft Factory 1 engine had *"split right down the centre, having evidently struck something very hard, concrete or stone."* Another officer who saw the incident was Lieutenant-Colonel Frederick Graham:

"[He] deposed that he was in the neighbourhood at the time and saw the airman flying. Just as the biplane was rising, he noticed the left plan flapping as if it was damaged through striking something, and the machine immediately went over on one side 'like a bird with a broken wing'. Witness could not see the flagstaff from where he was standing. Thompson appeared to have perfect control of the biplane. He knew the officer to be a careful and steady man."

In summing up, the coroner confirmed there were other witnesses that he could have summoned, but that their testimony would only be either similar or identical to those already called. He was glad to have dispelled rumours that Thompson had flown over Southwick especially for the meeting. Had that been true, then all parties concerned would have had a duty to keep the public safe by use of proper safeguards. After reviewing the evidence in detail, the coroner summed events up:

"...and observed that the airman had possibly misjudged the distance and knew nothing about the flagstaff until striking it. The striking disabled the machine, and he knew nothing more about it until finding himself against the Stores. In the course of descending, he killed two persons outright, and injured several others, three of who afterwards died. He was, however, glad to say that the injured were going on all right.

It was for the jury to say whether they considered there had been any criminal negligence on the part of the airman. For them to come to that conclusion they would have to be satisfied that he manoeuvred his machine in a reckless manner, regardless of all consequences. Now he thought it would be absurd to say that he did so, because he would be running a terrible risk to himself.

All the evidence seemed to point to the fact that the accident had resulted from flying too low in a limited space, where there was a crowd of people, and unexpectedly having to deal with a flagstaff. If it had not been for the flagstaff he would have been able to have risen high enough to clear all obstructions. Unfortunately, the machine just struck the top and became disabled. It seemed that it was the result of bad luck, and the sun caused him to misjudge the distance.

He appeared to have been a very clever aviator and had thorough control of the biplane. He had four months flying in France, which was a long life for an aviator there. He (Mr. Shepherd, the coroner) was quite sure nobody regretted the accident more than the airman."

The jury returned their verdict after a few minutes of deliberation, with the foreman's words being reported by the *Sunderland Daily Echo*:

"We find accidental death in both cases, and exonerate the airman from all blame, The jury would like to express their sympathy with the bereaved, also the airman. There has been a fund opened for the relief of the bereaved, and we would like to hand over our fees to that fund."

The jury of the second enquiry, held at the Police Court in Sunderland, arrived at the same verdict. However, the coroner had words of advice for No.36 Squadron's commanding officer:

"...there had been a great deal of attention drawn to airmen in the town and district by their flights, and he would suggest to those who were responsible for that kind of thing that they should make it a rule or an understanding that an airman should not descend below a height sufficient to clear buildings round about. They all knew it was a matter of necessity for airmen to practice manoeuvring under varied circumstances, but he would suggest that as far as possible, such should not be done over the crowded parts of the town, he thought that those in authority would understand and act in that matter."

There appeared to be little if any ramifications in terms of Lieutenant Thompson's career in the Royal Flying Corps. In March 1918 he was promoted to the rank of Temporary Captain, being posted back in France as the new Flight Commander of "C" Flight, No.22 Squadron, based at Serny. This unit flew two-seat Bristol F.2B Fighters (known to their crews as "Brisfits"). He carried out his first mission as flight commander on 20th March 1918.

A Bristol F.2B Fighter, similar to the aircraft that Captain Philp Thompson lost his life in over France in March 1918.

However, Captain Thompson's luck ran out just three days later. At around 0905 hours on the morning of the 23rd, he took off in Bristol Fighter B1171 with 2/Lt. D. W. Kent-Jones (who had formerly been with the Royal Engineers) as his observer. Their mission was an offensive patrol over the enemy lines. Last seen over Cambrai, the pilot was killed, and the observer taken as prisoner of war. Philip Thompson had been shot through the head whilst taking on three German aircraft in air-to-air combat over Prouville, near Le Quant. He was buried at Lebucquires, close to Bapaume. He was just a week away from celebrating his 20th birthday at time of his death.

```
                                                          3841.

THOMPSON, Philip
      24, Argyll Road, Kensington, W.


Born  30th March 1898         at    London
Nationality    British
Rank, Regiment, Profession   2nd Lieut.    R.F.C.
Certificate taken on
At
Date    14th July 1916
Killed in action 23rd March 1918
```

The Royal Aero Club index card for Philip Thompson. His promotion to the rank of Captain appears to have been omitted.

CAPTAIN PHILIP THOMPSON, who was reported missing on March 23, and is now believed to have been killed while fighting his machine on that date, was the only son of Mr. Whitaker Thompson, who was Chairman of the London County Council for 1910-11. Educated at St. Aubyn's, Rottingdean, and Winchester (Mr. Aris's house), he joined the R.F.C. in April, 1916. After some months in France he was chosen for night-flying defensive service in England, but soon after being promoted captain he was again posted to a squadron at the front. He was 19 years of age at the time of his death.

Capt. Thompson's death was announced in the 4th May 1918 edition of The Times, being included in the "Fallen Officers – The Times' list of Casualties".

Philip Thompson also came from a prominent family in London. His father, William Whitaker Thompson, a barrister, had previously served on London County Council, of which he was Chairman between 1910 and 1911. He then became the Mayor of Kensington from 1911 to 1912.

8. Aeroplane Tragedy. Location - Extreme west end of The Green

On Thursday May 24th 1917, at 8.25 pm 19 year old Lieutenant Philip Thompson took off from Usworth Aerodrome in a biplane to test a newly fitted gun. When he passed over Southwick he saw a large crowd on The Green and went down to see what was happening. An open air meeting was taking place to urge economy in food consumption. The crowd estimated at 500 were bemused by the rare spectacle of a Royal Flying Corps warplane, and after two swoops he proceeded towards the sea to test the gun. On his return to Usworth at about 8.45 pm he descended low over The Green travelling at about 105 mph. The Sun was low in the west and shone in his eyes and he did not see the 56ft flagstaff in the centre of The Green. The biplane's left wing hit the flagstaff and the plane went into a side spin, hit the Co-op Stores at the top of Stoney Lane, and dropped onto a portion of the crowd. Five people were killed and eight were injured. The pilot miraculously walked away from the smash uninjured.

At the inquest the jury returned a verdict that the deaths were accidental and the pilot wasn't guilty of any criminal negligence.

Ten months after the disaster on March 23rd 1918 Captain Philip Thompson was killed in action while flying at a height of 12,000 feet over the western front.

SVGPS Committee members and the owners of the former Co-op building Mr and Mrs Dhillon pictured after the plaque installation.

This blue plaque was funded by Andrew Carr and installed in September 2021.

One of the panels on an information board at Southwick Green gives more details about the tragedy and the installation of the blue plaque. (Author)

No longer a village a few miles from the centre of Sunderland, Southwick is now a bustling suburb of the city, and the Green still exists – but barely – among a mixture of older and newer buildings. The Co-Operative can still be found at the top of Stoney Lane, but it is now a Lifestyle Express with a Post Office inside. A blue plaque commemorating the May 1917 incident was affixed to the side of the building in September 2021, the event being mentioned on a panel on an information board across on the Green itself.

Watching so many people going about their business in Southwick on a cold but bright February morning in 2023, one suspects that few may know of the tragedy that unfolded at that very location 106 years previously. The existence of an information board and blue plaque demonstrates that at least some local people have an interest in keeping local history alive.

WOULD-BE ACE DOWN AT BISHOP AUCKLAND

An early Avro 504 training biplane fitted with an 80 hp Gnome Lambda engine. The early examples of this type were underpowered, although the design itself would be in service with the Royal Flying Corps and then the Royal Air Force for years, with production only ending in 1932. Other examples were used by the Royal Naval Air Service, one of which came to grief near Bishop Auckland in May 1917.

Mention flying activities during the First World War and the Royal Flying Corps (which became the Royal Air Force in April 1918) usually springs to mind. It was a branch of the Army, using army ranks and insignia. What is less well known is that prior to April 1918, the Navy had its own air arm, known as the Royal Naval Air Service (and would do again later). In the first two years of the war, aircraft from naval squadrons and training units often provided the sole aerial defence against Zeppelins and submarines operating off North East England. Aerodromes at Whitley Bay, Tynemouth, Marske and Redcar, along with a whole host of subsidiary landing grounds, were used by the Royal Naval Air Service.

Despite being the vanguard for much of the early part of the war, at least as far as Home Defence went, naval aircraft types left a lot to be desired in terms of performance, manoeuvrability and ease of flying. When good aeroplanes were acquired by the service, they were often let down by being fitted with underpowered engines.

At Redcar Aerodrome, east of Middlesbrough, Royal Naval Air Service aircraft had been stationed at a large grass area just to the west of Redcar Racecourse. A motley assortment of types was used for training purposes at the station, the aerodrome being one of four located across Britain which was used for naval pilot elementary flying training. Instructors were also trained there too. The station grew to accommodate four aircraft sheds (hangars) which were needed to house and maintain a large number of aircraft. However, due to a lack of accommodation on the site, trainee pilots and instructors had to be billeted in Redcar itself.

A Zeppelin attack on the aerodrome occurred on the night of 8th August 1916, although little damage resulted. However, it was quickly realised that the Royal Naval Air Service aircraft types based at Redcar were ineffective in night combat operations against enemy airships. The naval machines had proved to be unreliable, underpowered and under-gunned. Training was therefore the main priority for the station.

Crashes involved training aircraft during the First World War were very frequent. Redcar had the dubious honour of its own high attrition rate, with some 130 incidents being recorded involving aircraft based there between July 1915 and April 1918. One such event which thankfully did not result in the death of the pilot occurred on 26th May 1917, just two days after the disaster at Southwick.

Born in April 1897, Probationary Flying Officer Harold Day hailed from Abergavenny in Monmouthshire, and commenced his flying training at Redcar on 2nd March 1917. He had been promoted to that rank in January of that year at Crystal Palace before moving north to Redcar to begin his tuition. On 26th May, he took off from Redcar in Avro 504B N6149. His flight took him over the Bishop Auckland area. During the training sortie, the trainee pilot experienced engine failure and crash-landed some seven miles north-east of the town. The Avro was wrecked in the impact, but Day was unhurt.

The probationary pilot continued his flying training after this incident, and records state he moved to the naval air station at Cranwell, Lincolnshire, on 2nd June 1917. There, he was promoted to Flight Sub-Lieutenant before a further move to Dover in July. Harold Day finally graduated as a pilot on 27th July 1917, receiving 2nd Class marks in flying ability, aerial engines, navigation, gunnery and wireless telegraphy.

Posted initially to No.10 Naval Squadron and flying Sopwith Triplanes, he chalked up his first enemy aircraft on 12th August 1917, when a hostile machine was driven down "out of control". These usually meant that the German aircraft was not seen to crash or explode on impact, but such an event was likely, something that would be regarded as a "probable kill" during the Second World War.

A lull in terms of victories then followed, as did Flight Sub-Lieutenant Day's transfer to No.8 Naval Squadron by December. There, he converted to the Sopwith Camel and scored ten more kills using the type. A German DFW was forced down "out of control" near Lens on 6th December, a "kill" shared with Flight Commander Guy Price. By 6th January 1918, Day had notched up six victories and was posthumously awarded the Distinguished Service Cross, meriting an entry in a supplement to *The London Gazette* on 22nd February:

Flight Sub-Lieutenant Harold Day became a fighter ace, achieving no fewer than 11 aerial victories over the Western Front between August 1917 and February 1918. He died on 5th February 1918 whilst chasing what would have been his 13th "kill": his Sopwith Camel disintegrated during a steep dive on a German aircraft.

"In recognition of the skill and determination shown by him in aerial combats, in the course of which he has done much to stop enemy artillery machines from working.

On the 6th January 1918, he observed a new type enemy aeroplane. He immediately dived to attack, and after a short combat the enemy machine went down very steeply and was seen to crash.

On several other occasions he has brought down enemy machines out of control."

By the time *The London Gazette* published this, Harold Day had died in the course of his duties. On 5th February, he and three other No.8 Squadron pilots shared in the destruction of a German aircraft. Spotting another, he dived on it but while doing so, his Sopwith Camel disintegrated in mid-air. Without a parachute (such items were not routinely carried by Royal Flying Corps airmen), Day plummeted to his death. He was buried at St. Mary's Advanced Dressing Station Cemetery, Haisnes. The incident was listed in the Admiralty's records:

"A22151 5/2/18 Report from No.8 Naval Squadron. Total loss of Sopwith Camel Aeroplane N6379 on 5/2/18.
Telegram 367 Missing 6/2/18.
A136144 27/2/18 It is considered there is sufficient evidence to presume death.
3/3/18 Now officially presumed to have been killed on that date."

A trainee naval pilot who wrecked an aircraft during a forced landing in Country Durham had gone on to become an air ace, one awarded medals for his efforts against the enemy.

ROUGH LANDING AT ANNFIELD PLAIN

The Royal Aircraft Factory FE.2b had an engine mounted behind the pilot. It drove a "pusher" propeller which allowed the pilot and his observer unrestricted views and firing positions ahead of the aircraft. However, "pusher" types suffered from poor overall performance and similar designs were soon phased out in favour of more conventional "tractor" propeller-driven types. Note that the aircraft's "fuselage" was uncovered. (Public domain)

Only one Royal Flying Corps pilot came to grief in County Durham during the First World War before the service became the Royal Air Force on 1st April 1918. This was Sergeant Arthur John Joyce, a member of "A" Flight, No.36 (Home Defence) Squadron, the same unit that Lieutenant Thompson belonged to, based at Hylton Aerodrome near Sunderland. Sergeant Joyce, service number 9932, hailed from Clapham Common.

No.36 Squadron was organised into several Flights, each operating from its own aerodrome located in the North-East. They also employed a network of emergency landing grounds scattered across the region. Although nothing more than farmer's fields earmarked for the task, these landing grounds provided a place to set down on if pilots encountered mechanical difficulties or bad weather once airborne on training flights or routine patrols. Some of these fields were better than others, and if aircraft were forced down at night, the poor ones could be downright dangerous. In an emergency, pilots often elected to put down on the nearest adequately sized field they could find, sometimes with fatal consequences. This was the case with the No.36 Squadron pilot who came to grief near Annfield Plain in March 1918.

On the night of 13th March 1918, Sergeant Joyce was assigned to carry out a nocturnal patrol in A5740, an FE.2b aircraft. The military authorities had received information that an air raid over the North-East was imminent, and that air patrols should be sent up to protect the public from as much danger as possible. Although the FE.2b was a two-seater, Sergeant Joyce flew alone that evening. His flight took him westwards towards the Stanley area where he apparently got into difficulties, although the exact causes are unknown. Mist had covered Hylton so he may have been trying to find an alternative site to put down on. Witnesses on the ground observed him flying around Pontop Pike, the 1,023 feet high hilltop to the west of Annfield Plain (and later the site of a TV transmitter aerial), three times before he was seen attempting to land nearby.

Sergeant Joyce put his FE.2b down in a field at Loud Bank, Greencroft, just west of Annfield Plain, close to the present-day West Road leading from the latter across to the A693. It was a very rough landing and his aircraft overturned, bursting into flames and then exploding. The pilot was killed in the incident. The rough, steep slopes of Loud Bank had not been an ideal place to put an aircraft down on, although this may not have been apparent to Sergeant Joyce, even though there had been clear skies over Annfield Plain.

Mr. E. N. Carr, who lived at Loud Terrace, Greencroft, was standing just 50 feet or so from where the FE.2b crashed. Running to the scene, he tried to rescue Sergeant Joyce from the wreckage but as he did so, it caught fire and he was forced back by the heat and exploding ammunition. The aircraft's fuel tank then detonated. An inquest into the pilot's death was held at Annfield Plain Co-Operative Hall by the local Coroner, with Carr attending as the principal witness. Each person who gave evidence was issued a new half-crown for their participation, quite a sum of money for 1918.

> THIS MONUMENT IS ERECTED BY THE
> INHABITANTS OF ANNFIELD PLAIN AND
> DISTRICT IN GRATEFUL RECOGNITION
> OF THIS GALLANT AIRMAN'S
> GREAT SACRIFICE
> IN HIS OWN WORDS, "OUR LIVES ARE NOT
> OUR OWN, THEY BELONG TO OUR COUNTRY"

Part of the wording on the memorial commemorating Sergeant Joyce which was erected at Loud Bank in May 1919.

Arthur Joyce was buried at Earlsfield Cemetery, Wandsworth, not far from his home. However, he is also commemorated by a monument that was erected close to the site where he crashed in March 1918. Taking the form of a stone column with a memorial plaque, it was initially surrounded by three-foot-high palisade railings.

Sergeant Arthur Joyce's death is commemorated on the memorial on the roadside at Loud Bank, Greencroft, Annfield Plain.

The monument to Sergeant Joyce on Loud Bank, Annfield Plain, photographed in February 2023. (Author)

Costing the sum of £50, the memorial was paid for by a combination of public subscription and "schoolchildren's pennies", the fund being established by Mr. W. J. Mackay, the headmaster of Greencroft Council School, which lay adjacent to the crash site. The official unveiling by Mrs. Mackay, the headmaster's wife, took place on 14th May 1919. Local children sang hymns at the memorial service. Also in attendance were two of the pilot's former colleagues, Sergeant Waterman and Sergeant Harvey, who had travelled down from Hylton Aerodrome for the event. Sergeant Joyce's widow was unable to attend on the day but visited the memorial a fortnight later with her two sons and stayed in the area for a few days with a local family. She had sent a letter regarding her inability to attend the unveiling, which was published in the local press:

"Dear Sir, please accept my deepest regret at being unable to be present at the unveiling of the memorial on Wednesday. I intended being present, and daresay there will be some disappointment among you good people of Annfield. There seems to be no-one who can manage to get the free time to go with me, and I feel that the ceremony will be too much for me alone. I found it so hard to bear. If you will kindly permit me, I would like to come up to see the memorial soon when I can go quietly to it. I hardly know how to express my gratitude to you all for the honour you have shown to my dear husband's memory; it is very comforting to know that the great sacrifice he made was so appreciated by the people. My thoughts will be with you all on Wednesday and I shall hope to see you soon. I enclose photos of my two little ones. I am, yours sincerely, F. A. Joyce."

In the Second World War, the railings were removed as part of a scrap metal drive. However, the memorial was renovated by the Royal Air Force Association and rededicated in 1959: a low stone wall replaced the missing rail. In addition, the name of one of one of Sergeant Joyce's sons, Sergeant Dennis Arthur Joyce, was added to the base of the stone column. A member of No.44 Squadron based at Waddington in Lincolnshire, he had been listed as missing, presumed killed, whilst on a mission over Germany on the night of 13th September 1940. The Hampden he was a crew member in, X2913, had in fact crashed into the sea after being hit by anti-aircraft fire. His body was never found.

FAIREY FATALITY

A later mark Fairey IIIF pictured on the aircraft carrier HMS Furious off Gibraltar in the late 1920s. The design dated from 1917 and the last examples were withdrawn from service as target tug aircraft as late as 1941. An earlier Fairey IIIA was lost at Hylton Aerodrome, Sunderland, in July 1918. (Public domain)

Aircraft crashes continued to take its toll on airmen from the newly-formed Royal Air Force, which had absorbed both the Royal Flying Corps and the Royal Naval Air Service at its creation in April 1918. One such incident occurred near Sunderland in July of that year.

On the morning of 14th July 1918, Captain Arthur Leslie Simms took off from the Marine Aeroplane Depot at Royal Naval Air Station Grain, near Shoeburyness in Kent. He was delivering Fairey IIIA N2851 to the airfield at Renfrew near Glasgow. Designed as a reconnaissance aircraft to be flown from aircraft carriers, the type could be fitted with either wheels or a skid undercarriage. Other versions had floats to allow them to operate from the water as bombers. Some 50 Fairey IIIAs were constructed, each one powered by a single 260 hp Sunbeam Maori engine.

For some reason, whether due to mechanical difficulties or as a result of a pre-planned en route stop, Captain Simms attempted to land at Hylton Aerodrome. This did not go without incident; the pilot overshot his landing and then stalled the aircraft as he tried to gain height. The Fairey crashed on the landing ground and was wrecked, the unfortunate airmen succumbing to the injuries he sustained in the impact. His death was announced in *Flight* magazine's 25th July 1918 edition:

"Capt. Arthur Leslie Simms, D.S.C., RAF, who was killed on July 14th while flying, aged 20, was the younger son of Mr. and Mrs. G. F. Simms, the Farlands, Stourbridge. Educated at the Lickey Hills School and Malvern College, in June 1916 he was granted a commission in the RNAS. In October 1917, he was awarded the Distinguished Service Cross for valuable services in home waters, and was promoted to Flight Lieutenant.

Afterwards, he became an instructor, and later he was transferred to the Experimental Construction Department. Since the formation of the Royal Air Force he had made several applications for service at the Front, and at the time of his death was expecting orders to proceed there."

Captain Arthur Simms, pictured as a Royal Naval Air Service pilot.

Arthur Simms was buried at Stourbridge Cemetery. Hylton Aerodrome was renamed Usworth the day after the crash, and remained an airfield until the Nissan Car Factory was built on the site in 1984.

Simms had attended Malvern College between 1912 and 1916 and his death warranted mention in the institution's magazine, *The Malvernian*:

"He had repeatedly applied to be sent overseas, but his services were required at home. He was killed whilst flying on July 14th. The keeness, splendid nerves and absence of fear, which he proved himself to possees throughout his School career marked him out for the Air Service. He became a keen and daring officer, and was regarded as a Flying Officer who was likely to make a name. Many will grieve for the loss of a true friend and brave man."

TRAGEDY AT SEATON CAREW

The remains of Airco DH.6 B3087 were photographed at Seaton Carew Aerodrome the day after the fatal crash on 18th July 1918.

Charles David Danby was born in Manchester on 10th July 1887. His father, Charles Clemson Danby, who died in 1906, was an actor, singer and comedian who regularly appeared on stage at the Gaiety Theatre in London. Schooled in France and then educated at the School of Mines, the younger Danby travelled to Egypt to take up a government engineering appointment there. When war was declared in August 1914, Danby returned to Britain and soon obtained a commission in the Royal Tyne Engineers, becoming a Captain. He then transferred to the Royal Flying Corps in 1915 in order to become a pilot. Being awarded the Royal Aero Club's Certificate No. 1324 in May 1915 after training on Farman Biplanes at Shoreham, he initially served in Belgium.

Joining No.6 Squadron in November 1915, the then 2nd Lieutenant Danby flew BE.2c aircraft with this unit. On 4th November, whilst flying a reconnaissance mission in aircraft 1714, he was in combat with a couple of Albatross scouts at 9,000 feet over Westroosebeke. On 17th January 1916 he was flying BE.2c 4309 over Polygon Wood and scored an unconfirmed victory over one of three Aviatik aircraft. On the way back to Abeele, he was attacked by a Fokker Scout monoplane near Ypres, but managed to reach the squadron's home aerodrome without further incident. Another combat resulted on 20th January 1916 when Danby flew a sortie involving registering the fall of artillery fire on German positions. He entered combat with another Aviatik over Polygon Wood and almost certainly shot down the enemy aircraft, although again the "kill" was not confirmed.

An Airco DH.6 aircraft pictured during the First World War. A rigid aeroplane with enough strength to survive clumsy landings, it was an ideal machine for training.

Captain Danby returned to Britain due to illness, eventually joining 509 Flight, No.252 Squadron, based at Royal Naval Air Station Seaton Carew, south of Hartlepool on the Durham coast. On 18th July 1918 he was detailed to fly Airco DH.6 B3087, one of the Flight's aircraft. An aircraft type specifically designed as a trainer, the DH.6 had excellent flight characteristics for the time but was extremely underpowered and had a low maximum speed. In Royal Flying Corps service, this workhorse had been given a variety of unkind nicknames, "the Clutching Hand" and "Skyhook" being two of them. From 1917, several DH.6s were employed on anti-submarine patrols by units based in the North-East of England, although most sorties were flown without an observer onboard because the aircraft could not carry a second airman and offensive weaponry at the same time. The bombs carried were extremely small and largely ineffective, so such missions amounted to little more than scare tactics.

After being constructed, Airco DH.6 B3087 was delivered to the 2nd (Northern) Marine Aeroplane Depot sub-station at South Shields although as a seaplane base, it is likely that the naval unit was simply engaged in checking the airframe for defects prior to entry into service. The aircraft was allotted to No.256 Squadron by 25th May 1918 but delivered instead to 509 Flight, No.252 Squadron at Seaton Carew.

On 18th July 1918, Captain Danby, accompanied by Air Mechanic 1st Class E. A. Bannister, took off from Seaton Carew in B3087. Bannister's presence suggests that this may well have been an air test or some kind of air experience flight for the fitter. However, Bannister could have been acting as an observer for an anti-submarine patrol, which was No.256 Squadron's primary task. Over the aerodrome, Danby lost control of the Airco DH.6, and it spun into the ground, catching fire on impact. Both airmen were unfortunately killed.

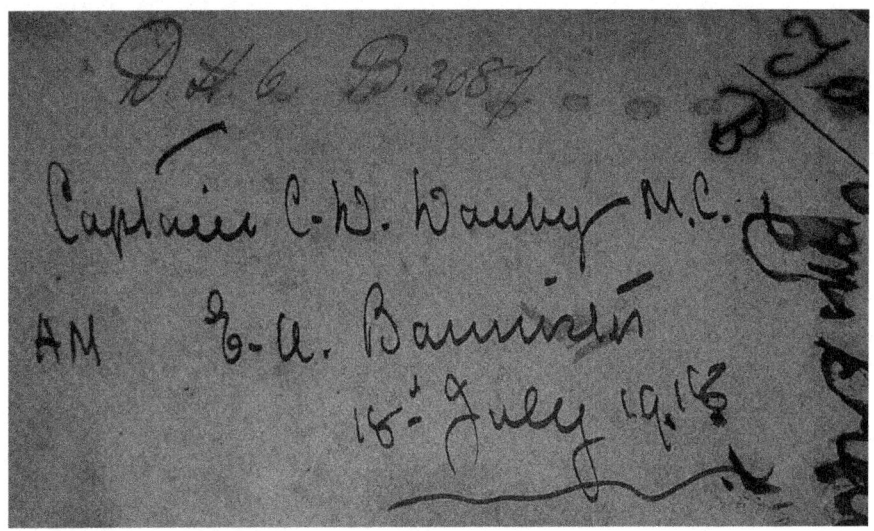

The reverse side of the photograph of the wrecked Airco DH.6.

A photograph taken the following day shows the burnt wreckage on the flying field at Seaton Carew. As per proper procedure, a Court of Enquiry was opened into the deaths of Captain Danby and Air Mechanic Bannister. Its verdict was entered into No.256 Squadron's official records:

"The cause of the accident was due to the pilot making a sharp turn on a slow machine out of a strong gusty wind, and losing flying speed, was unable to regain control owing to insufficient speed and height."

Flight magazine's 1st August 1918 edition carried Danby's obituary:

"He was one of the first to take photographs over the enemy lines and was awarded the Military Cross for a daring flight, from which he returned with valuable photographs. Invalided home through typhoid about a year ago, he had since been teaching and organising. He spoke French, Spanish and Arabic, and was a fine boxer."

Captain Charles David Danby, M.C., was interred at Hartlepool (Stranton) Cemetery, possibly due to there being no next-of-kin to claim his body for burial elsewhere.

CRASH AT CARRVILLE

Instone Air Line's de Havilland DH.34 G-EBBV was identical to an Imperial Airways aircraft that crashed into trees whilst force landing in a field near Carrville in July 1925. Note the open cockpit for the pilot and the enclosed passenger cabin which occupied the deep fuselage.

Early commercial aviation was fraught with danger. By the mid-1920s, the concept of powered flight was almost a quarter of a century old but aircraft in general were underpowered, had little or no safety equipment and there were no blind-flying or radio navigation aids. Bad weather could – and did – cause accidents, many of which were serious or involved fatalities. Of the entire production run of DH.34 airliners built in 1922, half of these were lost in crashes, all of which occurred during the first four years of operation. These incidents included one which happened near Durham in July 1925, this one happening without loss of life, something that could not be said of all four events.

DH.34 G-EBBY was completed in early 1922 and registered as such to the Air Council on 6th March that year. The aircraft was leased to Daimler Air Hire Limited. Two years later, this company was absorbed into Imperial Airways in a merger of the four largest British airlines. The hope was that the new organisation could compete with French and German concerns benefitting from government subsidies. By this point, three of the DH.34 fleet had already been lost in crashes, one of which involved fatalities.

On 3rd July 1925, Captain Frederick F. Minchin, his flight engineer and five passengers boarded G-EBBY at Croydon Airport, Surrey, in order to fly north to the Town Moor, Newcastle. The passengers were following the Kings Cup Air Race which was visiting the city.

Bad weather was encountered en route to Newcastle, which caused a landing accident that was described in detail by the *Yorkshire Post and Leeds Intelligencer* newspaper's 4th July 1925 edition:

"An airliner, which was following the competition and carrying a number of experts and newspaper men, made a forced landing shortly before eleven o'clock in the forenoon two miles north of Durham. The machine came down in a hayfield and ran into some trees at the edge of a wood. Although the wings were damaged no one on board was injured.

The forced landing was due entirely to the weather. Realising the impossibility of finding Newcastle aerodrome under the conditions the pilot selected what appeared to be a perfectly flat and suitable field on which to land. On coming down, however, he discovered that the ground was very uneven and sloped downwards in the direction he was proceeding. At the edge of the field, too, there was a wood.

The machine on landing ran downwards right into the trees, which, fortunately, prevented the machine from turning over.

There was a moment's silence on board when the pilot asked, 'Anybody hurt?' The answer came from the passengers, 'All safe.' The machine was left in charge of a mechanic, and after repair it was hoped that it would be able to fly back to London. On account of this accident, the scheme of witnessing the air race from the air came to an unfortunate end."

A representative from the *Manchester Evening Chronicle* was onboard the DH.34, and he provided an account of what happened near Carrville:

"We are enveloped in far the worst enemy of air craft. Our machine with its mean cruising speed of 80 miles per hour is helpless. We can hardly see beyond the wing tips as they brush across house tops and past trees. We are over hilly country.

The pilot suddenly tilts the machine up and turns, just to escape a tree-covered hill. Round we go again, this time in what seems an endless valley.

In front of us, a wood suddenly looms out of the fog. It is too late. Bump! The undercarriage strikes a ridge, but this cannot stay our mad flight. Then the wood – a ripping, roaring sound as we strike its outpost of shrubs.

Trees snap and then the sturdy ones bite into the fabric of the planes. A last rush; a grinding; and the last dreadful shock of impact as the weighty monster comes to rest!

We are flung forward. Then silence, broken at last by the cheery voice of Colonel Minchen, whose super airmanship undoubtedly diverted what might have been a dive of death into a mere thrill.

'All right?' he asked. And we scrambled out into the ditch and stood surveying 'G-EBBE' [sic], now most certainly unable to continue her splendid race.

Where were we? Presently a small boy from a nearby pit arrived and told us we were at Whitwell, near Durham. Thus ended the first day of our race round Britain. The fog had made what might have been a pleasant trip a gamble with death. A landing place had been a difficult thing to find. Our pilot had made the best of a bad job. Happily, no one was any the worse for the experience."

Despite optimistic forecasts that the aircraft could be repaired and flown down to London, the remains of the DH.34 were instead recovered by road to Croydon, the idea being to fix the damage properly and then return it to revenue service. This plan was soon scuppered when upon closer and professional examination, the airframe was deemed uneconomic to repair. It was officially withdrawn from use on 31st January 1926 and then scrapped later the following year. However, the Civil Aviation Authority did not get around to cancelling the aircraft's registration until January 1927.

Captain Frederick Frank Reilly Minchin, former Royal Flying Corps, Instone Air Line and subsequently Imperial Airways pilot, was involved in the Carrville crash.

Captain Minchin, known to his friends as "Dan", served in Egypt and Palestine with the Royal Flying Corps during the First World War, received the Distinguished Service Order in 1918 for leadership in directing raids against enemy armies and had reached the rank of Lieutenant-Colonel, went missing during a trans-Atlantic flight attempt on 31st August 1927. Together with Princess Anne of Löwenstein-Wertheim-Freudenberg and Captain Leslie Hamilton (a First World War ace known as "the Flying Gypsy", Minchin took off from Upavon in Fokker F.VIIA G-EBTQ in an attempt to become the first aviators to cross the Atlantic from east to west.

Last seen by the crew of an oil tanker sailing 800 miles west of Galway, Ireland, the aircraft was bound for Newfoundland but never arrived. Presumably something happened to the aircraft or its crew en route and the Fokker, with Minchin onboard, had crashed into the North Atlantic.

Back to 1925, and the air race itself was not without further incident in the region. Mr. J. D. Siddeley's Ajax aeroplane, piloted by Captain Courtney, crashed into a ditch on landing at Newcastle's Town Moor and was damaged, although the pilot was unhurt. A Siskin aircraft flown by Capt. Baggs also crashed on arrival at Newcastle. He came to rest just 100 yards from Courtney's machine. Captain F. L. Barnard, who departed Newcastle and was bound for Renfrew, near Glasgow, remarked on his trip north:

"The weather was filthy all the way after leaving Newcastle. I did not know where I was for two-thirds of the journey."

AN EXERCISE IN DISASTER: PART ONE

Fairey Gordon K1736 belonged to No.40 Squadron, Royal Air Force, the same unit involved in a string of forced landings and crashes in the North-East of England on 26th September 1933. Four aircraft from the squadron were heading back to their base at Abingdon, Oxfordshire from Scotland when the incidents occurred. (Flight magazine, 13th May 1932, public domain)

Forced landings and crashes due to bad weather were not uncommon in the 1930s but multiple events involving aircraft from the same squadron on the same day certainly were. A string of incidents which stretched all the way from Bamburgh in Northumberland right down to the sea off Hartlepool occurred on 28th September 1933, involving no fewer than 14 RAF aircraft from the same unit. The day ended with three machines lost and four pilots and crewmembers killed.

No.40 Squadron was based at Abingdon, Oxfordshire, equipped with Fairey Gordon two-seat light bombers. Even though the monoplane was starting to become the dominant design for aircraft, the Royal Air Force still operated biplane types such as the Gordon, the type first flying in 1931. In many ways, they were little better equipped for flying in bad weather than the Sopwith Camels and Royal Aircraft Factory SE.5As had been during the First World War.

In mid-September 1933, the unit sent 14 of its aircraft (almost certainly the whole complement) north to Leuchars, near St. Andrews. Its crews had been engaged in exercises over the Forth Estuary and these had finished by the 26th when the aircraft left Scotland on their long southbound flights back to Abingdon. Navigation for the first section of the trip was easy: they simply followed the coastline down to Middlesbrough, or the Edinburgh to Newcastle railway line from Dunbar. However, once the crews approached Berwick-upon-Tweed, they encountered poor visibility and fog lying along the coast.

Given the lack of radio aids and blind-flying apparatus available to pilots at that time, it was inevitable that they soon became lost when they could not see landmarks on the ground. For the aircrew of No.40 Squadron, this was to have fatal consequences. Sergeant John Christian and Corporal Aubrey Lewis were flying in Gordon K1742. They crashed into the North Sea off Hartlepool after presumably becoming lost in the fog. They were both feared lost, presumed drowned. Another Gordon had already crashed and burned out near Bamburgh, killing both its occupants, Flying Officer Norman Styche and Aircraftsman M. A. White. The other nine aircraft from the squadron overflew County Durham but were forced to turn back by increasingly poorer visibility and landed safely at Newcastle where they had to stay the night.

News of the tragedy was published in *The Sunderland Daily Echo* in its 27th September 1933 edition:

"It seems certain that the missing RAF bomber lies wrecked under the waters of Hartlepool Bay. Today, a motor boat fishing off the North Sands picked up an aircraft wheel. It bore the numbers, in red: 'Dunlop 37969 MU 61932', with the number '1' in red.

When the wheel was handed over to Hartlepool coastguards they immediately got into communication with the aerodrome at Catterick. It was at once decided to send an RAF officer to Hartlepool, and he will examine the wheel and other wreckage.

The plane passed over Hartlepool about 3.30 yesterday afternoon, some distance behind four which were flying south together. An hour and a half afterwards, people on the shore heard a crash out at sea. Pieces of wood resembling aeroplane struts and other wreckage were washed up on the beach.

The lost plane, which had apparently fallen behind the rest of the squadron, had been seen to turn in a north-easterly direction. The coast was covered by fog, and a few seconds after the plane had disappeared out of their sight, people on the beach and spectators watching a football match on a field near the shore were startled by a sudden thud.

This morning a large number of small light articles were picked up on the beach. Then a fisherman in a motor boat came across a rubber-tyred wheel, apparently from an aeroplane. No trace has yet been found of the bodies."

Witnesses heard and saw the aircraft looming out of the fog. They were flying extremely low, what seemed to be mere feet above the wavetops in some cases. A local resident, John Horsley, whose brother was the fisherman who retrieved the wheel at sea, recalled what he himself had seen whilst standing on the beach at Hartlepool:

"Visibility was no more than a quarter of a mile and the aeroplanes were being forced very low. The four had disappeared when the last one came in sight much lower than the others. He was so low that we had to duck as he came over the beach, and from the manner in which the engine was running he seemed to be having trouble with it. He struggled round as if

trying to pick up the direction taken by the others. Suddenly he seemed to set his engine away full pelt and shot away to the north-east. No more than five seconds afterwards we heard the bang."

Mr. J. Currall was another spectator to the events that unfolded. He told a representative from the newspaper that he believed the airmen in the formation of four aircraft were at risk of drowning, before seeing a fifth come out of the fog:

"Then the other plane came, and after it had disappeared, we heard a thud, just like a poss-stick in a tub of clothes, and the faint noise of the engine died very suddenly."

The fog bank had stretched from the Northumberland and Durham coasts right across to Westmorland, a distance of about 50 miles. It was estimated to reach about 6,000 feet so was a considerable handicap to flying.

Sergeant Christian's body was finally discovered when it washed up on a beach at Clacton-on-Sea in November 1933, two months after his aircraft had crashed into the sea. In their 1st December 1933 edition, *The Sunderland Echo* published details of the coroner's inquest into his death:

"A verdict of 'death by drowning' was returned at the inquest at Clacton-on-Sea today, on the body of the airman which was washed ashore there on Wednesday. It was identified as that of John William Eric Christian, a sergeant pilot in the Royal Air Force whose plane crashed off Hartlepool.

John Robert Christian, of Newark, identified articles produced as the property of his son and the signature on a driving licence. He received a telegram on September 27 from the RAF saying his son was missing and it was feared that he was drowned. PC Simpson said that when he found the body an unopened parachute was strapped to the back.

Flight Lieutenant Eric Charles Delamain said he knew Christian as a pilot sergeant in No.40 Bombing Squadron. He last saw him alive a few minutes before he crashed. The squadron had been taking part in exercises with the Fleet at Leuchars, Scotland, and was due to return to Abingdon.

On September 26 they started out. Witness was leading his flight of machines, and Christian was flying on his left with Corporal Lewis as a passenger. Off Belford they struck a bad patch [of weather] and lost one machine. Christian followed him until near The Hartlepools, when they ran into low cloud and were forced down to twenty feet off the water.

Just before emerging from the clouds, Christian's machine suddenly rose above and disappeared. Delamain added that he did not see Christian again, but presumably he turned back into the clouds and crashed into the sea. It was difficult to keep control in a cloud.

The coroner said that Christian met his death in the cause of duty and in the service of his country."

No.40 Squadron wasn't the only unit encountering bad weather over the region that day. Three Hawker Hart biplane bombers from No.33 Squadron put down at South Shields, part of a formation of 12 returning south from the same exercises in Scotland. One crashed on landing, the event also making the pages of the *Sunderland Daily Echo*, this time on 26th September 1933, the day of the incident:

"An RAF bomber in making a forced landing near Marsden today owing to fog struck a broken stone wall and crashed. The undercarriage was ripped away and as the machine fell forward the propeller snapped.

It was one of 12 machines returning from Edinburgh, three of which were forced to land at Marsden. The other nine, after circling round for some time, flew to Cramlington to await better conditions.

The plane which crashed at Marsden was the Hawker Hart Day Bomber K2437, attached to the 33rd Bomber Squadron of the Royal Air Force, stationed at Bicester, Oxfordshire. The pilot was Sergt. F. W. Cook, with Leading Aircraftsman T. Jones as gunner-observer."

A close-up of the damaged propeller and nose area of the Hawker Hart aircraft that crash-landed at South Shields on 26th September 1933.

"As the machine landed, the undercarriage struck the tumbled stones of a broken wall and was ripped off. The plane fell forward, and the propeller was snapped, while the fuselage was badly buckled and one of the wings was torn. Both Cook and Jones were able to jump clear without injury.

'It was fog which forced us down,' said Leading Aircraftman Jones to a Sunderland Echo representative. 'We have been up with the 33rd Bomber Squadron at Turnhouse Aerodrome, Edinburgh, taking part in the recent naval-aerial manoeuvres. At 8 am, when the Squadron's twelve planes left Edinburgh, the clouds were really low but there was no fog. It was not really bad flying weather. By the time we reached Tynemouth at 9 o'clock, however, we were in very thick fog, which had made us keep out to sea for quite a good part of the way down. Visibility at times was less than a hundred yards, and when we got over South Shields, we could not have been flying at much more than a hundred feet.'

'As the fog was getting worse, we were ordered to land and three of us came down in this field. The other two got down safely, but as we touched the ground and turned the undercarriage caught a large heap of stones. The plane lurched forward as the undercarriage gave way and the propeller hit the ground and snapped off. As soon as we pulled up, Cook and I jumped out. We weren't hurt at all, but the plane is pretty badly damaged.'

'The other nine planes circled round for a while and then decided that they better go to Cramlington to await better flying conditions.'

The wrecked plane has titled up on its nose on the remains of the wall in the middle of a large field, awaiting the arrival of road transport from Catterick Camp to remove it. Whitburn police and Marsden coastguard are on the scene together with the airmen who are standing by till the plane is moved."

Two squadrons had lost aircraft, one of them also losing four of its airmen. Bad weather could play havoc with the fragile machines that constituted the vast bulk of the Royal Air Force, there being no blind flying aids, radar or effective radio communication at that time. Crews were forced to keep in sight of each other and used hand signals to indicate their intentions. Add thick fog to the mix and it was a recipe for disaster.

A FAMILY TRAGEDY

De Havilland DH.60G Gypsy Moth G-ABRD was involved in a fatal accident near Knitsley, Consett, on 24th April 1935. Two brothers were flying in the aircraft at the time: one died, and the other was seriously injured. (Unknown)

Sir S. A. Sadler Limited was a coal company which owned and operated several mines located between Bishop Auckland and Consett before the Second World War. One of the partners in the business was Lieutenant Colonel Hereward Sprot. He had two sons, Alexander, who was a licenced civilian pilot and a mining engineer who was employed by the family firm, and Samuel ("Ted"), a Pilot Officer with No.607 Squadron which operated Westland Wapitis from Usworth, near Sunderland. Together with their father and sister, they lived at Woodlands Hall, Knitsley, near Consett.

On the evening of 24th April 1935, Alexander Sprot obtained the use of one of the Newcastle upon Tyne Aero Club's fleet of DH.60 Gypsy Moth aircraft. These two-seaters were used for pilot training and general flying. Alexander and his younger brother Samuel were soon airborne and bound for Knitsley. His intention was to land in the grounds of Woodlands Hall, but this would end in tragedy.

With both men waving to their father and sister as they performed a low pass over the grounds, the Gypsy Moth stalled during a steep turn, causing Alexander to lose control. The aircraft entered a spin and soon after crashed into a nearby wheat field, killing Samuel and badly injuring the pilot. Alexander Sprot was quickly taken to the Richard Murray Hospital at Blackhill, suffering from multiple injuries. An official from the Air Ministry travelled to Woodlands Hall to inspect the wrecked Gypsy Moth.

Samuel Edward ("Ted") Sprot was 22 years of age at the time of his unfortunate death in the grounds of his home.

Given the family's prominence in the area, local newspaper coverage of the accident was extensive. A story appeared the following day about the crash and the Air Ministry official's visit:

"Air Ministry officials today visited Woodlands Hall, Knitsley, near Consett, the home of Colonel and Mrs. Sprot, whose son Samuel Edward, an enthusiastic amateur airman, was killed in a crash in the grounds of the Hall last night.

Another son, Mr. Alexander Hereward Sprot, a 24-year-old instructor in mechanical transport in the Royal Artillery, stationed at Woolwich, who was piloting the machine, sustained critical injuries.

Mr. Samuel Sprot who was aged 22, and a mining engineer, died in hospital at Blackhill.

The machine, which belonged to the Cramlington Aero Club, Newcastle, was about to land when it suddenly took a nose dive into a field on the estate. The household staff heard the crash and rushed to the machine, from which they extracted the two brothers. They were sent to hospital by ambulance.

The wrecked machine was watched throughout the night by police officers.

Mr. Samuel Sprot, who was a popular member of the Cramlington Flying Club, who was a keen amateur aviator and had built an experimental glider and an aeroplane to his own design. A machine, partially constructed, lies in an outbuilding at the hall. At the age of 19 he built a glider at a cost of £20, with the assistance of his brother.

Colonel Sprot, the father of the two airmen, is a well-known north country mine and landowner, being associated with the firm of S. A. Sadler and Company.

Their uncle, Mr. Basil Sadler, is chairman of the Lanchester magistrates and is managing director of the Holmside and Southmoor Colliery Company.

Captain J. D. Irving, secretary of the Cramlington Club, told a reporter today that the two brothers had done a fair amount of flying and were competent airmen."

ORDEAL FOR FATHER

The two sons of Colonel Sprot, of Woodlands Hall, Knitsley, near Consett, Durham, flew from Cramlington, near Newcastle, to visit their father recently. Their father and sister were waiting for the areoplane to land in the grounds of the hall.

They saw it come nearer and lower. Then suddenly it nose-dived and crashed. Samuel Edward Sprot, aged 22, died in hospital from his injuries. His brother, Alexander Sprot, aged 24, was seriously injured.

News of the accident went around the world. This story appeared in the 21st June 1935 edition of the Otago Times of New Zealand.

Another story, titled *"Son's Fatal Flight, Father Refuses Invitation to Go with Him"*, was self-explanatory:

"It was revealed at the inquest last night on Samuel Edward Sprot (22), who was killed in an air crash in the grounds of his home, Woodlands Hall, Knitsley, near Consett, Durham, on Wednesday night, that his father, Colonel Hereward Sprot, declined his invitation to go flying.

'Shortly after lunch, Samuel asked me to go flying with him and Alexander,' said Colonel Sprot. 'I declined as I had some work to do. That was the last time I saw him.'

The inquest was adjourned until a day to be fixed later. It was reported that the condition of Lieut. Alexander Hereward Sprot, the pilot of the machine, who is lying critically ill in the Richard Murray Hospital, was much about the same, but that he was comfortable.

Both brothers, it is stated, held 'A' flying licences. That of Alexander expired at midnight on Wednesday, only a few hours after the accident.

A message of 'very deep sympathy' to Mrs. Sprot, wife of Colonel Hereward Sprot, was sent by the spring Council meeting of the County of Durham Federation of Women's Institutes at Stockton yesterday."

A contemporary photograph of Woodlands Hall, Knitsley, near Consett.

Samuel Sprot was buried in the family plot at Dunino Churchyard, St. Andrews, Fife. He was No.607 Squadron's first fatality, albeit as a result of a civilian aircraft accident. Following the tragic incident, the Sprot family moved from Woodlands to Colepike Hall, at Hollinside, near Lanchester, before finally settling in St. John's Hall, Wolsingham. The inquest, which was adjourned indefinitely as per the above newspaper report, resumed about a year later, as a follow-up article from the time revealed:

"A resumed inquest at Blackhill Hospital, Consett, today, was the final chapter of an air crash on April 24 last year.

A verdict of death from compression of the brain and shock from multiple injuries was returned in the case of Samuel Edward Sprot (22), mining engineer, of Woodlands Hall, Consett, the victim of the crash which was in the grounds of his home.

The jury added a rider that no blame was to be attached to the pilot, Lieut. Alexander Sprot, the dead man's brother, who left hospital only a few days ago."

Certificate No.	Full Name, Nationality and Address of Owner		Usual Station	Date of Registration	Change of Ownership of Aircraft	Destruction or Permanent Withdrawal from Use of Aircraft	Cancellation by the Secretary of State
	Full Name and Address	Nationality					
	THIS ENTRY COPIED, on 1st JANUARY, 1929, From FORMER REGISTER						
3448	The Newcastle-upon-Tyne Aero Club Ltd., Newcastle-upon-Tyne Municipal Airport, Woolsington, Kenton, Newcastle-upon-Tyne	British	Cramlington	7.10.31	6.7.39		
3448/2	W. S. Shackleton, Ltd., 175, Piccadilly, London, W.1.	British	Brooklands	29.7.39	1.8.39		
3448/3	Brooklands Flying Club Ltd., Brooklands Aerodrome, Weybridge, Surrey.	British	Brooklands Weybridge, Surrey.	4.8.39	23.6.40		

G-ABRD's logbook shows that it was owned by Newcastle upon Tyne Aero Club at Cramlington Aerodrome at the time of the crash in 1935.

What remained of the aircraft was not scrapped. Instead, G-ABRD was rebuilt and then purchased by the Brooklands Flying Club in 1939. Flown out of the company's Shoreham-on-Sea outstation, the Gypsy Moth was impressed into Royal Air Force service on 23rd June 1940 and ended up being used by No.8 Bombing & Gunnery School located at Evanton, north of Inverness. It was allocated the RAF serial AW134, which it wore instead of its pre-war civilian registration. AW134/G-ABRD was apparently written off in an unspecified accident on 11th August 1942.

THE MOTH AND THE SLURRY PIT

De Havilland DH.60G Gypsy Moth G-EBYV was initially built as a floatplane. This image of a Royal Canadian Air Force example shows the layout involved. Later converted to a landplane, 'YV was involved in a landing accident at Medomsley, near Consett, in June 1936.

Gypsy Moth G-EBYV was constructed in 1928 as a floatplane and may have been based at the seaplane station at Cattewater, Plymouth, whilst T. E. Lawrence (better known as Lawrence of Arabia) was serving there. Prior to sale to Iona National Airways of Ireland in June 1931, the aircraft was converted into a landplane. It also received a Gypsy engine at this time. Sold to the Newcastle upon Tyne Aero Club on 16th September 1932, it was based at Cramlington Aerodrome in Northumberland.

On 30th June 1936, the aircraft was being flown over the Derwent Valley by Mr. Samuel Smith, one of the sons of the founder of Rington's Tea. He had only gained his pilot's licence four days earlier, having trained at Cramlington Aerodrome. Encountering a combination of mist and rain over County Durham, he quickly lost his bearings. Attempting to make a forced landing in a field at Glebe Farm, about half a mile west of Medomsley, Smith stalled the aircraft just prior to touchdown. One of the Gypsy Moth's wings then clipped a stone wall close to a farm building as it hit the ground, overturning the aircraft and wrecking it.

Mrs. Armstrong, the farmer's wife, and the unfortunate pilot both ended up in the slurry pit, badly bruised and suffering from shock. Stories differ as to how they had ended up there. One version states that Smith was catapulted out of the cockpit, striking Mrs. Armstrong, who just happened to be standing outside at the time, and they both fell into the pit. Another tale has the farmer's wife being knocked into the slurry by one of the aircraft's wingtips, and after the machine came to rest inverted, Smith fell out of the cockpit and landed next to her.

Samuel Smith, pictured in the 1930s.

```
SMITH, Samuel,                                          13991
         17 Jesmond Vale Terrace,
              Newcastle-on-Tyne.


Born    8th July 1905        at    Leeds.
Nationality          British
Rank, Regiment, Profession  General Manager.
Certificate taken on   D.H.60G.Gipsy I, 85 h.p.
At      Newcastle-on-Tyne Aero Club.
Date         26.6.36
```

Samuel Smith's Junior Pilots' Licence. Note that the licence was only gained four days before the crash at Medomsley.

A local newspaper headline summed up the incident: *"Falling Plane Strikes Woman – Pushed in Pool with Craft on Top – Amazing Escapes".*

Flying was something of a family tradition. Sam Smith, Samuel's father, had been involved with the Newcastle upon Tyne Aero Club and had even been its president for some time. A founder member of the Newcastle Gliding Club, he had also invested in the creation of Dyce (now Aberdeen) Airport and was a director of Newcastle Air Training Limited. Smith Sr. also purchased two de Havilland DH.82s for the Aero Club, one of which was named "The Ringtonian". His son, Samuel, was the manager of Rington's subsidiary, Northern Coachworks.

The logbook record for "two-seater biplane" DH.60G Moth G-EBYV, showing its ownership by the Newcastle upon Tyne Aero Club at the time of the crash.

The wreckage of G-EBYV was photographed after the incident. Its proximity to the buildings at Glebe Farm is all too evident.

Although he survived the crash at Medomsley, Samuel Smith was not so lucky two years later. He and two friends were killed in May 1938 when their aircraft, Percival Gull G-AFGU, crashed on Brundholme Ghyll, located between Skiddaw and Latrigg, north of Keswick. Smith was piloting that day in poor weather conditions and may have banked hard to avoid high ground in front of him, resulting in part of the aircraft's rudder assembly breaking off.

DISASTER AT DAWDON

Pilot Officer Thomas Templar ("Timothy") Richardson served with No.607 Squadron based at RAF Usworth, near Sunderland (formerly known as Hylton Aerodrome). He was killed when his aircraft crashed onto the beach at Dawdon Colliery in bad weather in May 1937.

One of No.607 Squadron's Hawker Demon two-seat biplane fighters.

On 14th May 1937, an accident occurred on the beach Dawdon Colliery, one that involved an aircraft from No.607 Squadron based at Usworth and ended with the death of one of the unit's pilots. An official announcement on behalf of the Air Ministry was published in the 27th May edition of *Flight* magazine:

"The Ministry regrets to announce that P/O Thomas Templar Richardson lost his life in an accident which occurred at Seaham Harbour on May 14 to an aircraft of No.607 (Fighter) Squadron, Auxiliary Air Force. P/O Richardson was the pilot and sole occupant of the aircraft."

That evening, the pilot had been returning to Usworth after a cross country flight Sutton Bridge in Lincolnshire. He was piloting Hawker Demon K5690, one of the squadron's two-seat fighters. Encountering fog on the Durham coast, P/O Richardson circled overhead the beach at Dawdon Colliery, possibly in a vain attempt to locate a suitable landing spot.

Whilst flying over the beach, Richardson became disorientated, and the aircraft suddenly stalled. What happened next was recorded by the following day's *Sunderland Daily Echo*:

"In full view of a number of coal gatherers, Auxiliary Pilot Officer Timothy Richardson, of the Royal Air Force, attached to Usworth Aerodrome, was killed when the RAF machine in which he was flying solo crashed on the beach near Dawdon Colliery, Seaham Harbour, last night.

Mr. Richardson, who was a single man, 24 years of age, was the son of Judge Thomas Richardson, of Cliffe, Corbridge, Judge of Durham County Court and Deputy-Chairman of Durham Quarter Sessions.

Pilot Officer Richardson had been on a journey to another depot in the south-east of England and at the time of the accident was returning to Usworth. There was a thick fog at the time.

The machine, which was flying very low, appeared to nose-dive onto the beach and overturned. Those in the vicinity say there was a loud report and the aeroplane burst into flames.

A number of coal-gatherers on the beach threw wet sand onto the blazing machine and extricated the charred body of the pilot. The plane was a complete wreck. Word was sent to Dawdon Colliery ambulance room and a party of men descended from the cliffs, which are very high and steep, to the beach and brought with great difficulty the body to the top. The body was taken to Seaham Harbour mortuary."

The charred wreckage of Hawker Demon K5690 on the beach at Dawdon Colliery, County Durham.

As mentioned in the report, the coal gatherers had an unwanted close-up view of the tragedy. One of them was Martin Loughlin, an unemployed labourer from Sunderland:

"I heard an aeroplane overhead and looking up, I saw the machine coming towards the beach as though from the direction of the sea. The plane then turned southward towards Hawthorn, flying very low, and then it seemed to nose-dive onto the beach about ten yards from the water's edge.

I was about 300 yards south of Dawdon Colliery refuse heap, which is on the beach at the foot of the cliffs, and the plane came down about 300 yards further south. The machine turned over after striking the beach, there was a loud explosion, and it burst into flames. There were between 20 and

30 men gathering coal on the beach at the time, and we all rushed to the machine to render what help we could, but we could not get near for the fierce heat.

We threw wet sand on the plane and after ten minutes or so we subdued the flames to such an extent as to be able to extricate the pilot, but he was dead. The plane was smouldering more than an hour afterwards. It was a complete wreck."

Another witness to the incident was Sidney Horn, a blacksmith who lived in nearby Dawdon. He was standing in his garden when he heard the aircraft's engine:

"I heard a noise and saw a big flash of flame in the direction of the beach. I ran down to the beach where I saw the aeroplane on fire and men were trying to extricate the pilot. I think the petrol tank had been burst by the impact. The nose of the plane made a hole about four foot deep."

22-year-old Pilot Officer Thomas Templar Richardson was buried at St. Andrew's Cemetery, Corbridge.

URPETH FORGE CALAMITY

A line of Bristol Blenheims belonging to No.61 Squadron based at RAF Hemswell in Lincolnshire. An aircraft from the unit came to grief near Beamish in September 1938, killing two members of the three-man crew.

Bad weather was a factor in most of the cases included in this book so far. Another crash that occurred on 18th September 1938 added to the list, one that involved the crew of a Blenheim light bomber based at RAF Hemswell in Lincolnshire. Two of the three crewmembers onboard the aircraft were killed but the pilot miraculously survived. News of the incident was reported in the following day's edition of the *Hartlepool Northern Daily Mail*:

"Two members of the Royal Air Force were hurled to their deaths in a little dell in Durham yesterday when their machine, a Blenheim bomber, travelling through a rain and mist enshrouded countryside, crashed with terrific force in a field.

Their bodies were not recovered until later; as darkness was falling, local police and RAF men from Usworth were able to haul the wreckage away. A third occupant of the aircraft, the pilot, made a safe parachute landing. The two men killed were Corporal Henry Edward West and Aircraftsman James Stewart Grey. The officer that escaped by parachute was Pilot Officer A. G. Newton.

The accident occurred about 4.45 at Urpeth Forge, a group of cottages and a farm between Urpeth and Kibblesworth. The plane was first heard over Tinkler Fell, but prior to that, several planes had been flying over the neighbourhood, and no one appears to have paid much attention until a machine came down so low that occupiers of farmsteads rushed out expecting it to hit their roofs.

Several people in the vicinity stated last night that the machine was seen to turn over three times and throw the pilot out and his parachute opened not long before he alighted in the field.

In the conflicting reports which surged around the place it appears clear that the fog had brought the machine too low in a district of hills and dales, and the pilot had been attempting to land in a fairly big field adjoining the wood."

Once news of the tragedy spread, souvenir hunters descended on the site of the crash, their numbers simply too many to be thwarted by the single farm hand assigned to look after the wreckage of the Blenheim. Reports of their ghoulish behaviour appeared in the *Dundee Evening Telegraph* three days after the incident:

"Hundreds of souvenir hunters swarmed past a solitary guard into a field at Urpeth Forge, near Chester-Le-Street, to gather fragments of a plane which crashed on Sunday, killing two men.

Working behind a canvas screen, squads of men from Usworth Aerodrome removed the twisted remains of the plane to their headquarters. Their departure was the signal for the crowd to get to work. A local farmer placed one of his hands to guard the field to keep the people away. In spite of heavy rain, however, they continued to visit the scene, picking up fragments of the plane which the RAF men had overlooked."

An inquest into the deaths of the two victims was held on 20th September 1938 in the living room of Blue House Farm, Beamish, which was situated opposite the scene of the crash. As one of the two dead airmen came from Fochabers, near Elgin, it was natural that one of the newspapers covering that area would pick the story up. The *Aberdeen Press & Journal* provided its readers with details of the inquest in its 21st September edition:

"It was from this house that the only survivor of the tragedy, Flying Officer E. Newton [sic], the pilot of the machine, who escaped by parachute from the crashing plane, telephoned for assistance.

Pilot Officer J. Rawnsley Sullivan, of Birkenhead, who is attached to the Hemswell Military Aerodrome, Lincolnshire, gave evidence of identification. He said that both men were decapitated, and identification was made possible only by the uniforms the men were wearing and the private equipment in their possession.

The coroner said that it was impossible to proceed with the inquest at that stage, as there were innumerable inquiries to be made by the Air Ministry. He proposed adjourning the inquest until next Monday evening, when the pilot in charge of the ill-fated machine and a member of the maintenance team present when the plane left the aerodrome would be present to give evidence."

The inquest resumed on 26th September and a verdict was arrived at, as reported by the *Northern Whig* (Northern Ireland) newspaper the following day:

"A verdict of accidental death was returned at yesterday's resumed inquest on Corporal Henry Edward West (26), of Hemswell Aerodrome, Lincs., and Aircraftsman James Stewart Grey (18) of the Berks, Morayshire, who were killed in a bomber crash at Urpeth, near Stanley, County Durham, on September 18.

The jury exonerated from blame Pilot Officer Alner Charles Newton [sic], of Hemswell Aerodrome, who said that he was thrown out of the plane without knowledge of what height they were flying.

'Twice Corporal West and I were involuntarily thrown from our seats,' he said. 'We were flying through a storm and were unaware if we were upside down or not. When I saw it was hopeless, I gave orders to jump.'"

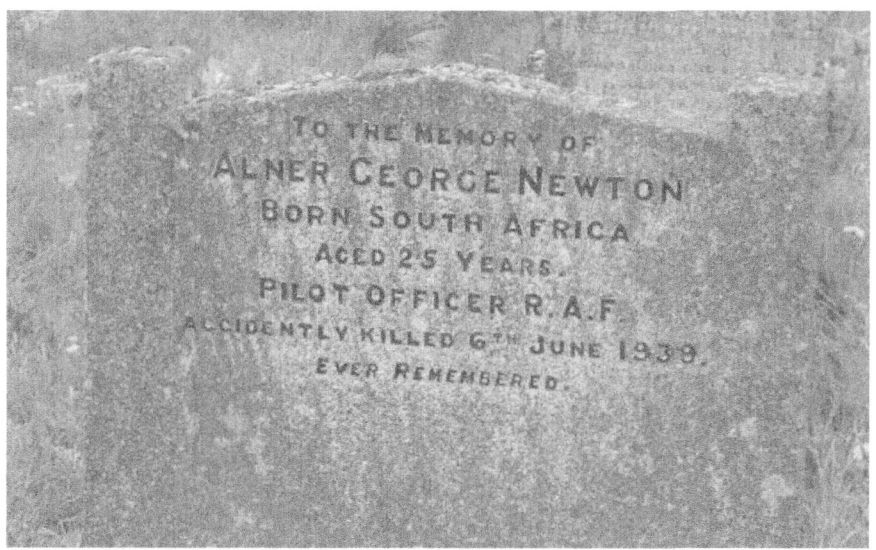

Alner George Newton is buried at St. Gregory's Churchyard, Seaton, Devon.

Alner George Newton's name had been given incorrectly in two different newspapers. He was born in South Africa but had grandparents who lived in Seaton, Devon. Although he survived the incident over County Durham, his luck would eventually run out. On 6th June 1939, he was piloting a Handley-Page Hampden bomber flying over the Tentsmuir Ranges, a practice bombing area located just south of the Tay Estuary near Dundee. His aircraft crashed into the sea during an air-firing exercise, with all three crewmembers onboard being killed. Flying Officer Newton was buried down at Seaton.

THE KING'S JOCKEY

De Havilland Dragon Rapide G-AGTM is pictured here at Kemble in May 2005. An identical aircraft, G-AERE, crashed near Ettersgill, not far from Forest-in-Teesdale, County Durham, back in June 1939. (Arpingstone, via Creative Commons licence)

Back in the 1930s, air travel was improving in terms of speed and comfort, and if you could afford it, flying to your destination in Britain or across on the Continent saved a lot of time and trouble. Unfortunately, safety needed a vast amount of improvement. Aircraft and their engines were unreliable, navigation was nothing more than compass headings, sighting features on the ground and if you were lucky, radio communications. Radar had been invented in the mid-1930s, but development was still in its infancy and the military naturally guarded it's use. Radar for civilian purposes had to wait until after World War II.

One of the most popular types used for passenger transport in Britain was the twin-engined de Havilland DH.89 Dragon Rapide, a biplane airliner capable of seating up to eight people. Although considered both reliable and durable, the aircraft (a faster and more comfortable version of the company's earlier DH.84 Dragon) was largely constructed from plywood, so still quite primitive. However, fitted with a couple of de Havilland's new Gipsy Six engines, the new design proved to be a huge success and over 700 were eventually completed.

DH.89 construction number 6355 was built in early 1937 and took up the registration G-AERE. It was sold to British-American Air Services Ltd. of Heston, Middlesex, on 18th March of that year. Although the title of the airline indicated trans-Atlantic schedules, the Dragon Rapide certainly did not have the range to undertake such flights!

John Crouch, the King's jockey, appeared on cigarette collectors' cards in the 1930s.

John Lionel Crouch was born in London in 1915. The young boy appeared to have a talent with horses. His father was a greengrocer and he looked after the ponies used to pull the cart to and from market. As a teenager, he was apprenticed to an Australian trainer, Stanley Wooton, at Epsom. John Crouch's name started to appear in newspaper lists of runners and riders in 1933. 1936 saw him riding no less than 31 winners, and in October of that year it was announced that he would become the King's jockey – at the tender age of 21. Crouch was paid a retainer so that he would always be available to ride the King's horses in preference to other owners. Over the winter of 1936/37, he travelled to India to ride in races at Madras.

On 20th June 1939, John Crouch was scheduled to ride at Newcastle Racecourse, located at High Gosforth Park, a few miles north of the city centre. He departed Heston Aerodrome near London at 1019 hours that morning in de Havilland Dragon Rapide G-AERE. The aircraft belonged to British-American Air Services Ltd. at Heston and had been acquired by the company in March 1937. Destination for the aircraft was the Newcastle aerodrome known as Woolsington, located to the north-west of the city.

Despite its name, British-American Air Services did not fly services to the United States and was only a charter airline that operated flights within Britain and to the near Continent. On that fateful day in June 1939, the Dragon Rapide was being flown by Ferruccio ("Frank") Appi. With him was his flight engineer, James Emslie, who came from Amble, Northumberland. Crouch was the only passenger onboard, so the aircraft was nowhere near fully loaded.

Passing York at around midday, Appi radioed his position and continued to fly northwards towards Newcastle. John Crouch was no doubt thinking about possibly winning on the King's horse "Mouzelle" in the Seaton Delaval Stakes race at Gosforth Park. However, as the time of the race drew near, there was no sign of the jockey. Worse still, his aircraft had not arrived at Woolsington aerodrome. No-one there knew where it was.

Indeed, there had been no news from the de Havilland Dragon Rapide after Appi's confirmation that he had reached York. It was assumed that the aircraft had crashed somewhere between there and Newcastle, and as a sign of respect, "Mouzelle" was withdrawn from the Seaton Delaval Stakes. To try and learn more about what might have happened, the authorities asked the BBC to broadcast an appeal for information about the missing aircraft, which was done the same evening. By then, it was too late in the day for an aerial search to be conducted and it had to wait until the following morning. The RAF sent out aircraft to search along the Dragon Rapide's predicted route, but nothing was found.

At around 1700 hours the following afternoon, two men found the burnt-out wreckage of an aircraft near the summit of Dora's Seat, Ettersgill Fell. Robert Redfearn from Forest-in-Teesdale had spotted something white on the hillside whilst on his postman's round, which led to the discovery of the charred remains of G-AERE. The full story appeared in a local newspaper:

"Teesdale was again the scene of an aerial tragedy when on Wednesday afternoon on Ettersgill Moor, near High Force, the remains of an aeroplane and the dead bodies of its three occupants were found lying on the hill side in a secluded part of the wide moorland between Teesdale and Weardale. It was later established that the aeroplane was that which vanished on

Tuesday while carrying John Crouch, the King's jockey, to Newcastle, with Mr F.S. Appi as pilot, and Mr J. Elmslie, as the wireless operator.

The first to sight the missing aeroplane was Mr Robert Redfearn, postman of Forest Post Office, who while on his round saw something white in the distance. He went home and got his field glasses and saw that what he had seen was the wreckage of the aeroplane. Later, Mr Walton, Lord Barnard's gamekeeper, become interested, and Mr M. Richardson, Middleton-in-Teesdale, who had got wind of the rumour, took his car up, and having no doubt that the heap was the wreckage of a plane, advised Sergeant Blake and P.C. Douglas at Middleton police station. The party then tramped from the end of the moor road leading from Newbiggin over boggy ground to the spot where the heap was lying and found that the aeroplane had been burned out after its nose had been embedded several feet in the fellside, and nearby, but clear of the wreckage, were three human bodies terribly mangled.

The inaccessibility by car to the place where the wreckage was found caused much delay in reaching the spot. The road from Newbiggin to Ettersgill, a typical moorland cart way, is not of the best, and when we had gone a mile past Moor House, where Mr Walton lives, there were still between two and three miles to be traversed on foot to the lonely spot on the hillside where the plane and its dead occupants had been lying for at least 24 hours.

It was in the weird half-light of departing day with the north wind blowing half a gale, and mist and clouds occasionally enveloping the hill tops that the task of moving the bodies of the ill-fated flyers was carried out. Sergeant Blake, of the Durham County police force who had charge of the proceedings, had secured a hay bogey on rubber wheels commonly called a sledge on account of its wide flat top, but this vehicle could not get within at least a mile of the place where the charred wreckage and the crushed bodies were lying on account of the boggy character of the ground. It was getting on for midnight when the bogie with its sad load was on its way to Moor House. Each body had to be separately lifted on to a stretcher borne by four men who when the gathering mist fell could hardly see a hand before them. They had to pick their way over the fenny ground to where the bogie, drawn by a sturdy dales pony, was waiting at the end of the moorland road to receive the bodies. The three parties of stretcher bearers occasionally lost sight of each other and one could only ascertain the whereabouts of the others by shouting and listening for a reply. At last the first party reached the stone wall which marked the beginning of the rough road to Moor House, where at nearly midnight the sad burdens were laid down in an improvised mortuary to await the inquest."

The 23rd June 1939 edition of the *Morpeth Herald* newspaper carried the following story about radio operator James Emslie's demise:

"There was a widespread regret and sorrow in Amble when it was learned that Mr. James Elmslie, an Amble man was one of the party of three who perished in the ill-fated aeroplane which crashed near Middleton-in-Teesdale, Co. Durham, on Tuesday.

After a widespread search the machine, wrecked and burned out was found on Wednesday night. The three occupants, who had all been thrown clear, were dead.

James Elmslie was 32 years of age, and his parents live at 19 Wellwood Street, Amble. He was educated at the Duke's School, Alnwick; many Old Boys will remember his cheery personality and pleasant disposition. He made many friends there, who will grieve at his untimely end. After leaving the Dukes School, 16 or 17 years ago, he became a wireless operator in the Merchant Service, a job which he seemed to enjoy. Later he transferred to British Airways, and about three years ago he joined British American Airways [sic] as their chief radio operator. He was clever and resourceful and had a bright future before him.

Sympathy will go out to Mr. and Mrs. Elmslie in their sad loss."

Wreckage of G-AERE lay near Dora's Seat, a secondary summit close to the top of Fendrith Hill, located between St. John's Chapel and Forest-in-Teesdale. All three people onboard the aircraft were unfortunately killed in the impact and ensuing fire.

With the aircraft being all but destroyed by the impact and its remains consumed by fire, there was little for those charged with investigating the crash to work with. Mist had covered the hilltops when the Dragon Rapide was flying northwards, and it was assumed that Appi had failed to realise how low he was flying or had strayed slightly off course and believed the ground below him was lower than it was. The probable cause was therefore listed as *"controlled flight into terrain"*. It is therefore likely that the pilot and his two companions had little or no warning of the fate that would befall them. News of the official verdict appeared in the *Yorkshire Post and Leeds Intelligencer* newspaper (1st July 1939 edition):

"A verdict of " Death by misadventure" was returned at the inquests here today on the three victims of the aeroplane crash on Ettersgill Fell, between Teesdale and Weardale, on Tuesday of last week. The occupants of the machine, all of whom were killed, were John Crouch (24), of Beech Way. Epsom, the King's jockey, who was a passenger; Ferruccio Sylvani

Appi (20), pilot, of Henlow Camp, Bedfordshire; and James Elmslie (33), wireless operator, of Amble.

Eric Raymond Taylor, chief engineer of British-American Air Services. Ltd., the owners of the machine, said he personally inspected the aeroplane, which was a De Havilland, and engines before signing the daily certificate of safety for flight. Everything was in perfect order and the pilot, Appi, also signed the certificate.

The machine was due to leave Heston about 10 a.m. It was the duty of the pilot or the traffic manager to obtain a weather report, and this was done. Appi was a highly skilled and perfectly reliable pilot.

Answering Mr. Andrew Balfour, representing the National Provincial Bank, Crouch's trustees, Taylor said it was highly improbable that the pilot had been cruising round for some time before the accident. Appi had informed Newcastle Airport that his estimated time of arrival was 12.25 p.m. The route was left entirely to the discretion of the pilot.

An Air Ministry Inspector of Accidents, Major S. J. Fill, in his report, stated that the marks on the ground and the distribution of the wreckage were consistent with the machine having flown into the hillside. It was evident the machine had not fallen or nose-dived to the ground. He found no evidence to suggest any part of the structure or controls had failed or developed defects in the air.

Major Fill said the weather conditions were not such as to stop regular air services, and the pilot had had a verbal weather forecast given to him. He was also in wireless communication with Newcastle.

Mr. Balfour asked for details of the wireless communications between the pilot and Newcastle Airport, and Major Fill then read several messages asking for bearings and replies from Newcastle which stated that there was haze, low clouds and that fog regulations were in operation there. At 12.11 the aeroplane received another instruction regarding its course, and a statement that fog regulations had been suspended at Newcastle.

In reply to a suggestion that Appi was exceptionally young for a commercial pilot, Taylor said Appi had amassed a considerable amount of experience and had had between 600 and 800 hours solo flying. Sergeant Charles Blake, of the Durham County Constabulary, Middleton-in-Teesdale, said a search for the missing machine was made on Wednesday, June 21. The fells were covered with mist and nothing was discovered. At 5.55 p.m. he received a telephone message that the wreckage of a machine had been found on Ettersgill Fell, and there he found the three occupants, who had been thrown clear, dead. They had all received multiple injuries.

'The aeroplane, which was burnt out, had apparently flown straight into the hillside. The appearance of the ground suggested that the machine had struck the ground 25 yards from the summit of the hill, ploughed it up for 15 yards, and then caught fire,' he said.

The place where the crash occurred was known as Dora's Seat and was 2,158 feet above sea level.

Major Fill added that these were purely normal communications to machines in flight, and there was nothing in the weather that made it inadvisable to fly.

Addressing the jury. the coroner (Mr. J. E. Brown-Humes) said the accident appeared to be a simple one. The pilot must have lost his bearings and crashed into the hillside because of bad visibility caused by fog. Until greater perfection was attained in air travel there was bound to be hazard. but there was nothing to suggest In this case criminal negligence, either by the pilot or the company. It was, In his opinion, purely a case of misadventure."

Nearly 84 years later, the site of the impact and fire can be determined from a scar on the hillside. Small fragments from the airframe still lie at the scene, small pieces of metal from what was once a de Havilland Dragon Rapide airliner.

LOST AT SEA

Lockheed Hudson Mk.I N7284 is pictured here on a test flight from the Burbank aircraft plant in California shortly before delivery to the Royal Air Force. The service purchased an initial 200 machines but nearly 3,000 examples of this miltary version of the Model 14 Electra airliner were eventually constructed. The first ones were delivered in February 1939 and by the outbreak of war, 78 were in service. This particular aircraft and its entire crew were lost off Seaham in November 1939.

War clouds gathered during the summer of 1939 and once it was finally declared at the beginning of September, the numbers of aircraft flying over and just off the coastline of County Durham grew massively. So did the amount of aircraft losses, the reasons ranging from bad luck, bad weather, mechanical failure, running out of fuel and enemy action. Squadrons and training units were robbed of valuable trained or potentially trained aircrew, plus aircraft which were always in short supply during those first vital years.

On 19th November 1939, Lockheed Hudson Mk.I N7284, which belonged to No.220 Squadron at RAF Thornaby, near Stockton, took off from its home base on a routine air gunnery practice sortie over a firing range located a few miles off Seaham. Hudsons had been bought from the United States to fulfil a requirement for a medium-range coastal patrol and anti-submarine aircraft. In the early years of the war, they proved to be extremely useful and versatile machines, and were subsequently used for training when replaced by more up-to-date types.

For such a mission, it is odd that only two crewmen were listed as onboard the Hudson that day. They were Pilot Officer Hubert John Keller, a 20-year-old New Zealander, and Pilot Officer John Whyte Crichton

Robertson, also 20. Normally, Hudsons had a crew of five, including a dedicated air gunner who sat in the gun turret mounted on top of the rear fuselage, just forward of the tail unit. It may be that for some unknown reason the remaining crewmembers were not listed.

After practicing firing the aircraft's guns against sea markers on the offshore ranges, Keller set course to return to Thornaby. For some reason that failed to be established, the aircraft was seen to crash into the sea and sink below the waves by witnesses onboard the armed trawler HMS *Dalmarron*. News of the incident prompted the Seaham Harbour lifeboat to be launched but no trace of the aircraft or those onboard was found. Later, a trawler reported locating wreckage from the Hudson but there was still no sign of the unfortunate Keller or Robertson.

As far as the official records go, the following entry appeared in their squadron's Operations Record Book:

"Met: little cloud: good visibility except in local smoke haze. Pilot Officer Keller and Pilot Officer Robertson (J. W. C.) killed in flying accident."

Because neither of the crew's bodies were ever retrieved from the sea, no burial ceremonies could be performed. Their names are therefore listed on the Runnymede Memorial in Surrey, which has the names of 20,267 men and women of the air forces who were lost in the Second World War and have no known grave. Pilot Officers Keller and Roberson were not the first airmen to fall into this category during the war and they certainly would not be the last.

GARDENING ON THE BEACH

A Handley Page HP.52 Hampden belonging to No.455 Squadron, Royal Australian Air Force is pictured here in May 1942, towards the end of the type's active service role in European skies. Back in April 1940, the type was still an important part of the Air Force's inventory. One of these bombers met its end on Ryhope Beach, just south of Sunderland during that month.

The Operations Record Book Summary for No.49 Squadron for April 1940 includes a brief entry which described a tragedy off the Durham coast. The aircraft involved was a Handley Page Hampden from RAF Scampton in Lincolnshire, serial number L4043, that was engaged in a "Gardening" sortie off the Danish coast. "Gardening" was the codename for dropping anti-shipping mines in coastal waters, the mine usually being referred to as a vegetable such as an asparagus or a carrot, which was "planted" in a specific area. The Operations Record Book entry read as follows:

"S/Ldr. Lowe and crew forced landed in L.4043 off the coast at Ryhope. P/O Bryan-Smith was killed."

More detail was found in the squadron's mission logs, located elsewhere in the Operations Record Book documentation for that month, provided by Squadron Leader Geoffrey Lowe himself:

"I took off at 1900 hours and set course down Corridor 'B' for the Target Area: the weather was extremely bad in parts.

Cloud over the target area was at 200/400 feet. The area could not be clearly discerned so it was decided to return to base after searching for 45 minutes.

On the way home, the weather deteriorated rapidly. Two fixes were obtained from Heston, but the second one could not be relied upon. From this period onwards the weather was very bad (cloud from 800 ft to 18,000 ft). All my Blind Flying instruments with the exception of the Reid and

Sigrist, went unserviceable. I changed over from pump to venturi but they were still useless. The only instruments available in the pilot's cockpit were the turn and bank indicator and the P.4 compass. Every time I wished to know what height I was, I had to ask my Navigator. Meanwhile, the W/T operator informed me that he was getting no reception on the set. Eventually, we managed to get through to Hemswell and asked for homing bearings, which afterwards proved to be inaccurate.

When the coast was sighted, I had left the Danish coast approximately four and [a] half hours ago. I could not identify the coast and by now I was beginning to mistrust my W/T slightly.

Whilst searching the coast for some prominent land marks, I found an aerodrome Beacon flashing a red 'D'. I flew over this and whilst circling round carried out the procedure laid down for requesting the direction to its parent aerodrome. No reply was given at all; SOSs were flashed by Aldis lamp several times and still no reply was given.

A red Verey light was then fired and a few minutes later numerous searchlights appeared to the North about 10 to 15 miles away. I immediately set course for these lights, realising that they were bringing in the searchlight organisation for me. While making for these lights one engine stopped but I managed to maintain a height of approximately 5,000 feet. After a minute or two's flying on my good engine, it began to spit and cough and came on in jerks. The aircraft was beginning to become uncontrollable, so I informed my crew to prepare for a landing in the sea just off the coast and I instructed them to collect in the compartment behind the pilot's seat.

I asked if any of them wished to jump out by parachute, but they all agreed to remain in the aircraft.

I made my forced landing approach up the coast, intending to land on the western edge. At 500 feet I put on my headlight, my wheels and flaps were up. As I was holding off to land, the aircraft suddenly swung violently towards the cliffs and rocks below them. I managed to correct this slightly but not enough to clear a bunch of rocks running into the sea. When I was holding off and practically stalled, I pulled the nose up and landed slightly on a tail slide with very little forward speed.

As already reported, before landing I had instructed my crew to all assemble amidships of the aircraft but owing to Pilot Officer A. Bryan-Smith being only halfway through the rear door, he was killed instantaneously. My navigator received very slight cuts on the hand, while my W/Operator received a bump on the head and was very slightly concussed. Myself, I received a split lip.

Despite his title, Squadron Leader Lowe was only one of the unit's Flight Commanders – Wing Commander Gillan was the commanding officer and had also flown on the same night (but to a different minelaying point). That night, Lowe's crew consisted of himself as pilot, Pilot Officer Kenneth Beauchamp as navigator, Corporal George Appleton as wireless operator and the unfortunate Anthony Bryan-Smith as air gunner. The 28-year-old was buried at Hylton (Castletown) Cemetery in Sunderland.

Anthony Bryan-Smith is buried at Hylton (Castletown) Cemetery, located on the western outskirts of Sunderland.

A rather blurry photograph of Pilot Officer Kenneth Henry Penrith Beauchamp, the navigator and occasional second pilot in Squadron Leader Lowe's crew.

Pilot Officer Bryan-Smith had not long been with No.49 Squadron, although both Appleton and Beauchamp had served in different crews in the unit for several months beforehand. They had gone on one previous mission together, on the night of 6th/7th April along the north German coast, encountering inaccurate anti-aircraft fire and searchlights. On the fateful night, only their second "trip" as a crew, they were one of three No.49 Squadron Hampdens to venture out over the North Sea. Two had no problems but Lowe's mission ended with the death of his gunner.

George Appleton, the wireless operator, had a secondary role as air gunner, as most members of his "trade" at that time did. Once his "tour" of operations at No.49 Squadron was up, he was transferred to a second-line training unit "for a rest". This posting was to the Central Gunnery School at Castle Kennedy, near Stranraer in south-west Scotland. On 27th July 1941 the Hampden he was flying as wireless operator/air gunner in for camera-gun trials stalled on take-off and crashed, killing all five onboard. Since the incident at Ryhope, Appleton had been awarded a Distinguished Flying Medal for gallantry in May 1940 and promoted to Flight Sergeant. His body was buried at the West Road Cemetery in Newcastle upon Tyne. He was just 20 years old at the time of his death.

Kenneth Beauchamp was awarded the Distinguished Flying Cross in May 1940. He remained with No.49 Squadron until November that year. During his time with the unit, he had gone on to captain his own aircraft, flying 38 operations in total, with nine as second pilot. He later served as a Squadron Leader (flight commander) with No.207 Squadron and then as a Wing Commander in 1945, taking charge of No.157 Squadron.

George Appleton, as drawn by Sir William Rothenstein and included in "Men of the RAF", published in 1942. By the time of publication, the airman had died in a flying accident in south-western Scotland.

Squadron Leader Geoffrey Lowe had been with No.49 Squadron since June 1936. By the time of his final "trip" with the unit in October 1940, he had flown 27 missions in Hampdens. He was presumably placed onto non-flying duties as he did not leave the squadron until February 1941.

The incident at Ryhope had not been the first involving aircraft from No.49 Squadron in the North-East – for the story of how one of its bombers crashed into a church in a small mining village near Amble, see my book *Northumberland Aviation Stories Vol.1-3*, page 121.

THE RED CROSS INCIDENT

What is believed to be the last photo taken of Heinkel He 59 floatplane D-ASAM, which belonged to Seenotflugkommando 3, a Luftwaffe air-sea-rescue unit. The picture was taken at Flushing on 30th June 1940. The following day, the aircraft was attacked by RAF Spitfires off the Durham coast.

Article 9 of the 1929 Geneva Agreement allowed the unhindered provision of humanitarian aid on the battlefield under the auspices of the Red Cross, which covered medical personnel wearing armbands and ambulances with the symbol marked on them. It would eventually include aircraft engaged on air-sea-rescue duties, provided they had the appropriate markings and did not carry out any other duties such as reconnaissance or photography. The agreement would be tested to its limit at the beginning of July 1940 off the coast of Durham.

The German *Seenotdienst* ("distress service") worked with naval units to pick up airmen who ditched or were shot down over the sea. Its aerial component comprised of *Seenotflug-Kommando*, air-sea-rescue flights that were equipped with various floatplanes and seaplanes. One of these, *Seenotflug-Kdo.3*, was based at Norderney in the summer of 1940, tasked with rescuing *Luftwaffe* crewmen over the North Sea. Most missions did not take place close to the English coast for fear that their aircraft might be fired upon, even though they were painted high-visibility white overall, wore Red Cross markings and also carried civilian registrations. In addition, their fleet of Heinkel He 59 twin-engined floatplanes were unarmed.

At about 0215 hours on the morning of 1st July 1940, a Heinkel He 115 floatplane belonging to the 3rd *Staffel* (squadron) of *Küstenfliegergruppe* 106 (3./KüFlGr. 106) crashed into the sea some 30 miles east of Whitby whilst its crew were performing a minelaying sortie. One of its two engines had failed, but *Unteroffizier* Siegfried Soest, the aircraft's wireless operator, had time to send out a distress message regarding their predicament.

Despite the *Luftwaffe* floatplane going down near the North-East coast, 9. *Fliegerdivision* Headquarters ordered that an aircraft from *Seenotflug-Kdo.3* be sent out to look for the He 115's crew. This was recognised by all as an extremely hazardous undertaking, but necessary if the three man crew were not to be taken prisoner or perish from drowning. The aircraft selected was He 59 D-ASAM and its crew consisted of *Unteroffizier* Ernst-Otto Nielsen, the pilot, *Leutnant* Hans-Joachim Fehske, the observer (the *Luftwaffe* term for navigator), *Obergefreiter* Erich Philipp, wireless operator, and *Unteroffizier* Fritz Stuckmann, flight mechanic. The pilot was outranked by the aircraft's observer, a common occurrence in the German air force.

Despite their supposed special status under the Geneva Agreement, He 59s from various *Seenotflug-Kommando* had been witnessed flying in the vicinity of British coastal convoys. Some of these sightings had taken place just before *Luftwaffe* bombers had attacked the vessels, so it was believed that the air-sea-rescue crews were radioing details of the ships' positions for targeting purposes. Whether this was true or not is unknown, but the suspicion was probably enough for RAF commanders to consider sanctioning attacks on such aircraft.

D-ASAM, which carried the manufacturer's plate *Werke nummer* 1994, had been built by Arado Flugzeugwerke, under licence from Heinkel, as a He 59D variant. It was later converted to an He 59N air-sea-rescue version by Walther Bachmann Flugzeugbau at Ribnitz and delivered to the unit on 26th April 1940. It took off from Norderney at 0305 hours on the morning of 1st July and Ernst Neilsen set course for an area off Whitby, where the downed He 115 crew had last reported their position.

Radar stations along the North-East coast presumably picked up the slow-moving contact as it made its way towards the area where the He 115 had gone down. No.72 Squadron based at Acklington in Northumberland was alerted at 0601 hours that a possible enemy aircraft was approaching the coast. *Luftwaffe* raiders had indeed been searching for isolated vessels to attack during the previous few months. These were mostly single Heinkel He 111 bombers, and a few of these had even been shot down. This was of course just prior to the start of the "Battle of Britain" and North-East England, although seeing some action, was on nowhere near the same scale as the other end of the country.

Clearly, Neilsen flew beyond the area where the He 115 had apparently gone down and proceeded north-westwards to a point just off the Durham coast near Sunderland. This sparked off a scramble from Acklington, one which involved Blue Section from No.72 Squadron. Three fighters roared off the airfield's grass runway shortly after the call came through. Flight Lieutenant Edward ("Ted") Graham ("Blue 1") led the section in Spitfire P9457, accompanied by Flying Officer Edgar Wilcox ("Blue 2") in K9959 and Flight Sergeant Harry Steere ("Blue 3") in K9935. F/Lt. Graham's two wingmen were flying somewhat older examples of the Spitfire, ones which were among the first ones that had been delivered to the RAF – but they were still potent machines, and much faster than the lumbering He 59.

Although not the aircraft in question, this photograph of a Heinkel He 59 air-sea-rescue floatplane shows its size and biplane layout quite well.

No.72 Squadron's Operations Record Book for that day describes what happened when the three Spitfires of Blue Section were scrambled:

"Blue Section were ordered off to intercept unidentified aircraft at 6,000 ft., 8 miles east of Sunderland. A few minutes later the height was given as 3,000 feet and later still as 'height unknown'.

At 0612 hours Blue 1 sighted a white two engined biplane with floats flying S.E. at about 500 feet 8 miles East of Sunderland. He circled this A/C three times until he was satisfied of its identity and recognised as a He 59. Large red, repeat, red crosses were seen on the upper surface of top plane and a black swastika on a red background on tail. Blue 1 then ordered No.1 attack and opened fire at 200 yards, closing to 30 yards with a burst of 4 secs. The speed of the E/A [enemy aircraft] was estimated at about 130 mph and it was therefore very rapidly overtaken.

Faint greyish smoke or vapour was observed coming from the fuselage as Blue 1 attacked; The E/A turned slowly to starboard as Blue 1 broke away and Blue 2 then attacked from 200 yards with a burst of 4 secs. The E/A was losing height when Blue 3 attacked with a simple deflection shot as the A/C wheeled to the right. Blue 3 fired a burst of 6 secs. Blue 2 began a second attack but only fired a burst of 1 sec when E/A landed on the water about 4 miles East of Hartlepool.

After Blue 2's first attack, Blue 3 observed a number of small articles strike the water. These he thought were fragments of the machine but Blue 2, on seeing them, thought they were small bombs. As soon as Blue 1 saw the E/A in the water he flew to the light cruiser which was leading a convoy in the vicinity and directed the ship to the spot. Meanwhile, Blue 2 and 3 circled the A/C which was slowing sinking, tail first. Three of the crew of the E/A were seen to leave in dinghy and row towards the cruiser, whose long boat took up its position by the sinking A/C which was now in a vertical position with the nose up and submerged as far as the trailing edge of planes.

No return fire was experienced by any of our pilots during the combat and the E/A took no evasive action. A long trail of oil on the water clearly marked the track of the A/C from the time it touched the water until it came to rest. A total of 2,590 rounds were fired. Blue 1 had one stoppage due to a split cartridge case. The letters D-ASAM were seen on the upper surface of the top plane of E/A.

Blue Section returned to Acklington and landed at 0700."

Flight Lieutenant Ted Graham was one of the flight commanders in No.72 Squadron. He is pictured here at Acklington in front of one of the unit's Spitfires which is fitted with glare deflectors just in front of the cockpit. These were installed to stop the pilot being blinded by flames from the Rolls-Royce Merlin engine's exhausts during night patrols. A starter trolley is parked next to the aircraft to aid starting during scrambles. (Unknown)

Combat reports from all three fighter pilots survive: Ted Graham's reads as follows:

"On receiving order from Control to intercept bandit [confirmed enemy aircraft] 8 miles E of Sunderland, I took 'X' Section off & bustered [used maximum throttle]. On the way Control informed me that bandit was close *in shore at height unknown. Approx. 8 miles E of Sunderland I spotted a twin engined biplane with floats, coloured white and with large red crosses on upper surface of upper plane, flying at 500 ft in SE direction. I circled floatplane two or three times close in, flashing the challenge. There was no reply & on my last circuit I got a good view of the black swastika with red background on fin and rudder. I ordered No.1 Attack at 0612 hrs & went in, overtaking very rapidly from above & behind. Fire was opened about 200 yds range & continued until about 30 yds. My incendiary bullets appeared to hit E/A & I saw faint greyish smoke coming from fuselage. Immediately the water below E/A was covered with splashes & this I took this to be petrol. As I broke away to port E/A turned slowly starboard & lost height slowly. I then saw No.2 & 3 deliver their attack, E/A settling on water during No.3's attack. No return fire was encountered, the E/A appeared to have both upper & lower gun emplacements.*

Leaving my 2 & 3 circling E/A, I flew off to leading cruiser of nearby convoy & diving low indicated direction of disabled E/A. Cruiser turned off in right direction. I then flew to coast & found that position of E/A was 4 miles E of Hartlepool. On my return to E/A I saw that she was going down fairly slowly by the stern. A rubber dinghy was launched as cruiser drew alongside. Three survivors were in dinghy which was rowed towards cruiser. Cruiser's longboat was beside sinking E/A, which by this time was standing straight up on tail, with trailing edge of planes submerged.

Blue Section then returned to base. N.B. A long trail of oil lay on surface of sea along track flown by E/A after attack was delivered."

There were other reasons to suggest the non-combative status of the enemy aircraft, as the ORB report detailed:

"No return fire was experienced by any of our pilots during the combat and the E/A took no evasive action. (...) The letters D-A SAM were seen on the upper surface of the top plane of E/A."

The registration had been written as "D-A SAM" with the space as "D-A" was painted on the port upper wing surfaces and "SAM" on the starboard one. Flight Sergeant Steere's combat report was as follows:

"Blue 1 ordered No.1 Attack. Blues 1 & 2 fired, I closed to 250 yards, the machine turned right, I had a simple deflection shot, the machine touched the water & I broke off my attack. The machine jettisoned several small articles after Blue 2 finished his attack (possibly pieces from the machine)."

Flying Officer Edgar Wilcox's original combat report also survives, being repeated in full here:

"No.1 Attack: I delivered one attack and fired a burst of 4 seconds from dead astern. I observed incendiary bullets going into enemy aircraft. After breaking away I saw E/A jettison some small objects which I thought were small bombs. I then delivered a second attack and was just opening fire when E/A touched down on water; after one second burst I ceased fire. At this time Blue 3 [Steere] was just ahead and above me. I continued circling E/A as it settled on water and stated to sink. Rubber dinghy was launched

with three occupants. A British light cruiser then appeared, and I joined up with my section leader. I clearly saw red crosses on the upper surfaces of top planes and the letters D-A SAM. A black swastika on a red background was on the rudder."

Fritz Stuckmann was badly wounded in the attacks. All four crewmen were picked up by HMS *Black Swan*, taken ashore and made prisoners of war. The aircraft was beached by the Navy so that air intelligence personnel could examine it for possible armament, mine-laying equipment or bomb racks. As far as can be determined, D-ASAM was unarmed, but the aircraft had been flying some distance beyond the potential search area for the missing *Luftwaffe* crewmen.

Naturally, when captured, *Leutnant* Fehske protested about how he and his crewmembers had been attacked by the RAF when they were flying in an aircraft marked with red crosses. News of the incident made headlines the same day, with the *Hartlepool Northern Daily Mail* being one of several local newspapers to carry the story. It is interesting to see what information was left out of the account and which details appear to have been changed or embellished, when compared with the official squadron records:

"Aircraft of the Fighter Command intercepted an enemy seaplane off the North-East England coast this morning and shot it down into the sea.

This was announced by the Air Ministry at noon today. Its crew of four were picked up, one injured, and brought to the shore.

A second raider, over after last night's 'desultory attacks' on Britain – this is how they are officially described – was attacked but flying low to avoid the shellfire. It reached the coast and was chased out to sea by three Spitfires, before noon today in the North-East England area.

The four rescued airmen were sighted floating in a rubber dinghy. They had been adrift about four and a half hours. One, who spoke a little English, asked for a cigarette. The pilot, a heavily built man, still wearing his flying outfit, smiled broadly at a section of the crowd as he left."

He 59 D-ASAM had been the first to suffer at the hands of RAF fighter pilots, but it would not be the last. Another He 59 was lost just eight days later, this time off Kent. The aircraft was forced down by British pilots, its crew beaching it on a sand bank. After capture, it was examined by RAF personnel. They found the pilot's log, which had notes of the position and direction taken by British naval convoys – something which was in direct contravention of the 1929 Geneva Agreement. The Air Ministry spared no time in issuing a briefing notice ordering pilots to shoot down German air-sea-rescue aircraft wherever they were seen. Fehske and his colleagues had been extremely lucky to survive.

BLACK THURSDAY OVER COUNTY DURHAM

A He 111 belonging to KG 26 is pictured here flying over Norway. Aircraft from this Kampfgeschwader were part of a large formation of aircraft that attempted to raid targets in the North-East of England on 15th August 1940. German Air Intelligence believed that the RAF fighter force in the region had been stripped of fighters in order to shore up the defenders based in South-Eastern England. Events would prove their assessment to be wildly inaccurate.

In early August 1940, the *Luftwaffe's* air intelligence branch fooled itself into thinking that RAF fighter defences based in the North-East of England had been reduced to practically nothing. This assumption was due to their belief that aircraft must have been sent south to bolster the squadrons tackling German raids over the South Coast. Their thinking may have been clouded by the fact that, unlike the RAF, the *Luftwaffe* did not "rest" its fighter pilots by rotating them out of the line every so often. Senior staff *Luftwaffe* intelligence officers were therefore convinced that No.13 Group, responsible for the air defence of Scotland and North-East England, had very few operational fighters. The fact that *Luftwaffe* bombers had been flying just offshore and over the region for the past month or so largely free of interception by RAF fighters may have also reinforced those beliefs. However, whatever the reasons, it was decided that the time was now right to mount a large attack on the North-East on the morning of 15th August.

Luftflotte 5 ("Air Fleet 5") based in Norway and Denmark were selected to provide the Heinkel He 111 medium bombers that would comprise the force's attack element. However, unlike the battles over the Channel, the bombers would be denied the protection of their fighter escort of single-engined Messerschmitts. The Bf 109E simply did not have the range to fly across the North Sea from Norway or Denmark to the North-East, loiter for enough time to defend the bombers and then return to base safely, even with drop tanks fitted, which were not in regular use at that time. Instead, the Heinkels would have to rely upon larger, twin-engined "escort" fighters. Whilst the Messerschmitt Bf 110 was designed as a multi-purpose, long-range fighter, and was used to good effect in Poland and Norway, its lack of agility was discovered to be a weakness, one exploited during the early phase of the Battle of Britain. It reached the point where Bf 110s needed their own escorting single-seat fighters, but as *Luftwaffe* air intelligence believed the RAF air defences were weak, they did not believe their aircraft would meet serious opposition. This would prove to be a fatal error.

Some 63 Heinkel He 111H bombers from *Kampfgeschwader 26 "Löwe"* (KG 26, or "Bomber Wing 26 'Lion'") had been prepared at Stavanger-Sola airbase in Norway. Primary targets for the bombers were the aerodromes at Dishforth and Leeming in North Yorkshire, with secondary aiming points listed as Newcastle, Sunderland and also Middlesbrough if the former were hidden by bad weather. Each Heinkel carried 2,000 kg of bombs, a mixture of high-explosive and incendiary devices. From the identities of the aircraft shot down off the North-East coast, the bombers were drawn from at least three separate *Staffeln* from KG 26 - 1./KG 26, 8./KG 26 and 9./KG 26.

One of Zerstörergeschwader 76's Messerschmitt Bf 110 heavy fighters with its distinctive "shark's mouth" nose insignia. Note the long cockpit in which two or three crew could be easily accommodated. (Bundesarchiv, Bild 101I-382-0211-011 / Wundshammer, Benno / CC-BY-SA 3.0)

A smaller force of around 40 Junkers Ju 88D bombers belonging to *Kampfgeschwader 30* were also part of the attack. Other aircraft from this bomber wing comprised part of another formation that flew independently towards targets located in East Yorkshire.

The Messerschmitt Bf 110D escorts were drawn from *I. Gruppe, Zerstörergeschwader 76* (I./ZG 76, "1st Group of Destroyer-Fighter Wing 76") based at Stavanger-Forus aerodrome. I./ZG 76 was made up of three *Staffeln*, 1./ZG76, 2./ZG 76 and 3./ZG76, plus a *Stabschwarm* ("Staff flight"). All four elements would lose aircraft and crews on that fateful morning. Some 21 Bf 110s were allocated to the raid, and the combined number of German bombers and fighters was in the region of 125. Given that their air intelligence believed there would be little if any opposition, the *Luftwaffe* commanders must have thought this was an overwhelming show of force.

However, as far as the mission itself went, things started to go awry from an early stage. After the bombers and fighters had assembled into their unit formations and were proceeding across the North Sea, whoever determined their overall navigation was at serious fault. Instead of the planned landfall between Sunderland and Middlesbrough, from where some would wheel south and then attack Yorkshire bases, their actual route took them directly towards the Farne Islands, some 70 miles to the north. The *Luftwaffe* formation was still well to the east of the islands when it was picked up by radar and the alert was immediately raised. At Acklington, every available Spitfire from No.72 Squadron was ordered into the air. No.79 Squadron's Hurricanes were also readied for action, and the Spitfires were to have further back up from aircraft based at Drem (No.605 Squadron) and Usworth (No.607 Squadron), which would also be thrown into the coming battle. Before describing the latter unit's part in Black Thursday, the events that led up to its participation should be summarised.

No less than 11 Spitfires from No.72 Squadron at Acklington were soon airborne after the call to scramble came through. All of their pilots would claim German aircraft as damaged, destroyed or "probables" - intense air battles occurring all the way down the Northumberland coast from a point off the Farne Islands down to Tynemouth. Rather than actively defending the Heinkels, the crews of the Bf 110 escorts had formed themselves into a tight defensive circle, which had become standard *Luftwaffe* doctrine for this type when it came under sustained attack from an overwhelming force. Although the types of aircraft had been misidentified in the heat of battle, the circle was referred to by Flight Lieutenant Smith, who as "Red Leader" was at the head of the four Spitfires immediately behind the front three:

"When sighting E/A, Leader ordered attack. Red Section formed echelon starboard and attacked rear section of 6 Ju 88. Red 1 [Smith] opened fire at about 250 yards and closed to 100 yards. Port engine observed to smoke & bits fell away from fuselage. Broke away and fired burst at another a/c which caused several bits to fall from E/A. The a/c dived steeply, apparently seriously damaged and Red 1 broke away. Red 1 then attacked rear a/c of 6 Ju 88 flying in circle. Upon closing to approx. 50 yds, E/A exploded. Attack broken off and Me 110 sighted attacking head on. Short burst fired at E/A with no visible result. Red 1 then attacked rear a/c of circle of 6 Me 110s, firing remainder of rounds with no visible effect. Rounds then expended so returned to base."

The Bf 110 escorts were clearly completely ineffectual in the battle, their crews concentrating on their own survival rather than looking after the bombers, which were left to fend for themselves. At about this time, the formation split into three separate groups. One flew down the coast whilst the other two made landfall, the first near Amble and the second further south. Meanwhile, the pilots of the rearguard of four Spitfires from No.72 Squadron had established that there were no escorts apart from the Bf 110s, so decided to attack them.

A Messerschmitt Bf 110D heavy fighter pictured with a jettisonable Dackelbäuch ("Dachshund belly") fuel tank fitted underneath the aircraft. Although streamlined, the extra tank created drag and was unpopular with crews. A Luftwaffe group commander was killed on 15th August 1940 when his Dackelbäuch release mechanism jammed. The aircraft exploded when the tank was struck by machine gun fire. (Crown Copyright expired)

The *Luftwaffe* Bf 110 escorts had large, jettisonable fuel tanks fitted under their fuselages. These were bulbous in shape and extended from halfway underneath the nose to a point directly below the rear of the long cockpit canopy and could carry 1,050 litres of fuel. It created plenty of additional "drag" on the airframe and the German crews nicknamed the tanks *Dackelbäuche* ("Dachshunds' bellies") due to their appearance. The aircraft were carrying two crewmen each, as the loss reports indicate. The second member was a wireless operator who also acted as a gunner, a machine gun being fitted in the cockpit's rear. However, it is possible that these weapons were removed to save weight and increase range for this mission. *Hauptmann* Restmeyer, one of the Bf 110 pilots, was unable to release his *Dackelbäuch* and it exploded by hit by machine gun fire.

It had not been a good day for the *Luftwaffe* crews assigned to this mission. No.72 Squadron, having expended their ammunition, had to return to Acklington to refuel and re-arm, allowing the German formations to carry on southwards. Any thoughts that this was the end of the RAF response were quickly dispelled though. No.79 Squadron's Hurricanes were also airborne from Acklington and soon entered the fray. Their pilots spotted around 60 bombers flying south over the sea off Amble, plus a group of Bf 110s which were attacked, two being shot down. Approaching Newcastle, the squadron encountered a large formation of enemy aircraft which they engaged. One of the Hurricanes was damaged, but no less than three He 111s were claimed as shot down. The Germans were paying a heavy price for the faulty air intelligence that they had used in the mission planning.

No.605 Squadron, based up at Drem near North Berwick, also scrambled fighters, which were vectored towards the engagement. "B" Flight's Hurricanes joined the air battle near Newcastle and its pilots claimed seven confirmed "kills", Flight Lieutenant McKellar bagging three. "A" Flight were also dispatched but failed to make contact with the enemy.

The *Luftwaffe* attacking force and its ineffective defenders had already been mauled by the time the surviving machines reached the Tynemouth area. Now it was the turn of the Hawker Hurricanes from No.607 (County of Durham) Squadron, based at RAF Usworth.

Flight Lieutenant W. F. Blackadder pictured at the time of his wedding in Sunderland in November 1940.

No.607 (County of Durham) Squadron's crest. The unit belonged to the Royal Auxiliary Air Force and had been formed in March 1930, equipped with Westland Wapiti light bombers. In 1936, its role changed to that of a fighter squadron and the Wapitis were exchanged for Hawker Demon biplanes. In December 1938, No.607 Squadron received the much faster Gloster Gladiator single-seat biplane, but these proved to be outclassed by most Luftwaffe monoplane fighters once war broke out. Deployed to France in November 1939, the unit received its first Hurricanes in March 1940 and flew the type until September 1943, after its move to India.

Acting Flight Lieutenant Blackadder poses with other pilots from No.607 Squadron in front of one of the unit's Hurricane fighters at Tangmere in autumn 1940.

As the *Luftwaffe* formations, somewhat depleted in their numbers, neared Tynemouth, the order was given. 14 Hurricanes clawed their way into the air, split up into five separate sections. These were as follows:

"A" Flight, No.607 Squadron:
    Red Section:
        Red 1:   Acting Flight Lieutenant W. F. Blackadder
        Red 2:   Pilot Officer C. H. E. Welford
        Red 3:   Sergeant W. G. Cunnington
    Yellow Section:
        Yellow 1:   Flying Officer W. E. Gore, DFC
        Yellow 2:   Sergeant P. A. Burnell-Phillips
        Yellow 3:   Pilot Officer G. J. Drake

"B" Flight, No.607 Squadron:
    Blue Section:
        Blue 1:   Acting Flight Lieutenant J. M. Bazin
        Blue 2:   Pilot Officer S. B. Parnall
        Blue 3:   Sergeant G. A. Hewitt
    Green Section:
        Green 1:   Flying Officer G. D. Craig
        Green 2:   Flying Officer W. H. R. Whitty
        Green 3:   Pilot Officer J. D. Lenahan
    White Section:
        White 1:   Flying Officer C. E. Bowen
        White 2:   Pilot Officer J. E. Sulman

Sergeant George Drake was one of three pilots from Yellow Section, "A" Flight, No.607 Squadron, which attacked the German bombers off the North-East coast on 15th August 1940. He was killed in combat with enemy fighters over Kent less than a month later, but his body was not recovered until 1972.

The pilots from No.607 Squadron were already at readiness, having been ordered to "Stand To" in preparation to scramble if the enemy came within range. There was also a real possibility that the attack, although large in terms of the number of bombers involved, was just a feint to draw attention – and defending fighters – away from the main group which had yet to be detected. The Usworth pilots were therefore held back until the enemy's true intentions were better known. At some stage, No.607 Squadron's pilots would be hurled into the fray to assist the pilots from their fellow units already airborne, and that point had now been reached.

No.607's Hurricanes were scrambled at 1315 hours as the German raiders flew past Tynemouth. The fighters engaged the *Luftwaffe* formations about eight miles east of Tynemouth. A graphic description of the defenders' actions appeared in the *Shields Daily News* the following day:

"About lunch time, the Nazi attempted an immense attack on the North East Coast. Two patrolling Spitfire and Hurricane squadrons caught the raiders before they reached the coast. The British pilots estimated that there were at least 100 bombers, protected by more than 50 fighters. These two squadrons engaged both enemy bomber and fighter formations, with the result that Spitfire pilots shot down eleven of the raiders and the Hurricane pilots seven.

A twenty-three-years-old Australian pilot, in action for the second time, had a remarkable escape.

'I went up with my section to about eight thousand feet when my hydraulic pipe line burst, spraying me with oil', he said. 'I immediately landed, jumped into another fighter and within three minutes was in the air again climbing to a height of 13,000 feet.'

'Through the haze I saw two large formations of Heinkel 111 bombers stepped up above each other. There must have been at least 30 in each formation.'

'I had to think pretty quickly. I picked out a Heinkel on the left side of the rear formation and dived down on his tail, spraying it with machine gun bullets. The Heinkel went down in flames. I then attacked a straggler. After two or three burst of fire this bomber also burst into flames.'

'Then across my bows flew another Heinkel. I fired two short bursts and when I last saw it, smoke was coming from the fuselage.'

Another pilot from this Spitfire squadron after firing a short burst at a Junkers 88, saw it explode in mid-air. The pilot believes his bullets hit the bomb rack. An Australian pilot whose life was saved by his earphones when he was hit by a machine-gun bullet during an action in December, shot down a Junkers 88 and a Messerschmitt 110.

The Squadron Leader of the Hurricanes said: 'It was a terrific battle. For a while the air was filled with diving and zooming aircraft. We caught the protecting Messerschmitt fighters about ten miles from the coast. Immediately we attacked they sheared off and they were never seen again.

'One of my pilots blew the tail plane off a German fighter. It was just like a balloon bursting. Pieces hit my Hurricane.'

The Heinkel He 111H-4s belonging to 8./KG 26 apparently had the airfield at Usworth as their target, although by this point the enemy crews may have just been looking for the first site of military or industrial value to hit. Two bombers were shot down into the sea before they even reached the coast, the first with three of its four crew being taken prisoner (the fourth died from wounds sustained in combat) and the second with the loss of its entire crew of five. The latter incident saw *Unteroffizier* Heinz Puschstein (pilot), *Leutnant* Wolfgang Burck (observer), *Unteroffizier* Hans Klug (wireless operator), *Unteroffizier* Hans Hoffman (air mechanic) and *Unteroffizier* Karl Lotz (air gunner) all being listed as missing.

A third 8th *Staffel* machine ditched off Sunderland after dropping bombs on the city. The aircraft had been attacked by fighters immediately afterwards and heavily damaged. The crew of the Heinkel, consisting of *Oberleutnant* Herman Riedel (pilot), *Feldwebel* Willi Scholl (observer), *Feldwebel* Paul Süssenbach (wireless operator) and *Oberfeldwebel* Karl Müller (air mechanic) all survived but that was not the end of the drama as far as they were concerned. D-AFFK, an air-sea-rescue Heinkel He 59 belonging to *Seenotflug-Staffel*.4 was dispatched from Norderney and managed to pick up the ditched crew. However, on the return flight to Germany, the rescue plane itself was attacked and badly damaged by a Lockheed Hudson patrol machine. The He 59 crew had to put their stricken aircraft down onto the water and so the 8th *Staffel* men endured another ditching. They also had to climb onto the wing of the air-sea-rescue machine to stop it from turning turtle in the rough seas. A three-engined Dornier Do 24 flying boat landed nearby in an attempt to rescue both crews but was itself damaged in the process. Now all three sets of airmen needed to be picked up. A cold night on the high seas was suffered before a German Navy minesweeper arrived to rescue them all – but the airmen had to wait until their He 59 drifted out of a minefield before it could be taken in tow. The minesweeper crew also picked up the Do 24 crew. The final ignominy was that the air-sea-rescue aircraft finally turned turtle as it was being towed into Norderney Harbour and had to be sunk by gunfire from the minesweeper to avoid becoming a navigation hazard!

No.607 Squadron claimed the following victories against the *Luftwaffe* raiders on 15th August 1940:

Confirmed:	6 Heinkel He 111
	2 Dornier Do 17
Probable	5 Heinkel He 111
	1 Dornier Do 17
Damaged	4 Heinkel He 111
	1 Dornier 17

No.41 Squadron's Spitfire Mk.Is had only arrived at RAF Catterick in North Yorkshire on 9th August. Their pilots had previously been stationed at Hornchurch in Essex and had seen plenty of action, so were due for a "rest" somewhere quieter. Six days later, their recent combat experience would be drawn upon once more.

As the depleted force of Heinkels and Messerschmitts were being attacked off the Northumberland coast, a call came through to Catterick: *"Squadron scramble!"* However, rather than head straight for the melee occurring to the north, their pilots were ordered to patrol the Durham area, to intercept any *Luftwaffe* raiders that escaped the RAF defenders over Tyneside and Wearside or were part of a second force coming in over the North Sea. No less than 13 Spitfires were airborne at 1235 hours, a great effort since the unit only had 17 serviceable aircraft out of a total of 19, and 25 pilots on strength to fly them. The names of the pilots and their machines were as follows:

No.41 Squadron, RAF Catterick:
Yellow Section:
- Yellow 1: R6604 Pilot Officer Bennions
- Yellow 2: P9428 Pilot Officer Ryder
- Yellow 3: P9430 Pilot Officer Morragh-Ryan
- Yellow 4: R6605 Pilot Officer Boret

Red Section:
- Red 1: R6756 Flying Officer Mackenzie
- Red 2: R6611 Sergeant Ford
- Red 3: R6885 Pilot Officer Lock

Blue Section:
- Blue 1: X4201 Pilot Officer Lovell
- Blue 2: N3108 Sergeant Howitt
- Blue 3: N3123 Pilot Officer Langley

Green Section:
- Green 1: N3126 Pilot Officer Shipman
- Green 2: N3266 Pilot Officer Wallens
- Green 3: N3162 Sergeant Usmar

The No.41 Squadron Operations Record Book reported that many German aircraft were encountered, and engagements with the enemy took place:

"Squadron ordered to patrol. About 50 enemy Bombers and 40 Me 110s were sighted and attacked. Enemy casualties, 4 destroyed, 5 probably destroyed and 4 damaged."

Hans Kettling, the Messerschmitt Bf 110D pilot attacked by Ted Shipman, set fire to his aircraft after he had force landed it near Barnard Castle. It was coded "M8+CH" and wore the Werke nummer (construction number) 3155.

Patrolling the Durham area at 18,000 feet, the No.41 Squadron pilots were awaiting the arrival of the German attack force. They didn't have very long to wait. Pilot Officer Ted "Shippy" Shipman and his section of Spitfires watched a formation of Bf 110s turning to head towards them:

"Before getting into firing range, the targets turned hard to port and came straight for us, closing speed probably in excess of 600 mph. One moment the windscreen was full of enemy aircraft approaching at an alarming speed, and then a second later the sky appeared empty as the Me 110 disappeared behind me."

Pilot Officer Edward "Ted" Shipman, who damaged a Messerschmitt Bf 110 over County Durham on 15th August 1940, one which came down near Barnard Castle.

Shipman and his section of three Spitfires had stumbled across the escort fighters of 1./ZG 76, including *Oberleutnant* Hans-Ulrich Kettling's Bf 110, which was encumbered by its *Dackelbäuch* fuel tank. The German pilot, together with his radio operator, *Obergefreiter* Volk, tried desperately to evade the fighters but their aircraft was at a severe handicap with the oversized ventral tank fitted. Shipman passed the Messerschmitt head-on and then turned hard to pursue it:

"Picking up another Me 110, which evaded violently in steep turns to the left with some climbing, followed by some diving. I then attacked the aircraft from astern at about 200 yards. This was a prolonged engagement which used up the remainder of my ammunition. The starboard engine of the Me 110 belched clouds of smoke and appeared to be on fire. I believe I had put it out of action."

A close-up of Messerschmitt Bf 110 W/Nr.3155's fuselage, showing the code letters "M8+CH". The "C" was painted in a different colour, signifying an individual aircraft within the 1st Staffel (denoted by the "H"), belonging to Zerstörergeschwader 76 ("M8"). The werke nummer (left) was not always so prominently painted. Bf110 W/Nr. 3155 ad force landed at Streatlam, a mile or so north-east of Barnard Castle.

Kettling had no choice but to put the stricken machine down in a field next to Streatlam Camp, just north-east of Barnard Castle. Volk had wounds to his leg, but the pilot was unharmed. He managed to set fire to his aircraft before they were both apprehended.

No.41 Squadron's pilots claimed the following against the opposition:

Destroyed: 4
Probable: 5
Damaged: 4

The squadron landed back at Catterick at 1335 hours. Shipman, Wallens and Usmar were airborne again on patrol 35 minutes later and up for a third time about three hours later, but no more enemy aircraft were spotted.

No.219 Squadron's Blenheim Mk.IF twin-engined fighters (light bombers converted into night-fighters with limited day operation capabilities), which were also based at Catterick at the time, were scrambled against the 30 or so Junkers Ju 88 bombers that were attacking Driffield and other airfields in North and East Yorkshire, but the actions that ensued are outside the scope of this book.

The numbers of aircraft claimed shot down was huge, although many of the bombers and escort fighters were attacked by multiple pilots and therefore the true number of "kills" was far lower. However, the Germans had just suffered a huge defeat without being able to inflict much damage upon the North-East, nor attack any of the assigned targets. However, they had caused civilian deaths, for some bombs landed on populated areas.

The survivors turned for home, many with damaged engines and others with injured or dead crewmen onboard. It had been a horrific ordeal for the *Luftwaffe* crew assigned to this mission and a daylight raid on this scale over the North East of England was never attempted again.

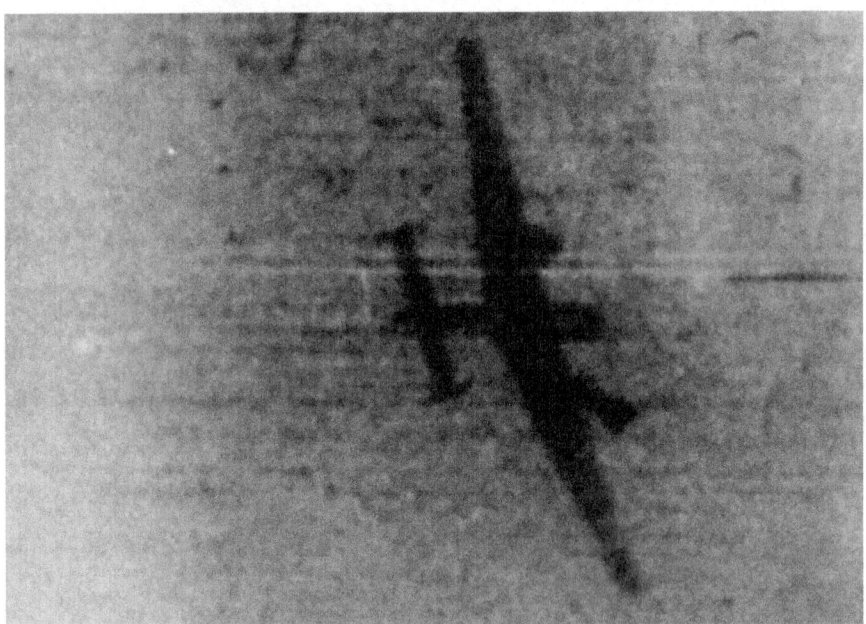

Pilot Officer Bennions' Spitfire was fitted with a camera which operated every time its wing-mounted machine-guns were fired. Strikes were recorded on a Bf 110 over County Durham, shown (not very clearly) in this image taken from the actual film.

8./KG 26, which belonged to the *Geschwader's III. Gruppe* (III./KG 26), lost no less than five Heinkels, the last being shot down into the sea off Middlesbrough. 9./KG 26 lost two bombers, bringing the total from a single *Gruppe* to seven. The force of Junkers Ju 88s from KG 30 fared little better in terms of the overall proportion lost. One aircraft belonging to III./KG 30 was confirmed as shot down and a further two crashed on landing at bases in Denmark and Holland due to the damage they sustained.

Pilot Officer George ("Ben") Bennions was serving with No.41 Squadron in August 1940 and took part in the scramble on 15th August 1940. His gun-camera recorded hits on a Bf 110D escort fighter. He had joined the RAF as an aircraft fitter back in 1929 and trained to be a pilot in 1936, joining the unit in Aden. Severely wounded on 1st October 1940, he lost sight in his left eye and became a fighter controller, serving in North Africa, Corsica and finally back in North-East England.

Two Spitfires from No.41 Squadron, with a starting trolley for the engine of the one nearest the camera. The unit used the fuselage identification code "EB-".

I./ZG 76's *Stabschwarm* ("Staff Flight") of three Bf 110s lost two during the battle, including its *Gruppenkommandeur*, *Hauptmann* Restmeyer, (the 1st *Gruppe's* commanding officer, responsible for three *Staffeln*). Among other aircrew lost included the *Gruppe* intelligence officer, *Oberleutnant* Loobes. 1./ZG 76 had a single aircraft shot down (Hans Kettling's machine) whilst 2./ZG 76 lost two and 3./ZG 76 three, with a fourth returning to base badly shot up by fighters. As far as the RAF defenders were concerned, they suffered only minor losses. A single Hurricane from No.607 Squadron had to belly-land near Hartlepool due to damage inflicted by defensive fire from one of the bombers and two No.605 Squadron Hurricanes were hit by return fire, force landing in County Durham. The stories of the latter unit's exploits during "Black Thursday" will be told in a sequel to this book.

NIGHTMARE ON SUFFOLK STREET

Although retrieved from a crash site in Dumfries & Galloway, the North East Land Sea & Air Museum have used the tail section from a Heinkel He 111 bomber to represent the wreckage that fell on a house in Sunderland during a raid on the city in September 1940.

Although the North-East of England did not suffer bombing raids night after night, something that Londoners became all too accustomed to over the winter of 1940/41, the region did experience some notable events. The author's own mother, who lived on a farm in South Shields at that time, remembered seeing German bombers heading over the coast, bound for targets across in Newcastle, and the anti-aircraft batteries situated along the coast opening fire at them. Indeed, Sunderland became the seventh most bombed in the country with over 250 residents being killed. For some residents of the city, 5th September 1940 would stick in the memory.

Despite the mauling that the *Luftwaffe* bombers from KG 26 had been given over the North-East back in August 1940, the Germans still believed that there were still sufficient reasons to attack Newcastle and Sunderland by night at that time. Night-fighters were still in their infancy and few if any were operating over the region each evening. Airborne radar was only just being developed, and none of the aircraft that did carry out night patrols in the North-East were fitted with the first sets. Pilots assigned to such sorties were reduced to spotting bombers caught by searchlights, although flying over such areas ran the risk of "friendly fire" from anti-aircraft batteries.

Anti-aircraft guns themselves were emplaced along the coast and at other strategic sites in the North-East, but there were always gaps in the areas that they could cover. Even when they fired at a bomber, it didn't mean that the enemy aircraft would be brought down. A lot of shells had to be fired for that to happen. As far as the defenders were concerned, their only "ace in the hole" was radar: the RAF and the army anti-aircraft gunners often knew in advance when raiders were approaching and could organise defences to the best of their ability. Yet bombers still got through to attack targets in the North-East, and civilian casualties resulted.

On the evening of 5th September 1940, the *Luftwaffe* mounted a large raid on Sunderland. Heinkel He 111s from *Kampfgeschwader* 4 *"General Wever"* were among the aircraft involved, and one of them would end up in pieces in a back street just south of the city centre. The 2nd *Gruppe* of KG 4 was based in the Netherlands, and among its four *Staffeln* was 6./KG 4, which operated from Soesterberg aerodrome. It was this squadron which lost an aircraft in so dramatic fashion over Sunderland.

Dockyards, heavy industry and transportation were no doubt the official targets for the raid but inevitably civilians bore the brunt of such attacks on built up areas. The September 1940 raid on Sunderland was no different.

Heinkel He 111P-4 *werke nummer* 3065 was one of the 6./KG 4 aircraft assigned to the raid on Sunderland. Coded "5J+JP" ("5J" signifying KG 4, "P" the 6th *Staffel* and the second "J" the individual aircraft in the *Staffel*), it had four crew onboard: *Oberleutnant* Hans Schröeder, (pilot), *Unteroffizier* Franz Reitz (observer), Obergefreiter Rudolf Marten (wireless operator) and *Gefreiter* Josef Wich (air mechanic). Both Marten and Wich were trained in air gunnery and would man machine-guns fitted in dorsal and ventral positions if necessary. Reitz would have been similarly trained and could fire the weapon mounted in the glazed cockpit's nose position.

The *Luftwaffe* bombers did not fly in formation at night but arrived over their targets in ones and twos. Crossing the North Sea from Holland was uneventful, but as Schröeder's Heinkel was crossing the coast just south of the mouth of the River Wear, local searchlight batteries caught the bomber in their beams. Almost immediately, the guns of the Grangemouth battery opened fire on the intruder, the shell detonations inflicting severe damage to the airframe. The Heinkel's tail detached as it dived down out of control, the aircraft itself becoming a mass of flames.

Werke nummer 3065 smashed into 55 Suffolk Street at around 2318 hours, less than a mile south of Sunderland city centre. As it did so, its fuel tanks exploded, which sent burning fuel and falling masonry on top of a garden air raid shelter, trapping the three members of a family inside. Mrs. Rachel Stormont was killed, her husband John injured and their 15-year-old daughter Jean losing both hands.

The bomber crew did not live to see a prisoner of war camp. The bodies of *Obergefreiter* Marten and *Gefreiter* Wich were found in the wreckage. Franz Reitz had presumably tried to jump to safety as the Heinkel fell out of the sky. His body was discovered on top of an air raid shelter located in Bede Towers, on nearby Ryhope Road. His parachute had opened but the observer's body had suffered horrific injuries. Schröeder's body was found in a garden on Grange Crescent, again having sustained huge injuries as his parachute had not deployed. The bodies of all four *Luftwaffe* crew were buried at Hylton (Castletown) Cemetery, where their gravestones can be seen today.

The two mainwheels from Heinkel He 111P-4 werke nummer 3065 (coded "5J+JP") lie in the back street behind Suffolk Street, Sunderland.

STORMONT.—Mr Stormont, daughter, of 55½ Suffolk Street, Sunderland, and relations of Murton, etc., desire to express their sincere thanks and appreciation to the directors, nurses, and staff of the Royal Infirmary, Rev. W. Walton, Young Women's Christian Association, Herrington Street Church Mothers' Union, Grangetown Women's and Men's Swimming Club, Sunderland; and other friends and neighbours, for kindness and sympathy shown during their sad bereavement, and for floral tributes. D

A thank you message printed in a local newspaper on behalf of Jean Stormont and her relatives in the wake of the Suffolk Street tragedy in September 1940.

There was a postscript to this tragic event 62 years later. On 14th October 2002, workmen carrying out excavation work at the rear of Deerness Park Medical Centre on Suffolk Street discovered an unexploded bomb.

The body of Gefreiter Josef Wich, the Heinkel's air mechanic, was found in the wreckage in Suffolk Street. He was buried at Hylton (Castletown) Cemetery along with his colleagues. (Author)

Work was immediately suspended. After the local police were notified and had cordoned off the immediate area, the Army's bomb disposal team was called out to examine the find. It was an *Sprengbombe Cylindrisch* 1000, a standard *Luftwaffe* thin-walled, high-explosive bomb, something carried by Heinkel He 111s and therefore very likely to have been onboard the aircraft that crashed behind Suffolk Street. The SC 1000 had presumably not been dropped or jettisoned as the bomber came down but had been buried by earth and masonry. As the bomb was not dropped, it was never armed and therefore did not explode on impact. The likelihood was that the SC 1000 was hidden underground during the clear-up operation in and around Suffolk Street. An assumption that the bomber had already dropped its lethal cargo may have been made – especially if no bombs were found in the remains of the Heinkel.

It was not a case of Army explosive "boffins" crouching over a bomb in a water-filled crater, with stethoscopes and pliers at the ready. When the experts from the bomb disposal unit had concluded their initial examination of the scene, they believed that detonation on site was the only solution. Of course, this was easier said than done. Although changed drastically from wartime days, Suffolk Street was still an area with residential properties. Trees and fencing were removed to prevent pieces causing further issues due to potential blast. Large skips were filled with a mixture of water and sand to minimise the impact of the explosion and situated to surround the site. In its 16th October 2002 edition, the *Sunderland Echo* printed the following story:

"Army chiefs revealed that an attempt to disarm the bomb last night had failed. The disposal team is now in discussions with experts and examining the options that could be used to end the situation.

Police chiefs have urged people to leave the area around Suffolk Street following fears that if the bomb exploded, it would leave a 25-foot-wide crater, damaging buildings up to 650 feet away.

The area was closed off for three days, the situation finally being resolved when the Army very carefully moved the bomb onto a trailer and towed it to Hendon Beach where it was remotely detonated. One can imagine nerves of steel being employed by the driver volunteering to transport it across the city to the shoreline!

NO.43 SQUADRON AT USWORTH, AUTUMN 1940

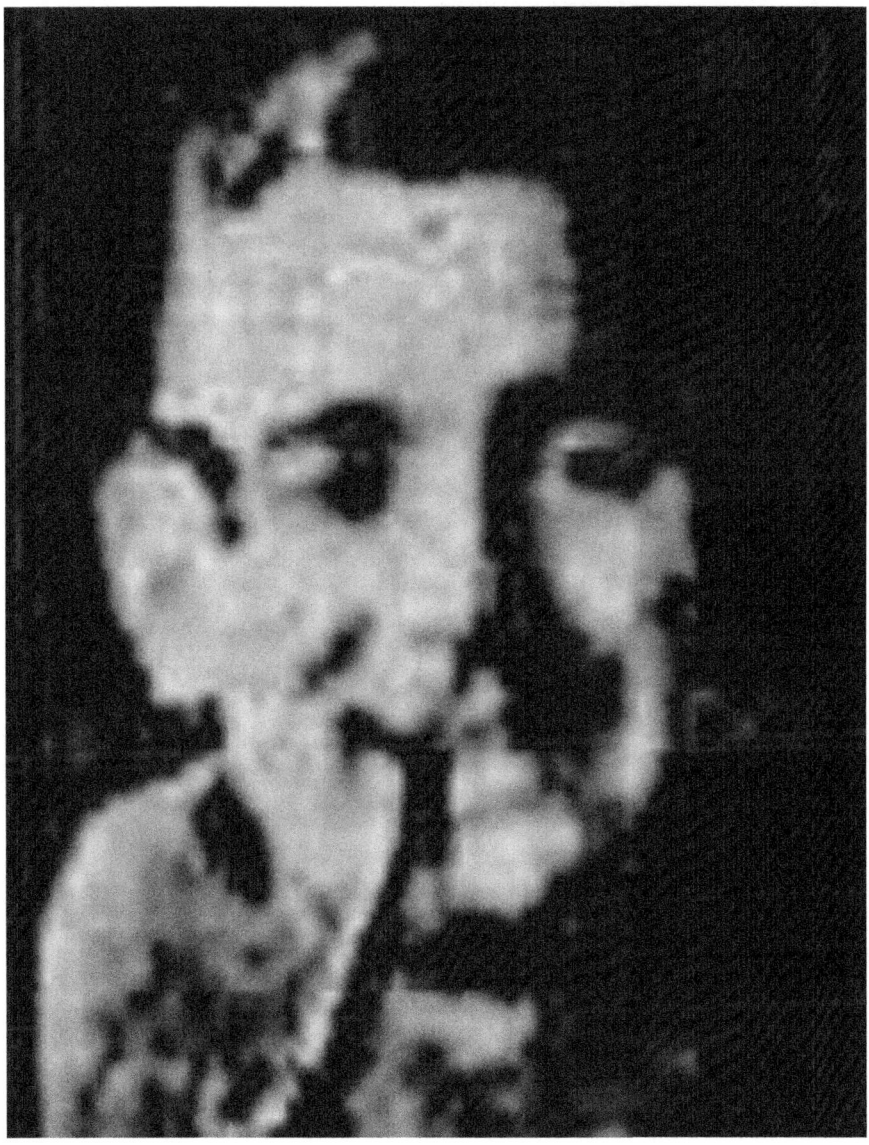

A member of No.43 Squadron, Sergeant Donald Stoodley was killed in a landing accident at RAF Usworth on 24th October 1940. This incident was one of a number that involved Hurricanes from this unit between mid-September and November of that year.

We have already seen how RAF squadrons which were in the "thick of it" down south during the Battle of Britain were rotated out of the line to allow their pilots "rest". No.43 Squadron had a particular difficult time as it was based at Tangmere on the south coast of England, slap bang in the middle of the daily aerial battles with the *Luftwaffe*. Its personnel were due a break and this occurred in September 1940.

11 No.43 Squadron Hawker Hurricanes moved north from Tangmere to Usworth on 8th September 1940. Pilots without fighters to ferry and ground crews were transported to their new home in a couple of Handley-Page Harrow transports belonging to No.276 Squadron. Harrow K7024 had arrived at Usworth empty on the morning of the 8th, in order to pick up 15 men, their kit and assorted tool boxes bound for Tangmere. The personnel were from No.607 Squadron, which was replacing No.43 at the south coast airfield. K7024 returned to Usworth, transporting 15 men from No.43 Squadron north together with all their kit and tool boxes. Harrow K6998 arrived from Bicester at 1725 hours with 20 more men from No.607. The Harrow took on 17 men from No.43 Squadron plus their kit, and flew north, stopping for the night at Doncaster en route to Usworth.

Pilot Officer Clifford K. Gray (centre) had an eventful landing on 14th September 1940 which led to his Hurricane being substantially damaged.

No.43 Squadron's Hurricanes had only been at their new aerodrome for a few days before losing one of them to a landing accident. On 14th September, Pilot Officer Clifford Gray got into difficulties arriving back at Usworth. His Hurricane, P2682, became caught in his leader's slipstream and he was unable to correct his machine in time due to an arm injury he had sustained the previous month. The aircraft landed rather heavily and was substantially damaged. However, once examined, the full extent of the damage was declared insufficient to scrap the Hurricane and it was repaired, then transferred to a training unit. Gray was unhurt.

On 16th September, Flight Lieutenant T. F. Dalton-Morgan was promoted to Acting Squadron Leader and assumed command of No.43 Squadron at Usworth. The same day, the remaining personnel from the unit who remained at Tangmere travelled north by train to Sunderland, and from the railway station there to Usworth by road transport from the base. Two days later, the squadron was activated in a "training state".

Flight Lieutenant John Simpson claimed a Ju 88 as a "probable" kill off Tynemouth, although there is some confusion over the precise date this occurred.

No.43 Squadron's pilots might have been classed as "training", but at least one of them would apparently see action almost as soon as they arrived in the North-East. An entry in the unit's Operations Record Book states that on 18th September 1940, Flight Lieutenant Simpson was flying solo as "Blue Section", patrolling around 20 miles east of Tynemouth. The pilot spotted a Junkers Ju 88 bomber flying east and decided to attack it. He claimed the enemy aircraft as a "probable" loss. However, sources usually list this "kill" as occurring on 30th November the same year, as John Simpson had been shot down and wounded on 19th July, only returning to No.43 Squadron at Usworth on 8th October, something also confirmed by the Operations Record Book. It is possible that another pilot was involved, and the name was written down incorrectly.

The squadron soon settled down at Usworth into a routine of training flights, air combat practice and formation flying. Some sorties involved the pilots landing at Acklington for a quick break, sometimes for lunch and then returning south down the coast. A few of their colleagues who had been temporarily detached to Tangmere and had remained there when their unit moved north, re-joined the squadron, and others returned from sick leave.

Pilot Officer Charles Langdon was involved in a forced landing at Hetton-le-Hole in the final week of September 1940. He was killed in action in February 1941 whilst serving in Malta with No.261 Squadron.

Another Hurricane was lost on 25th September 1940 when Pilot Officer Charles Langdon, flying P5191, carried out a wheels-up landing in a field at Hetton-le-Hole. The aircraft's engine had cut out due to the mishandling of a fuel cock. P5191 was damaged in the incident but deemed repairable. Langdon had arrived at the squadron with little or no experience on the Hurricane and had to be "converted" to (trained on) the type at Usworth. He flew just five operational sorties before moving on, becoming a staff pilot at an air gunners' school in November 1940, but only lasted two days there before joining No.145 Squadron at Tangmere. Pilot Officer Langdon then transferred to Egypt, ending up in Malta with No.261 Squadron. He failed to return from a sortie in February 1941.

No.43 Squadron's complement of pilots as at the end of September 1940 appears to have been as follows:

"A" Flight, No.43 Squadron:

Pilot Officer Chaffe
Pilot Officer Gorrie
Pilot Officer Gunter
Sergeant Jarrett
Flight Lieutenant Kilmartin
Pilot Officer Langdon

Pilot Officer Mackenzie
Sergeant Stoodley
Sergeant Twichett
Pilot Officer Westlake
Pilot Officer Wrazk
Pilot Office Yapp

"B" Flight, No.43 Squadron:

Sergeant Allen
Flight Lieutenant Atkinson
Sergeant Barrow
Flight Lieutenant Carey
Sergeant Cukr
Flying Officer Gill
Pilot Officer Gray
Sergeant Jeffreys
Pilot Officer Jerezek
Sergeant Jessop

Squadron Leader Morgan
Sergeant Morrison
Sergeant Page
Sergeant Palliser
Pilot Officer Pritchard
Pilot Officer Redman
Sergeant Russell
Pilot Officer Schwind
Sergeant Toogood

Squadron Leader Neale flew with both flights at various times, as did some of the other pilots. Wing Commander Thyne is also listed as flying a couple of aircraft from the squadron during the last few weeks of September, but it appears he was borrowing aircraft from the unit.

Several accidents occurred in October 1940, including the unfortunate deaths of two No.43 Squadron pilots. The first (non-fatal) event took place on the 10th, when Sergeant Josef Pipa, a newly arrived Czech pilot, was coming into land at Usworth at 1130 hours. The pilot had been carrying out practice aerobatics with Sergeant Ptacek, one of his countrymen who was also a new pilot at the unit. Making only his sixth landing in Hurricanes, Josef Pipa bounced on touchdown in a high wind, rising to about 20 feet before stalling and landing on one wheel, collapsing the main undercarriage. The aircraft, Hurricane Mk.I L2143, coded "FT-D", was substantially damaged.

Although Pipa lacked experience on Hurricane fighters, he had plenty of flying hours. He had trained as a pilot in 1938 and joined the Czech Air Force before fleeing to Poland when the Germans marched into his country in March 1939. In September 1939, when Poland was invaded, Pipa had to flee once more, first joining the French Foreign Legion before transferring to the French Air Force. Flying Potez fighters, he shot down one *Luftwaffe* bomber and had another classed as a "probable" before the French capitulation in June 1940. Once again, Josef Pipa had to leave the country, arriving in Britain via North Africa in July 1940, whereupon he joined the RAF. He arrived at No.43 Squadron at Usworth on 4th October 1940. Pipa survived the war, flew Spitfires to Prague for the reconstituted

Czech Air Force but returned to England in July 1946. He re-joined the RAF in 1952, converting to jets in 1955 and eventually becoming a test pilot with first No.20 and then No.33 Maintenance Units. Pipa finally retired from the service in July 1962, but still found a flying role as he became a tug pilot with the Swindon Gliding Club. He died in January 1977.

Sergeant Josef Pipa had served with the Czech and French air forces before he arrived in Britain in July 1940 to join the RAF. Having little experience of the latter's Hawker Hurricane fighters, he was involved in a landing accident at Usworth on 10th October 1940 – and a second exactly a month afterwards.

The first fatality occurred just a fortnight later. Sergeant Donald Stoodley, another recently arrived pilot on the squadron, had taken off in V7303 with Sergeant Jefferson in V7206 at 1825 hours on 24th October 1940 on a dusk flying sortie. Stoodley had already flown up to Turnhouse (Edinburgh) in the squadron's Miles Magister that morning and had returned to Usworth at 1630 hours, possibly to gain some experience or local orientation. After returning to the aerodrome from his dusk sortie, the pilot appeared to have trouble landing in a crosswind. He was observed to make six attempts to put V7303 down at dusk on the runway. On his seventh try, Stoodley closed the aircraft's throttle at 300 feet and put the machine into a steep glide, pulling out at just 50 feet. However, as he did so, the Hurricane stalled and then dived into an aircraft dispersal area located 80 degrees off the runway flarepath. Sergeant Donald Stoodley was killed instantly. Only joining the squadron on 28th September, the pilot was buried at London

Road Cemetery in Salisbury, the town in which he was born. Stoodley was just 21 at the time of his death.

No.43 Squadron's second fatality whilst in the North-East occurred on 27th October 1940. Sergeant Leonard Toogood took off from Usworth at 0945 hours in Hurricane L1963 to carry out "high flying and aerobatics". He was briefed to climb to a height of 25,000 feet before performing the manoeuvres. Either during the climb itself or once the pilot had commenced his aerobatics, other pilots operating in the same area saw his Hurricane entering a steep dive from about 20,000 feet, one which he did not recover from. The aircraft crashed into the ground close to Congburn Wood, half a mile to the north-west of Edmondsley, between Stanley and Sacriston. Sergeant Toogood's body was found in the wreckage. When the Hurricane's remains were examined, no definite cause for the accident could be found. Oxygen system failure was therefore suspected. The pilot had only joined the unit on 28th September. The 20-year-old was buried ay Kingston Cemetery, Portsmouth.

Another No.43 Squadron Hurricane suffered damage on 3rd November 1940. Sergeant R. A. Johnson, a pilot assigned to "B" Flight, took off from Usworth in P3809 at 1045 hours on an interception ("X Plot") sortie along with Flight Lieutenant Simpson in P2826 and Sergeant Sika in P3466. The plot turned out to be false or "friendly", as the trio returned to base just 15 minutes later. Simpson and Sika landed at 1100 hours, but Johnson may have had some trouble as he was recorded touching down five minutes later. However, "touching down" proved to be an event, as the unfortunate pilot suffered from what would come to be known in the RAF as "finger trouble". He forgot to lower the undercarriage and Hurricane P3809 belly-landed on the airfield, sustaining heavy damage in the process.

Josef Pipa was involved in a second incident exactly a month after his first at Usworth, although this one involved a forced landing well away from the aerodrome. On 10th October 1940 he was assigned Hurricane R4225 for several sorties in the local area. At 1345 hours he took off together with Sergeants Fiala and Preucil (the latter later becoming famous for defecting to the Germans with a Hurricane from Ouston in Northumberland) to carry out formation flying. He was back on the ground at 1500 hours and took off again alone at 1530 hours for aerobatics practice. Half an hour later, Pipa was back at Usworth, but his day was not yet over. He was tasked with flying a dusk patrol at 1710 hours, together with Pilot Officer Chaffe and Pilot Officer May. On the return flight to the aerodrome, R4225's engine failed, and Sergeant Pipa had to make a forced landing at Cold Heselden, near Seaham Harbour. The Hurricane was written off.

New pilots continued to be posted to No.43 Squadron and whilst their arrival was welcomed in terms of new blood, they occasionally provided headaches for the maintenance crews and administration staff, especially when aircraft were lost or badly damaged. Sergeant Wacław Giermer, a Polish pilot who like Pipa had served in France before arriving in Britain, might have been in this category. He turned up at Usworth in November and carried out his first flight with No.43 Squadron on the 24th, a sector reconnaissance sortie. A formation practice training sortie occurred on the following day, Giermer flying Hurricane N2665 in the morning. After lunch, the Pole was assigned a different aircraft, P3527, in which he was tasked with flying aerobatics. He took off from Usworth at 1430 hours on the 25th. At some stage during the flight, the Hurricane's Merlin engine failed and the pilot was forced to land wheels-up in a field three miles to the south of Usworth aerodrome. Sergeant Giermer was unhurt, but the aircraft was badly damaged.

No.43 Squadron moved to Drem, East Lothian, in December 1940. Its time at Usworth had been somewhat quiet in terms of intercepting German raiders but overall was certainly eventful.

THE MIDDLE END MOOR BLENHEIM

A line up of eight No.82 Squadron Bristol Blenheim Mk.IV bombers pictured at RAF Watton, Norfolk, in 1940. The large tail fin markings are indicative of the early part of the Second World War. A Blenheim Mk.IV from No.21 Squadron at Watton in Norfolk hit a hillside near Middleton-in-Teesdale at the end of November 1940.

Bomber crews engaged in operations over Germany had to contend with anti-aircraft guns, barrage balloons, night-fighters and equipment failure. In addition, there was also the weather factor, with winds being able to make aircraft drift off course and poor visibility denying the usual navigation by use of landmarks. Blind-flying aids were not in widespread existence by the end of 1940, and if crews found themselves over the Pennine Hills with a layer of low cloud below them, descending through the latter to see where they were could often be – and frequently was – a fatal course of action.

No.21 Squadron at RAF Watton in Norfolk was equipped with Bristol Blenheim Mk.IV light bombers. Although they could not carry a huge bomb load, they were available in numbers and therefore vital in taking the fight to the enemy's homeland. At 1715 hours on 26th November 1940, R3914 took off bound for Cologne in Germany. Onboard were the pilot, Sergeant Harry Collinge, his navigator/observer Sergeant Douglas Osborne and his wireless operator/air gunner, Sergeant Albert Moore.

Middle End Moor as seen from the B6278 Middleton-in-Teesdale to Stanhope road. Blenheim R3914 crashed on its eastern slopes at 2335 hours on the evening of 26th November 1940. There were no survivors from the three-man crew.

One of seven aircraft detailed to attack a power station in Cologne, Harry Collinge's aircraft appeared to be one of only three to do so. Three others bombed "military objectives in Germany" and the remaining bomber crew failed to locate any worthwhile targets.

On the return trip to Watton, Collinge's aircraft wandered well off course to the north. Landfall was probably made somewhere over North Yorkshire and their Blenheim flew westwards, possibly running low on fuel. The exact reason for their track over southern County Durham was unknown but just before midnight, R3914 flew into the eastern side of Middle End Moor, just west of the B6278 Middleton-in-Teesdale to Stanhope road, above Middle End Farm. The Blenheim exploded on impact and all three crewmembers were killed outright. As far as RAF officials were concerned, the following events had taken place that night prior to the crash occurring:

"The aircraft took off at 1711 hours on 26th November 1940. It was identified at 2031 when a bearing of 128° 1st class was taken. Aircraft requested QDM [magnetic bearing to the station] at 2033, no priority. DF [Direction Finding] Station replied QDM 318° 1st class 2034 and acknowledged by aircraft. At 2042 aircraft requested QDM, no priority, and DF replied 321° 1st class at 2043 and aircraft acknowledged receipt. On both occasions QDM had to be transmitted twice. Nothing further was heard but DF Station continued to call aircraft at intervals. No reports of Regional Control or other DF Stations having heard aircraft received."

A further note on the flying accident report reads as follows:

"In view of the fact that the wreckage covers an area of 400 square yards, a specialist officer's report is considered unnecessary as it could serve no useful purpose."

In other words, there were no sizeable chunks of airframe large enough to allow a detailed examination to be carried out by specialist personnel.

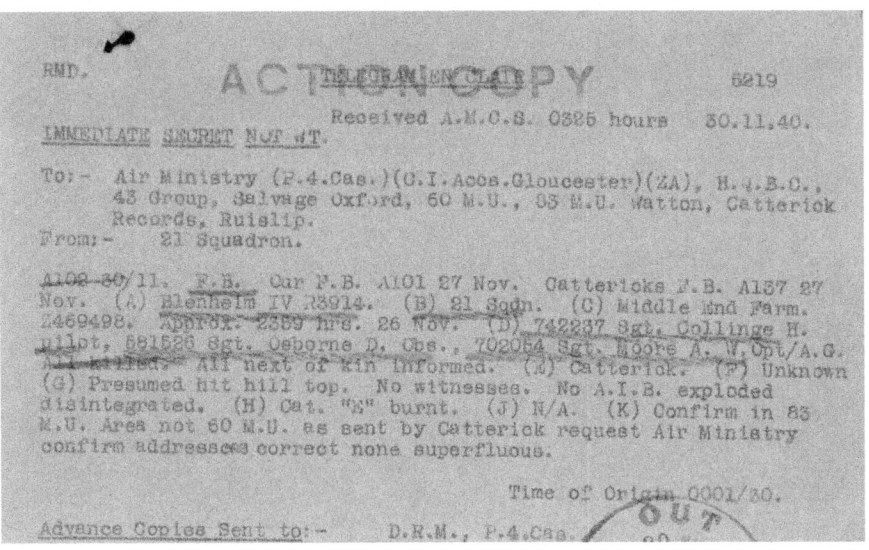

A telegram sent by No.21 Squadron to No.43 Group (Salvage) at Oxford, informing them of the loss of Blenheim R3914. The latter would have instructed one of the Maintenance Units under their command to salvage what equipment and materials they could from the crash site. As for those units listed above, No.60 MU, based at Rufforth (North Yorkshire), appears to have been originally requested by the unit the Blenheim belonged to, but the crash site lay under the jurisdiction of No.83 MU at Woolsington (Newcastle).

There were no witnesses to the crash that night, and officialdom assumed that the pilot had simply flown into the hillside at an altitude of 1,500 feet. As the aircraft had disintegrated in the impact, no real investigation took place at the site and the aircraft was officially written off as Category "E" (burnt). Middle End Moor fell under No.83 Maintenance Unit's purview. The unit was based at Woolsington (now Newcastle International Airport) but it is unlikely that much effort was expended at the site other than collecting the bodies of the unfortunate crewmembers, although there is a record of a piece of equipment with a serial number stamped on it being salvaged from the hillside. However, it is likely that this was picked up by local people or police officers who attended the scene before the RAF were involved.

20-year-old Harry Collinge had worked at Williams Deacon's Bank in Stockport before joining the RAF Volunteer Reserve. He is commemorated on a bank war memorial at Hardman Boulevard in Manchester.

Over eighty years later, some extremely small pieces of wreckage can still be found at the crash site. Some still bear traces of paint although the metal parts are rather corroded after their time out in the elements.

HUDSON DOWN OFF HARTLEPOOL

An unidentified Lockheed Hudson from No.224 Squadron, which operated the type on coastal patrol and anti-submarine sorties from bases in Scotland, Cornwall and Northern Ireland before converting to long-range four-engined aircraft. A machine belonging to No.220 Squadron at RAF Thornaby got into difficulties off the coast at Hartlepool on return from a patrol near the Danish coast in December 1940.

High ground wasn't the only hazard faced by RAF aircrew returning from operations over Occupied Europe and Germany during the Second World War. Damaged aircraft or those running low on fuel were susceptible to ditching or crashing into the sea, often with the loss of everyone onboard. Some machines were simply lost without trace or explanation. The crew of a Hudson from Thornaby near Stockton flying an armed reconnaissance patrol in December 1940 fell into this latter category.

No.220 Squadron at Thornaby was equipped with Lockheed Hudsons, which were employed in maritime patrol, anti-submarine and anti-shipping sorties over the North Sea. In early December 1940, bad weather curtailed the number of missions the unit could fly, but at 1050 hours on the morning of the 4th, a crew of four was assigned to carry out a sortie despite the poor conditions.

Flying Officer David Lingwood had been allocated Hudson Mk.I P5135 for a "Hornli" patrol, this codename using the first letters from the two end points involved, namely the Horns Rocks off Denmark and Lista on the south-western tip of Norway. These patrols were on the lookout for enemy vessels using the Kattegat or the Kiel Canal. Even submerged submarines could be spotted if conditions were right, and ones that were spotted on the surface recharging their batteries could be forced to dive when an aircraft was sighted. Depth charges could even be dropped on them if Hudsons were carrying such weapons.

David Lingwood's crew consisted of his navigator, Flying Officer Royffe Masters, wireless operator Sergeant Derek Taylor, and his air gunner,

Sergeant Edward Pritchard. They were all 20 years of age or under at the time of the mission.

By all accounts, the "Hornli" patrol was uneventful, and at the end of the mission Lingwood set course for Thornaby. Messages were received from Sergeant Taylor that provided estimated times of arrival back at base. At 1735 hours, a direction-finding signal was received from the Hudson – the last communication sent from the aircraft. Lingwood and his crew never arrived at Thornaby. In fact, they – and Hudson P5135 – were not seen or heard of again.

David Lingwood had trained as a pilot in 1938. His brother John also died on active service and his father was an RAF squadron leader. Edward Pritchard originally joined the RAF as an apprentice at Halton, learning a maintenance trade. Although trained as either an engine fitter, rigger or electrician, all highly skilled roles, he was selected for aircrew despite the obvious need for ground tradesmen to keep aircraft operational.

With no known graves, the names of all four aircrew onboard Hudson P5135 are listed on the Runnymede Memorial. No one will ever likely know what happened to them as they were returning to Thornaby on a cold, dark December evening in 1940.

HURRICANE HORROR

Pictured here is Hawker Hurricane Mk.I W9232 – a similar if not identical aircraft to Z7062, the machine which crashed on Parliament Street, Consett in August 1941.

John Heron Wire was a Pilot Officer serving with No.232 Squadron during the summer of 1941 at RAF Ouston, an aerodrome located to the west of Newcastle. Equipped with Hurricane Mk.I fighters, the unit was slated for a move to the Middle East in May of that year but had been retained at home for the time being. Meanwhile, its pilots were learning how to perform ground-attack duties in addition to air defence. As the war went on, the Hurricane became more and more obsolete as a front-line fighter aircraft, although its sturdiness compared with the Spitfire meant that it was suited to the ground-attack role and would fulfil that role for some time to come before being replaced by the Hawker Typhoon.

Learning the ground-attack role meant participation in what were called army co-operation flights, these entailing dummy attacks on road convoys, groups of soldiers on exercises and fixed emplacements. It would be one of the latter mock attacks that Pilot Officer Wire met his end at Consett.

On 30th August 1941, Wire and another No.232 Squadron pilot were assigned to fly an army co-operation sortie, the aim of which was to test the Consett defences. Although the town was well inland and away from any potential German coastal landing, it was home to an important steel-making industry and therefore considered to be a strategic location. Wire's brief was to carry out mock attacks on gun positions situated in and around Consett town centre. The gunners belonged to 205 Light Anti-Aircraft Battery, a Territorial Army unit which was part of 68 Light Anti-Aircraft Regiment. Formed in Cark, Cumbria, in December 1940 as part of the 7th Anti-Aircraft Division, 30th Anti-Aircraft Brigade, the unit was immediately moved to Tyneside but its elements were spread out across the region.

One of Pilot Officer Wire's duties during his fateful flight was to carry out a mock attack on a machine-gun post located on Parliament Street, just west of the town centre. However, witnesses saw his aircraft dive so low that its starboard wing struck the wall of sandbags that had been put up to protect the gun and the Royal Artillery soldiers manning it.

As the Hurricane's wing smashed through the machine-gun post, it hit Gunner Harry Seekins, decapitating him. One of his colleagues, Gunner G. Wilmin, and a civilian, Mr. J. Bell, were also injured in the incident. The aircraft then crashed into a wooden garage at the end of Parliament Street and burst into flames. Pilot Officer Wire was found dead in the wreckage of the cockpit. The No.232 Squadron Operations Record Book described the incident as follows:

"A fatal accident occurred today. 66493 P/O J. H. Wire was flying Hurricane I No.Z.7062 in company with another machine, in practice dive attacks on gun posts at Consett at the request of the Anti-Aircraft Battery concerned. He flew too low and hit the gun post, killing himself and a gunner at the post and completely destroyed the plane, which was burnt out."

The Station Commander at RAF Ouston, where Pilot Officer Wire was based, described him as *"an extremely promising pilot, though perhaps a little on the wild side."* Squadron Leader A.W. Pennington-Leigh, Wire's immediate superior, had the following to say about him:

"P/O Wire was above average as a pilot and had recently obtained a commission. He was a little bit 'daredevil' and I have had to censure him before for low flying around the aerodrome."

When the crash was investigated, it was found that Pilot Officer Wire had carried out several exceedingly low passes prior to the one that led to his death – and that the Army had not believed this to be much of a problem, at least until one of their soldiers was killed:

"There seems little doubt that not only the fatal dive was right down to ground level, but also several preceding dives. The Army seemed to have considered this 'a good show' until he hit the gun post, and I agree with the Squadron Commander that the Army could help by reporting flagrant cases of disobedience of orders, whether fatal or not."

The official report into the accident laid out a recommendation regarding future mock attacks of this nature:

"Recommended that the minimum height of 300 feet be increased to 500 feet and that the Anti-Aircraft Commanders should report any cases of low or dangerous flying. It appears that the Army do not object to really low ground strafing."

The Ouston Station Commander had his own additional recommendation:

"I also consider that a maximum angle of 45° should be laid down, since if a Pilot misjudges the start of the dive and gets too steep, even 500 feet will not be sufficient."

No.83 Maintenance Unit at RAF Woolsington (now Newcastle International Airport) were tasked with removing the wreckage from the scene. What little remained appeared to have been burnt beyond recognition.

Four days after the incident, John Heron Wire was buried at St. Mary's Churchyard in Stamfordham, a mile or so from Ouston aerodrome. Formerly a sergeant pilot with No.232 Squadron, he had become a Pilot Officer on 9th May 1941. When the unit's ground echelon was embarked for transport to the Middle East (which in the event never took place), Wire was detached to No.3 Delivery Flight, RAF Grangemouth, located between Edinburgh and Stirling. He re-joined his squadron at Abbotsinch on 19th July 1941, two days before it moved south to Ouston.

Gunner Harry Seekins was buried in the churchyard of St. Mary Magdalene, East Keswick, Cumbria. He was 35 years of age at the time of his death in Consett.

MASTERS MID-AIR COLLISION

Miles Master Mk.I T8559 was one of almost 3,250 examples of this trainer aircraft built for the RAF during the early part of the Second World War. Several examples served with No.55 Operational Training Unit at RAF Usworth and two were lost in a mid-air collision near the aerodrome on 30th December 1941.

Aircraft were lost through pilot error, mechanical failure and damage from enemy action during the Second World War, but another cause was one of mid-air collision. Though less frequent, when such events occurred there was inevitably more loss of life involved. One of these incidents happened in December 1941 close to the aerodrome at Usworth.

No.55 Operational Training Unit had moved to the Sunderland airfield in March 1941 from Aston Down in Gloucestershire. Its role was to train new pilots how to fly the Hawker Hurricane in an operational environment, preparing them for life on a front-line squadron. Apart from the Hurricanes, No.55 OTU also had a number of two-seat Miles Master basic trainers on hand, which were used to give the newly qualified pilots, most of whom had learned to fly on slow de Havilland Tiger Moth biplanes, experience of much faster monoplane aircraft of metal construction, fitted with retractable landing gear and possessing a fully enclosed cockpit.

Two Master Mk.Is from the unit at Sunderland were lost in a mid-air collision on 30th December 1941. Four newly qualified pilots who had started the operational training syllabus at Usworth had been detailed to carry out flights that afternoon. Their instructor, Flight Sergeant Goode, split them up into two pairs, Pilot Officer Arthur Kirby and Sergeant Leonard Wright being assigned to T8567 and Sergeants Peter Piggott and William Bothe in N8076. Their detail was to take off, return to base after 30 minutes and exchange seats. One man would act as Safety Pilot whilst the other was "under the hood", flying on instruments only without reference to the ground.

Clarendon Airman Killed

MELBOURNE.—The death of Sgt.-Pilot Peter Morphett Piggott, formerly of Clarendon, in an aircraft accident, is reported in an Air Force casualty list issued today, which contains the names of 31 members of the R.A.A.F. serving overseas.

South Australians included are:
Killed in Aircraft Accident.—Sgt. P. M. Piggott, Clarendon.
Missing in Air Operations.—Sgt. R. H. Nitschke, Hiltaba Station, via Port Augusta.
Seriously Injured in Accident.—Sgt. B. E. Hack, View road, Blackwood.
Injured in Air Operations.—Sgt. R. A. Borchers, Berri.
Previously Reported Injured, Now Reported Not Injured.—Sgt. D. G. Scott, Berri.

Sgt. Piggott's parents Mr. and Mrs. S. L. Piggott, of Clarendon, received advice that he was buried at Castlemaine Cemetery, Sunderland, England. He was aged 21.

Before he enlisted in the R.A.A.F. in October 1940 Sgt. Piggott assisted in his father's vineyard and later studied for the woolclassing diploma at the Adelaide School of Mines. In February last he went to Rhodesia to complete his training as a pilot and there he married a South African girl in September.

Pilot Officer Arthur Kirby was buried at Hylton Cemetery. Next to his gravestone, someone has placed a framed copy of a Canadian newspaper article from the time, titled "In England 5 Weeks, Arthur Kirby Killed". (Author)

T8567 with Kirby and Wright onboard took off from Usworth at 1430 hours, and N8076 with Piggott and Bothe departed 35 minutes later. They were seen to collide in mid-air over the Ford housing estate just off Hylton Road, at about 1550 hours. One crashed into the garden of a different house and the other into a residential street, all four airmen being killed. It was sheer luck that nobody on the ground was injured or worse. Their bodies were buried at Hylton (Castletown) Cemetery, where their graves can be seen today. Kirby, a Canadian, had only been in England for five weeks prior to the accident. Peter Piggott was Australian and had travelled to Rhodesia (now Zimbabwe) to complete his initial pilot training under what was known as the Commonwealth Air Training Plan.

THE RODDYMOOR CRASH: A SACRIFICIAL ACT?

Born in South Shields, Flight Sergeant Angus Roberts was one of two airmen with the same surname onboard Wellington DV841 that crashed at Crook in May 1942.

In May 1942, No.25 Operational Training Unit was based at Finningley in South Yorkshire. Its role was to bond newly formed bomber crews together and train them to fly and fight together as a disciplined team, for teamwork was often the difference between surviving or being shot down over enemy territory. Although not sent out on operations, their training flights ranged right across the length and breadth of Britain, with cross-country navigation missions being carried out at night, ones which usually involved a practice attack on a nominated city or town (the local defences having been warned previously). Some crews never returned, being the victims of high ground, bad weather or mechanical difficulty.

Vickers Wellington Mk.IC W5621 was identical to the aircraft that crashed close to Crook in May 1942.

On 21st May 1942, Wellington Mk.IC DV841 was readied at Finningley for a daytime cross-country navigation exercise, to get the crew ready for the night-time training flights that would follow. The training task was to fly over to the Isle of Man and return to base via a dogleg to York. This involved crossing the Pennines in both directions. DV841 was practically brand-new at the time of the flight as it had less than 15 flying hours "on the clock".

The crew assigned to fly this navigation had travelled across the world to fight the Germans in Europe. Two of the five-man crew were Australian: they were Flight Sergeant Rambler D. Roberts, the pilot, and Sergeant Rae Groom, the wireless operator (and second pilot in training). The other three were from Canada: Flight Sergeant William Reeves, the observer (navigator), and Flight Sergeants Angus Roberts and Robert Boates, both air gunners. At 27 years of age, William Reeves was the "old man" of the new crew. He had joined up in Winnipeg in January 1941, arrived in Britain in November and then died in a crash in County Durham just six months later. Angus Roberts had been born in South Shields, but his parents emigrated to Canada when he was very young.

The initial stages of the navigation exercise seemed to go as planned, and the return flight from the Isle of Man to York took Rambler Roberts and his new crew over the Crook area. It is possible that they were lost, trying to make sense of where they were from ground landmarks, as instead of flying south-east or south towards York, witnesses on the ground watched as the Wellington headed westwards towards Weardale at about 8,000 feet altitude. At 1755 hours, residents in Crook and surrounding villages saw the bomber heading south-east, flying over St. Thomas' Church in Stanley Crook. The aircraft was trailing smoke from one engine and losing height.

Suddenly, the Wellington veered off and headed south-west, as if its pilot was attempting to avoid flying into houses in its original path. A few of the witnesses believed that its pilot was trying to steer the stricken bomber through the gap between the houses in Crook and Roddymoor. Ernest Smooker was one of these onlookers. In 1942 he lived at High Terrace, Roddymoor, and had seen the Wellington flying over the church:

"They swerved out of the way to miss Crook."

Killed Overseas

According to word received by his wife, living at 120 Angus st., SGT. - OBSERVER WILLIAM REEVES, R.C.A.F., has been killed overseas. Sgt. Reeves joined up in January, 1941, and went overseas in November.

Ernst Smooker watched in horror as the Wellington bomber's trailing aerial caught a 30,000-volt high tension cable which supplied power to the local colliery. He believed this caused the aircraft to fall out of the sky, as it then came down next to Emma Pits Road, West Roddymoor, a mile north-west of Crook. Royal Observer Corps personnel in the area reckoned that it had spun into the ground after flying straight and level at 8,000 feet. Still more witnesses said that they saw the bomber heading from the direction of Stanley Crook and flying over Billy Row, to the north of Roddymoor, with one of its two engines on fire.

A farmer's son, John Burn, was busy ploughing a field nearby when the Wellington flew directly over his head. He watched as its port wing hit the ground first, then the aircraft crashed through a fence and came to rest at a drunken angle in the trees. One man was lying injured on the ground next to the bomber and another could be seen inside, seemingly trapped. The farmer rushed over to see if he could help, and people who lived in nearby Roddymoor were doing the same. There may already have been a fire onboard: bullets were "cooking off" and whizzing in the direction of the would-be rescuers.

Before any of the onlookers could get too close to the downed aircraft, it suddenly exploded. The tail gun turret, with its helpless gunner still inside, was blown upwards and landed dozens of yards away. The mainwheels were similarly sent flying a great distance. What hadn't been destroyed by the explosion was rapidly consumed by the fire that ensued. An hour later, the smell of burning Perspex remained amidst the smouldering wreckage. None of the crew were found alive. When the fire had died down enough to allow their bodies to be retrieved for identification purposes, they were laid out in a nearby byre. The local Home Guard unit was initially called upon to guard the wreckage and look after the bodies of the crew, but they were eventually relieved by an Army detachment.

All five were buried in Darlington West Cemetery. The pilot's unusual first name caused some problems at the time, as it was initially recorded as "Ambler". His parents therefore did not learn of his demise until after he was buried in Darlington. Flight Sergeant Roberts hailed from the town of Mitcham, South Australia. Wear Valley Council commissioned a plaque to commemorate the deaths of the crew. It is unclear where the council were intending to place it, or why it ended up in the main exhibition hall at the North East Aircraft Museum (now the North East Land Sea & Air Museum), near the Nissan Car Factory at Sunderland (once the site of RAF Usworth).

Although many decades have passed since the crash, small items are still brought to the surface in the field where the crew perished. Canadian coins were found some years ago, along with tiny fragments of metal from what was once a Wellington bomber. A new plaque was commissioned for the grounds of Crook Community Leisure Centre, not far from the scene of the crash. A memorial service, attended by members of the Canadian Forces, the Lord Lieutenant of Darlington and the town's Mayor, was held at its unveiling on 21st May 2019, exactly 77 years to the day following the tragic loss of DV841 and its crew.

The old: the original commemorative plaque commissioned by Wear Valley Council some years ago. It can be found inside the main exhibition building at the North East Land Sea & Air Museum next to the Nissan Car Factory near Sunderland.

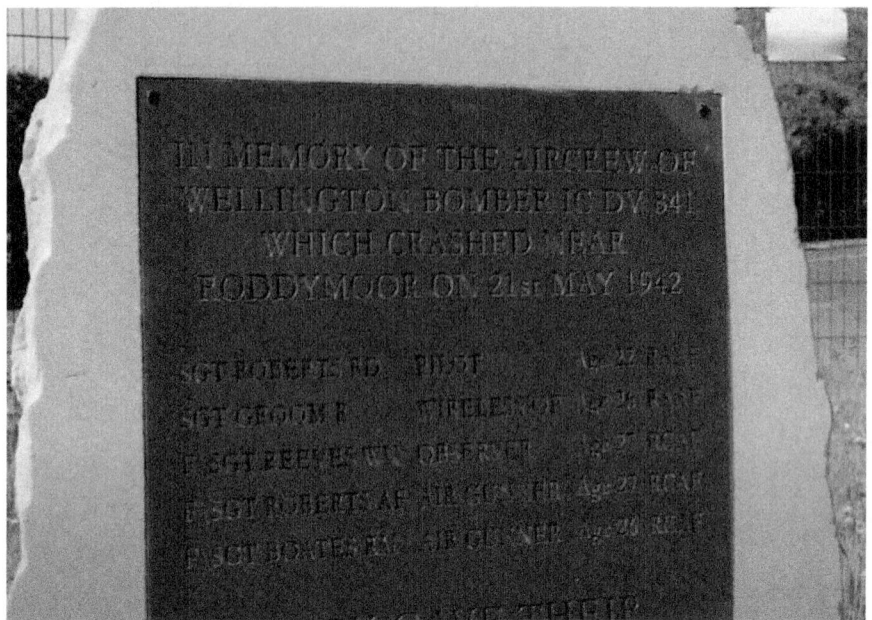

A newer commemorative plaque was unveiled on the 77th anniversary of the crash. It can be found inside the grounds of the Crook Community Leisure Centre.

Did Flight Sergeant Roberts intentionally put himself and his crew in mortal danger to prevent his damaged aircraft from crashing into houses in either Roddymoor or Crook? People who saw the bomber turning to avoid them believed that was true. The phrase "they gave their tomorrow for our today" had a special resonance with people who lived in Roddymoor.

SNOWY OWLS AT MIDDLETON ST GEORGE

Vickers Wellington N2887 is representative of the bombers that No.420 Squadron operated from RAF Middleton St. George between October and December 1942 whilst the unit was part of No.6 Group, Royal Canadian Air Force.

This chapter focusses on the missions and activities carried out by a single Royal Canadian Air Force bomber unit based at RAF Middleton St. George between October and December 1942. It was stationed there in 1943 as well but transferred to the control of another group in January of that year.

No.420 ("Snowy Owl") Squadron was formed at RAF Waddington, near Lincoln, in December 1941. It initially operated Hampden and Manchester bombers, but by August 1942 had converted to the more capable Vickers Wellington Mk.III. By this time, RAF Bomber Command was taking the fight to the enemy's homeland, with almost nightly raids on German cities and other targets being carried out when weather conditions allowed. When the squadron obtained its Wellingtons, it moved to Skipton-on-Swale in North Yorkshire, but the stay there was a brief one, for another move, this time to Middleton St. George (now Teesside International Airport) was imminent.

Wing Commander Douglas Bradshaw commanded No.420 Squadron during the period covered by this chapter. Born in Ontario in 1912, he had joined the Royal Canadian Air Force in 1935, received his pilot's licence the following year and served as an instructor until 1939. Posted overseas in December 1941, he took command of the Snowy Owls in March 1942.

The first official mention of the move to Middleton St. George in the unit records appeared on 9th October 1942:

"W/C Bradshaw, Sqn. Commander, accompanied by Adjutant and Section Heads proceeded by road to Middleton-St-George to look over the new location of 420 Sqn, after the move on the 15th of Oct. No day flying being carried out."

The squadron's advance party set out by road for Middleton St. George on the 12th, the remainder of the unit preparing at Skipton-on-Swale for when they would eventually transfer the short distance north into County Durham to their new base of operations. Bombing raids were still carried out while this work was being carried out, but the squadron lost two aircraft on the night of the 13th, one in a forced landing and the other which crashed into a house whilst climbing away after a missed approach in bad weather.

14th October 1942 saw the unit loading equipment at RAF Topcliffe for transportation to their new home. Most of the squadron's ground element then moved north the following day by train at 1130 hours, preceded by the air party which left at 1115 hours. The unit's vehicles departed Skipton-on-Swale at 1500 hours. No sooner had the Wellington bombers arrived at Middleton St. George when seven of their number were allocated to a raid on Cologne that night. The aircraft and their pilots were as follows:

X3808/B	Flight Sergeant L. E. White
X3809/O	Flight Sergeant W. W. Kennedy
BJ717/Q	Flight Lieutenant R. G. Cook
BK235/T	Flight Lieutenant L. S. Anderson
BK297/J	Sergeant D. A. Wilson
BK330/K	Pilot Officer W. J. Maitland
BK331/W	Pilot Officer J. Hudson

Flight Sergeant White and his crew were pronounced missing as no radio messages were received and the aircraft never returned to base or landed at another station. It was believed that they were shot down over Germany. To give an idea of what happened during a raid at this time, the mission log details given by Flight Lieutenant Cook and his crew provide an example. They took off from Middleton St. George at 1955 hours on the 15th and landed back at base at 0054 hours the following morning. The mission was detailed as follows:

"Primary target, Aiming Point 'A' Cologne, attacked from 12,500 feet 300°M at 21.05 hours. 8-10/10th thin cloud - fairly dark- visibility very poor. Saw River Rhine and bridges and PFF [Pathfinder Force] flares. Target was in sight and bombs were believed to drop in vicinity of aiming point. Own bursts not identifiable. Attack was not a conspicuous success, fires being very scattered and small. Bombs 6 x 500GP [500lb General Purpose, high explosive]. Photograph – technical success – 10/10th cloud."

A look at the list of pilots detailed to fly the raid shows that not every crew from the squadron took part. Missing are the Squadron Leaders (the rank being something of a misnomer in Bomber Command as they commanded flights, not squadrons) and Wing Commander Bradshaw. The commanding officer did not participate in every mission, nor did the flight commanders. It was rare to see a Wing Commander take part in more than two or three raids each month. The Squadron Leaders, like the other officers and crew, were occasionally "rested" during their "tour" of operations, which involved flying 30 missions over enemy territory. Flights that were abandoned due to mechanical problems or aircrew sickness were often not added to their individual totals of raids flown. The completion rate for those 30 missions was not great, as all sorts of hazards confronted bomber crews in addition to enemy action. Flight Lieutenant White and his crew became just another grim statistic on a lengthening list of casualties.

16th October 1942 saw No.420 Squadron unloading their equipment at Middleton St. George and settling into their new home. Due to the amount of work needed, the unit was not required for operations that night and was stood down. The following day saw the arrival of the squadron's rear party by road from Skipton-on-Swale. Once again, no operations were flown but the unit's aircraft were sent out on daytime navigation training missions. Crews needed to know how to find Middleton St. George and learning the local landmarks was one of the procedures when moving to a new airbase. Further training flights were carried out on the 19th and 20th, although it was only a matter of time before Bomber Command needed the Canadians back in the fight.

22nd October 1942 saw preparations being made for a daylight raid on the port city of Emden, located on the River Ems, close to the North Sea. This was a risky enterprise, given the *Luftwaffe's* day fighter defences, but two Wellingtons were detailed to fly the mission. However, reconnaissance aircraft sent to the Emden area before the mission took place showed that there was clear weather off the Dutch coast. As this meant interception of the bombers was much more likely, the planned raid was abandoned.

Another daylight raid was planned for the following day, the 23rd. This time, the target was Krefeld, an industrial city in the Ruhr Valley, and five of No.420 Squadron's Wellington Mk.IIIs were assigned to the mission. Four of these aircraft were as follows: (the fifth is not listed in the unit records):

BJ717/Q	Flight Sergeant C. P. Lundeen
BK297/J	Pilot Officer J. D. Craton
BK330/K	Squadron Leader D. S. Jacobs
BK331/W	Pilot Officer J. B. Burt

Clear weather en route caused four of the five to turn back, as the enemy *flak* and fighter defences would have been much more effective. Lundeen and his crew managed to reach Emden and dropped their bombs using "Dead Reckoning" because the city itself was covered in cloud – a far cry from the clear conditions encountered over the English Channel and over in Belgium. Lundeen's mission report read as follows:

"Primary target, Aiming Point 'A' Krefeld, attacked on D.R. at 15.24 hours from 2,000 feet, 093°M. 10/10th cloud 700-3,000 feet. Bombed on D.R., only cloud from English coast. No flak encountered either at target or en route. No results of bombing could be observed owing to cloud, but aircraft violently shaken by blast. No photograph attempted owing to cloud. Bombs 2 x 1,000 and 2 x 500 GP."

What wasn't included in the report was that the crew landed at Waddington on their return flight, possibly due to lack of fuel or weather forcing them off course. Diversions were simply part and parcel of bomber operations, but crews landing at unfamiliar stations occasionally came a cropper.

24th October 1942 saw the Middleton St. George station commander (a Group Captain) hold his first weekly parade. This was followed by a prayer service rendered by the Station Chaplain. Once again, the Snowy Owls were not required for operations, but this changed the following day. The planned mission was however cancelled, presumably due to bad weather. The same occurred on both the 26th and 27th, although night navigation training flights were carried out on the first evening. Poor flying conditions were recorded for the 28th but the squadron was not required for ops, and the same happened the following day – although three Wellingtons were scheduled for a daytime raid. However, once again, this operation was cancelled before it could take place. Crews bided their time by carrying out a series of cross-country navigation exercises over Britain during the hours of darkness, these flights consisting of overland routes to a town or city where a mock bombing attack was performed, followed by a different route back to base.

Oddly enough, whilst poor weather was preventing night bombing raids, clear weather en route to planned targets was doing the same to daytime missions. This was the case on 30th October 1942. However, conditions improved enough on the last day of the month to allow three Wellingtons to be readied for a daylight raid on Emden. In the end, only two bombers took off but their crews successfully bombed targets – although not necessarily the primary one. The aircraft involved were as follows:

BJ717/Q   Sergeant H. A. Hansen
BK330/K   Pilot Officer W. J. Maitland

Hansen's mission report read as follows:

"Primary target, Emden, not attacked. Unidentified town believed North of Emden attacked at 13.36 hours from 1,700 feet, 277°M, 10/10th cloud, base 1,400 feet, tops 2,500/3,000 feet, about 4/10th at 8/10,000 feet. Target not identified, last 'G' fix 54°08'N 04°36'E. Town seen at 800 feet. Climbed into cloud and bombed. Explosion of bombs felt in aircraft. Return trip without incident. Photograph technical success, no ground detail."

"G" was *Gee*, a blind-bombing radio navigation system which pinpointed an aircraft's position to within a few hundred metres by measuring the time delay between two signals sent by widely separated radio transmitters, the maximum range being around 350 miles. Note that the crew attacked what would have been classed as "a target of opportunity" rather than bring their bombs home or jettison them over the sea. Pilot Officer Maitland's crew bombed Emden through cloud, based on an estimated time of arrival.

As of 31st October 1942, No.420 Squadron had the following strength:

Royal Canadian Air Force	Officers	Aircrew	= 34
		Ground Crew	= 3
Royal Canadian Air Force	Airmen	Aircrew	= 76
		Ground Crew	= 201
Royal Air Force	Officers	Aircrew	= 6
		Ground Crew	= 1

Royal Air Force	Airmen	Aircrew	= 20
		Ground Crew	= 131
Royal Australian Air Force	Airmen	Aircrew	= 3

In addition, there were 17 Women's Auxiliary Air Force personnel on the unit's strength.

A Wellington Mk.III is readied for a bombing raid in wintry conditions at an unknown location in Britain.

November 1942 saw the Snowy Owls settled into their new surroundings and eager to resume the fight against the Germans. However, they would have been chomping at the bit for the first three days of the month, since despite the squadron being stood up for operations each day, the missions were cancelled due to weather. Fog and poor visibility were to blame.

4th November saw no less than 11 Wellingtons being required for night operations. This was the first occasion that so many of the unit's aircraft had been assigned to a mission since it converted to the Mk.III at Skipton-on-Swale. None of the squadron's machines were undergoing repair or maintenance at the time, so it reported a 100% serviceability rate, almost unheard of at that point in the war.

Heavy fog put paid to any operations on the 5th, so it was not until the following day when three Snowy Owl Wellingtons were prepared for a raid, although the name of the target does not appear in the squadron records. The mission was a daylight one, bombs being dropped on the secondary targets, possibly due to the primary being obscured by cloud. All three flew safely back to Middleton St. George although one had *flak* damage. The 7th was a repeat of previous days where the unit was stood up and then down again when operations were cancelled due to bad weather.

The records for a mission carried out on the night of the 8th are also missing from the squadron records, but ten aircraft were sent out to drop sea mines around the Friesian Islands off northern Holland. These flights were known as "Gardening" sorties, with the sea mines themselves often being referred to by a variety of vegetable names. One of the Wellingtons was hit by *flak* and its wireless operator injured in the right leg.

Missing records are a feature of all but the final week in November 1942 as far as No.420 Squadron is concerned. Another raid occurred on the night of the 9th, with no less than 15 crews and their aircraft being readied for a raid. In the end, just 11 became airborne and only two bombed the target. One of the Wellingtons failed to return, the crew being reported missing. This was Z1679, flown by Sergeant W. S. Beale. A subsequent raid occurred the following evening, this time only involving five machines. Their crews dropped their bombs succesfully, but the aircraft had to divert to Swinderby in Lincolnshire on their return to Britain. Further "Gardening" sorties were attempted on the night of the 11th, but none of the five bombers sent out on this mission managed to lay any sea mines at all.

Away from the grind of operations, the No.420 Squadron hockey team played against a team from No.424 Squadron (another Canadian unit) at Durham on the 12th. The Snowy Owls were victorious, winning 4-0, their second victory notched up.

Back to the bombing campaign, the unit was stood up for the night of the 13th and aircraft prepared for flight, but the mission was cancelled. The five aircraft that had diverted to RAF Swinderby early the previous morning returned to the fold. The stand up/stand down pattern was repeated on the 14th and 15th. In the meantime, the Snowy Owls received visits from Wing Commander Burnside, commanding officer of No.427 Squadron and Group Captain McCaul from Bomber Command. Operational matters did improve on the 16th when six Wellingtons were readied for cross-country "Navex" (navigation exercises) and two more for "Gardening" sorties. In the end, four took part in the navigation flights and the two allocated to mining successfully dropped their "vegetables" in the assigned areas. "Bullseye" training flights were also carried out, precision attacks on mock targets across Britain. Even though actual missions could not be flown, there was plenty of opportunity to train – crews needed the practice.

Events occurred away from the operational aspect of squadron life. On 17th November 1942, Leading Aircraftsman Broad, a motor transport driver serving with the Snowy Owls, was fined the princely sum of £1 after being convicted of reckless driving. He had been the driver of a coach which was involved in an accident on the night of 1st October. According to the unit's record book, the following incident had occurred in North Yorkshire:

"Bus returning from Leeming at night with personnel from ENSA show ran into back of parked truck on highway and killed Aircraftsman Reid of SHQ, a waiter in the Sergeants' Mess and seriously injured Sergeant Gagan of 429 Squadron and four other Sergeants less seriously. Sergeant Gagan taken to Catterick Military Hospital and others to Station Sick Quarters, RAF Leeming."

Another daylight operation was cancelled on the 18th, as were that night's "Gardening" sorties. Bad weather around Middleton St. George and in the Vale of York was hampering availability for raids, but there was another reason for sending nine Wellingtons south to Harwell, an aerodrome near Oxford, together with 20 ground crew on 20th November 1942.

A Wellington Mk.III belonging to No.419 Squadron, carrying the unit code letters "VR". The Snowy Owls at Middleton St. George were assigned the letters "PT".

Eight aircraft took part in a mission against the Fiat engine factory in Turin, northern Italy, that evening. The Snowy Owl crews successfully bombed the target and returned safely. They were *"greatly thrilled over first trip over the Alps."* Middleton St. George was outside the effective range to Turin, at least with any kind of worthwhile bombload, thus the reason for sending aircraft south to fly from Oxfordshire. The crews taking part in the Italian raid returned to County Durham on the 21st.

Their experience at Harwell must have been a positive one as another ten Wellingtons flew down there on the 22nd, two to pick up the ground crews and eight to participate in a raid on Stuttgart or "Gardening" sorties that night. The aircraft and pilots detailed to fly the raid on Stuttgart were as follows (only five machines being listed in the squadron records):

X3392/O	Pilot Officer J. B. Burt	Stuttgart
X3800/X	Sergeant R. E. Taylor	Stuttgart
BK235/T	Flight Lieutenant L. S. Anderson	Stuttgart
BK330/K	Pilot Officer V. M. Adilman	Stuttgart
BK331/W	Flight Sergeant C. P. Lundeen	Stuttgart

Pilot Officer Burt and his crew had an eventful flight, crash-landing on their return to Britain. Their mission report read as follows:

"Attacked primary. 2201 hours, 13,000 feet, 360 degrees M [magnetic]. 2 to 3/10ths cloud over target. Bright moon, haze. Good visibility. Target identified by Autobahn south, also River Neckar observed running parallel to the east on bombing run. Marker flares seen. Target in bomb sight. Bombs believed in target area close to Aiming Point. Incendiaries seen starting but had not properly caught hold while A/C was over target but large glow from what must have been large conflagration seen from more than 100 miles away on return journey.

Hydraulics shot away, all flying instruments, and all engine instruments except port rev counter by flak. Pilot states: 'Second pilot was flying home when we ran over Paris. I took over and descended to 50' to get out of searchlights and light flak and received a direct hit on my nose of aircraft, smashing hydraulics and causing wheels to come down. A direct hit behind instrument panel made all flying instruments and engine instruments u/s [unserviceable], except port rev counter. Starboard engine was hit which caused rough running and loss of engine oil. Rear Gunner put out searchlights and stopped guns by fire from rear turret. Squadron Leader Williams, 2nd pilot, was hit slightly on leg by flak. Crash landed at Runsden [sic – may have meant 'Rushden']."

Squadron Leader Williams had been seconded from No.427 Squadron. Although classed as beyond repair, Wellington Mk.III X3392 did not suffer serious damage as it was subsequently repaired and returned to service. However, the aircraft was lost on the night of 27th January 1944 whilst with No.84 Operational Training Unit, crashing half-an-hour into a six-hour-long night navigation exercise. The entire trainee crew was killed.

The 24th saw the familiar standing up of crews, followed by cancellation of their missions due to bad weather. The following day saw three aircraft being prepared for night operations. All of them took off, but one (X3335) was forced to return due to a problem with the intercom. The machines involved were as follows:

X3335/D	Pilot Officer V. M. Adilman	Gardening
X3926/A	Flight Sergeant W. W. Kennedy	Gardening
BJ966/R	Flight Sergeant C. P. Lundeen	Gardening

Only one of the remaining aircraft (X3926) was successful in its gardening exploits, as mentioned in the official No.420 Squadron records:

"Successful trip. Planted 2 vegetables [mines] 2001 hrs. 500 ft. 354°M ½ minute. 9-10/10ths cloud from English coast to garden [mining region] and in [specific] area. Pointe de Toulinguet identified by rear gunner as A/C left area. Parachutes [from sea mines dropped] seen to open. Conditions en route and around target very poor."

The squadron had 14 aircrew up for commissions on 26th November 1942, and Air Vice Marshal Carr arrived to interview the prospective officers. A daylight raid was planned for that day, but it was cancelled, although just two out of seven Wellingtons sent on "Gardening" missions that evening successfully dropped their sea mines in poor weather conditions. Four of the aircraft had to divert to Dishforth in North Yorkshire on the return flight, presumably due to weather at Middleton St. George. The aircraft involved were as follows:

BJ966/R	Flight Sergeant C. P. Lundeen	Gardening
BK235/T	Flight Lieutenant L. S. Anderson	Gardening
BK295/H	Squadron Leader D. S. Jacobs	Gardening
BK330/K	Pilot Officer J. B. Burt	Gardening

Wellington Mk.III X3763 belonged to No.429 Squadron, another Canadian unit but was identical to the aircraft flown by the Snowy Owls at Middleton St. George.

Squadron Leader Jacobs' mission was recorded thus:

"Successful. Planted 2 vegetables 2138 hrs. 300 ft. 330°. Traces of low cloud. Bright moon. Visual pinpoint made on Herbaudiere Pointe and D.R. run from there. Parachute seen to open. Pilot states: 'Weather on trip was exceedingly poor until Belle Isle was reached. Over garden bright moonlight and no cloud made pinpointing fairly easy. Vegetables definitely in correct position. Very good D. R. navigation.'"

However, Flight Lieutenant Anderson had a different story to tell:

"Unsuccessful. Furthest point reached 49 10'N 04 00'W 1,800 feet. 1914 hours. Vegetables brought back to base. Pilot states: 'Very unsuccessful trip. We flew in and out of 8/10ths cloud over England. The trip out in the Channel was below 10/10ths cloud and we were unable to see the sea. I flew for another hour and due to the lack of Gee fixes I assumed that we could be unable to pinpoint the islands in such conditions. Thus, knowing we couldn't drop our mines on D.R., I turned and set course for Predannack [in south-west Cornwall].'"

No further operations were carried out in November 1942 by the squadron. No.6 Group's commanding officer, Air Vice Marshal Barker, arrived at the station on the 28th for an informal inspection and stayed for two days. By the end of the month, the unit had one less Canadian officer and 30 less airmen and had flown a total of 104.50 operational flying hours, plus 62.05 hours on non-operational tasking.

No.420 Squadron's Operations Record Book summary for the first half of December 1942 is missing, but the information regarding the raids that were carried out during this period still exists. Mannheim was attacked by three Wellington Mk.IIIs from the unit on the night of the 6th, the aircraft involved being listed here:

X3809	Sergeant J. S. Thomson
BK235	Flight Lieutenant L. S. Anderson
BK331	Sergeant W. A. Horborenko

Sergeant Thomson's crews brought their bombs back to base as they only reached Dungeness Point before having to turn back due to thick cloud. Flight Lieutenant Anderson fared little better, his bomb-aimer being unable to identify the primary target due to 10/10ths cloud cover. They did drop their bombs but only using an estimated time of arrival and were not sure whether they had even attacked Mannheim. Only Sergeant Horborenko and his crew stated they had hit the primary:

"Primary, Mannheim 'A', attacked at 20.10 hours, 14,000 feet. Results not observed. 10/10th cloud, tops 10,000 feet. Many fires observed burning through cloud. Negative pitch control on port engine unserviceable."

Two Wellingtons participated in minelaying sorties off Point du Toulinguet on the evening of 7th December, both crews successfully dropping their "vegetables" at their assigned positions. Sergeant D. Wilson flew X3809, and Sergeant R. R. Taylor piloted BK365. The latter encountered accurate *flak* from a flakship (a naval barge or vessel armed with anti-aircraft guns) but survived unscathed. No less than seven No.420 Squadron Wellingtons were readied for the following night's "Gardening" sorties, and all flew:

X3335	Sergeant J. S. Thomson
X3800	Flight Sergeant W. W. Kennedy
X3926	Flight Sergeant H. G. Townsend
BJ966	Pilot Officer J. D. Craton
BK235	Flight Lieutenant L. S. Anderson
BK295	Flight Lieutenant R. G. Cock
BK297	Sergeant T. C. Lawson

Three of the crews were unsuccessful, failing to locate two islands that were near their assigned dropping points. As per standing instructions, the mines were brought back to base. Flight Sergeant Kennedy's raid report gives some idea of what a successful mission had been like, and just how low the crews flew over the sea in the dark to drop their "vegetables":

"Two mines successfully laid at 19.40 hours, 500 feet, 000°M, 1½ miles. Visibility poor, cloud 10/10th, base 1,000 feet to sea level. Neuwerk and Scharnhorn [the two islands near the mouth of the River Elbe, required for identification purposes] definitely identified. Parachutes seen to open."

There was another raid on Turin in northern Italy, this time on the evening of the 9th. The Snowy Owls put up seven bombers, nowhere near its full complement but more than had been dispatched at once for some days. Once again, the aircraft – with ground crew parties travelling separately – flew down to Harwell in Oxfordshire as it was within range of the target. These flights routed across France and round the western fringe of neutral Switzerland before heading towards Turin over the Dauphiné Alps. It was a long way in a Wellington and the mountains posed an extra danger.

No.420 Squadron were nicknamed the "Snowy Owls", the bird appearing on the unit's official crest. Their motto, "Pugnatius Finitum", means "We fight to the finish." The Canadian unit was based at Middleton St. George from October 1942 until the early summer of 1943 when it was transferred to North Africa.

The following No.420 Squadron Wellingtons participated in this second raid on Turin, and the unit's commanding officer was one of the pilots involved:

X3800	Flight Sergeant W. W. Kennedy
X3926	Sergeant R. E. Taylor
BJ966	Flight Sergeant C. P. Lundeen
BK235	Flight Lieutenant L. S. Anderson
BK295	Squadron Leader D. S. Jacobs
BK331	Pilot Officer J. D. Craton
BK365	Wing Commander D. A. Bradshaw

Wing Commander Bradshaw's mission report read as follows:

"Primary, Turin 'B' attacked at 21.37 hours, 14,500 feet. Bombs, 2 x 500 GP and 4 SBC (90 x 4) [incendiaries]. No individual bursts seen, but many fires in target area. Bombed on fires in centre of town. Fairly intense light flak and 6 or 8 ineffective searchlights. Port oil temperature broke on way in."

The Snowy Owls landed at Manston in Kent on their return to Britain. They arrived back at Middleton St. George later on the 10th or even during the morning of the 11th but were needed for a minelaying operation that night. Six aircraft were required for the "Gardening" sorties:

X3800	Sergeant S. J. Gerkley
BJ966	Sergeant P. G. McDuffee
BK235	Sergeant D, Sanderson
BK297	Sergeant T. C. Lawson
BK330	Sergeant D. J. Cozens
BK365	Sergeant J. S. Thomson

Three of the Wellingtons had to divert to Acklington in Northumberland on their return trips, arriving there around 0500 hours the following morning. These missions appeared to be "milk runs" for some of the new pilots that had been posted to the squadron. "Gardening" sorties had their own risks, but they were easier on new crews who would benefit from getting two or three of these operational flights under their belts prior to being sent out over Germany. Sergeant McDuffee was one of the pilots who diverted to Acklington, and his log summed up the frustration felt by crews who had to return with their "vegetables" still onboard:

"[Dep. 23.20 hours, landed 05.06 Acklington] Unable to pinpoint. Weather in target area, 7-8/10th cloud, base 1,500 feet. Visibility poor, Gee of no use. Aircraft badly rigged and very difficult to hold on course."

Sergeant Sanderson's crew was one of the successful ones that night:

"Two mines successfully planted at 01.16 hours, 800 feet, 100°M. Electric storm 30 miles from English coast. Visibility poor. Mist and thin cloud, very dark. Parachutes seen to open."

Five aircraft were laid on for further minelaying flights on the late afternoon of the 14th, with only one of them successfully "planting" their "vegetables" in the assigned area. The aircraft and pilots involved were as follows:

X3800	Sergeant S, J. Gerkley
X3809	Flight Sergeant P. G. McDuffee
BK297	Sergeant D. Wilson
BK330	Sergeant J. S. Thomson
BK331	Sergeant D. Sanderson

The official summary records for the squadron resume on 15th December 1942, with a note stating that the unit stood by to participate in day ops that were scrubbed. An unknown number of Wellington bombers were bombed up for a night raid but this too was cancelled. The same happened the next day, as mentioned in the official report, which gave a hint of the frustration the crews and their commanders must have felt regarding their inaction:

"Again, stood by for day operations but this was cancelled. Exceedingly high wind all day long. The Beaufighter aircraft which had been forced in on the fourteenth of this month finally took off to return to its base. Preparation undergone for gardening. Six aircraft lined up for take-off, but one was non-starter. Five got away, three are unsuccessful, two laid mines successfully. All aircraft returned safely to Harwell where they were to be diverted. The whole operation was not very successful due chiefly to poor visibility over the target area."

The five that "got away" on the evening of the 16th were listed as follows:

X3809	Sergeant T. C. Lawson
X3926	Flight Sergeant H. G. Townsend
BJ966	Flight Sergeant C. P. Lundeen
BK295	Pilot Officer J. A. Burt
BK330	Sergeant D. J. Cozens

The weather was not conducive to successful operations, with just two of the three crews being able to drop their mines in their allocated areas. One of them was Sergeant Cozen's crew, who reported the following:

"Successful. Two mines planted as ordered at 23.56 hours, 900 feet, 267°M. 8/10th cloud, visibility poor, electrical storm encountered. Islands and coastline identified. Mines seen to hit water."

The pattern of sporadic successful "Gardening" sorties and cancelled raids continued into mid-December 1942, scrubbed missions being recorded on the 18th and 19th. In terms of operations, things improved drastically on the 20th as preparations took place for a late afternoon attack on Duisburg, one of the industrial cities in the Ruhr Valley. It seemed to be a "maximum effort" by the squadron, as their Operations Record Book reported:

"Thirteen aircraft bombed up and took off for operations on Duisburg. Ten aircraft attacked and bombed target under good visibility. One aircraft returned due to engine catching on fire. Navigator of another aircraft went

unconscious at 18,000 feet. This navigator had sufficient oxygen but was apparently physically incapable of the height. It was rather an unusual case since he had completed twenty-three operational trips under similar conditions; he has since been admitted to hospital for thorough examination. The other aircraft returned due to the navigator accidentally catching his foot on the oxygen economiser and cutting off the oxygen. The whole operation was considered very successful. All aircraft returned safely."

The aircraft detailed for the mission were listed as follows:

X3809	Sergeant W. A. Horborenko
X3926	Flight Sergeant W. G. Townsend
BJ915	Sergeant J. S. Thomson
BJ917	Flight Lieutenant R. G. Cock
BK235	Flight Lieutenant L. S. Anderson
BK295	Squadron Leader D. S. Jacobs
BK331	Sergeant D. Sanderson
BK365	Sergeant D. J. Cozens
DF615	Pilot Officer J. D. Craton
DF626	Flight Sergeant D. Wilson
DF657	Pilot Officer W. J. Maitland
(not listed)	Squadron Leader L. K. Smith
(not listed)	Sergeant T. C. Lawson

Sergeant Lawson and his crew had a difficult time, as evidenced by their mission report:

"Primary Duisburg not attacked. Bombs and incendiaries jettisoned 53 40'N 09 26'E, 1845 hours, 17,000 feet. Port motor caught fire. Pilot states: Trip incomplete. Fire could not be extinguished till engine stopped after restarting 30 minutes later, motor very rough and after landing caught fire again."

As for the unfortunate navigator who passed out, he was part of Squadron Leader Smith's crew. A description of their mission was also entered into the official records:

"Primary Duisburg not attacked. Reached 52 45'N 04 55'E and returned with Navigator sick. Bombs jettisoned safe 53 30'N 01 10'E. Half our incendiaries brought back. Pilot states: Navigator passed out at 18,000 feet – all symptoms of oxygen lack although supply perfect. The W/OP [wireless operator] changed supply pipes with Navigator and found all OK. Navigator was quite incapable until we descended below 10,000 feet."

No less than ten Lancasters from other squadrons descended on No.420 Squadron's home airfield on the morning of 21st December 1942 due to bad weather at their own stations. The familiar pattern of the Snowy Owls' aircraft being assigned to a mission, bombed up and then the raid being scrubbed continued. Operational matters improved somewhat the following day, at least according to the Operations Record Book:

"Stood by for daylight [raid] and six aircraft and a 'Recce' carried out an operation on Emden. Four successfully attacked the Primary Target. Two were unsuccessful, one of which attacked a town named Pilsum, according to Pin Point, and the other went out of control temporarily, due to aileron jamming."

As mentioned above, Pilot Officer Maitland's crew didn't hit the primary, instead dropping their bombs on another location:

"Primary Essen not attacked. Attacked town, believed Pilsum, 1625 hours, 500 feet, 176°. Aircraft had been hit. 10/10ths cloud, base 500 feet. Very poor visibility, fog, rain. Bombed on ETA Air plot. No results observed, bombs dropped as soon as A/C was hit by flak. Hole in tail due to flak. Photograph not attempted."

It had been a frustrating time for the Canadians at Middleton St. George. Mission after mission was scrubbed, largely due to the weather although clear conditions had put paid to some of the planned daylight raids. The bombing campaign against Nazi Germany was still something of a work in progress, with twin-engined types such as the Wellington still in service alongside Halifaxes and Lancasters, the newer four-engined "heavies" that could deliver a much larger bombload to the enemy. Things would improve significantly during the next two years, although No.420 Squadron would be transferred to the Mediterranean theatre during the summer of 1943. Other Canadian bomber units would arrive at Middleton St. George to take their place.

WELLINGTON DOWN AT ST. JOHN'S CHAPEL

A Vickers Wellington Mk.III belonging to No.115 Squadron is pictured here – a similar machine used by No.29 Operational Training Unit at RAF North Luffenham to train night bomber crews crashed just south of St. John's Chapel in Weardale on 8th May 1943. None of the seven crew onboard the Wellington survived the impact.

The survival rate for RAF night bomber crews during World War II was not very good. 60 per cent of operational airmen were either killed, wounded or taken prisoner – the death rate alone was 46 per cent of the 125,000 or so aircrew that flew raids. Yet even before reaching an operational unit, these airmen had to fly numerous training missions, firstly whilst learning their own individual "trade" (either pilot, navigator, bomb aimer, flight engineer or gunner), and then further flights once they were put together as a crew.

One of the latter training sorties ended in tragedy for one newly formed bomber crew who were stationed at RAF North Luffenham in Rutland. The names of the individual members were as follows:

Sergeant William Mason	Pilot
Sergeant Walter G. Hutchinson	Co-Pilot
Flight Sergeant Alan Darby (RCAF)	Navigator
Pilot Officer Michael J. Meatyard	Bomb Aimer (and Nose Gunner)
Sergeant Ronald A. Page	Wireless Operator
Sergeant Stanley M. Marfleet	Air Gunner (Mid-Upper Turret)
Sergeant Ronald E. Stephens	Air Gunner (Tail Turret)

Note that crews could be led (or "skippered") by personnel holding lower ranks than other airmen on the same aircraft held. "Pilot Officer" was also a rank, not an indication that the individual was a qualified pilot.

Pictured here is the 26-year-old pilot of Wellington Mk.III BK441, Sergeant William Mason.

26-year-old Sergeant Mason took off from North Luffenham at around 2215 hours on the night of 7th May 1943 for a night cross-country exercise. The aircraft allocated to him that evening was Vickers Wellington Mk.III BK441. The "Wimpey" (as it was often affectionately known by its crews) had been a mainstay of RAF Bomber Command during the early years of World War II, but with the arrival of newer and larger four-engined types such as the Avro Lancaster and Handley-Page Halifax, Wellingtons were increasingly being relegated to second line and training duties. With recent participation in the night offensive against Germany, these aircraft were ideal machines with which to train newly formed bomber crews.

Some two hours into the cross-country flight, it is very likely that William Mason found himself flying into a blanket of low cloud sitting over the North Pennines. At around 0015 hours on the morning of the 8th, residents living in St. John's Chapel, a small village in Weardale, were suddenly woken by a loud explosion, one they believed to be the result of an aircraft crashing into the surrounding hills. Later that same morning, the wreckage of Sergeant Mason's Wellington was discovered at Greenlaws Hush, about a mile south of the village. The bomber had struck the hillside there at an altitude of 1,400 feet, the entire seven-man crew perishing in the impact.

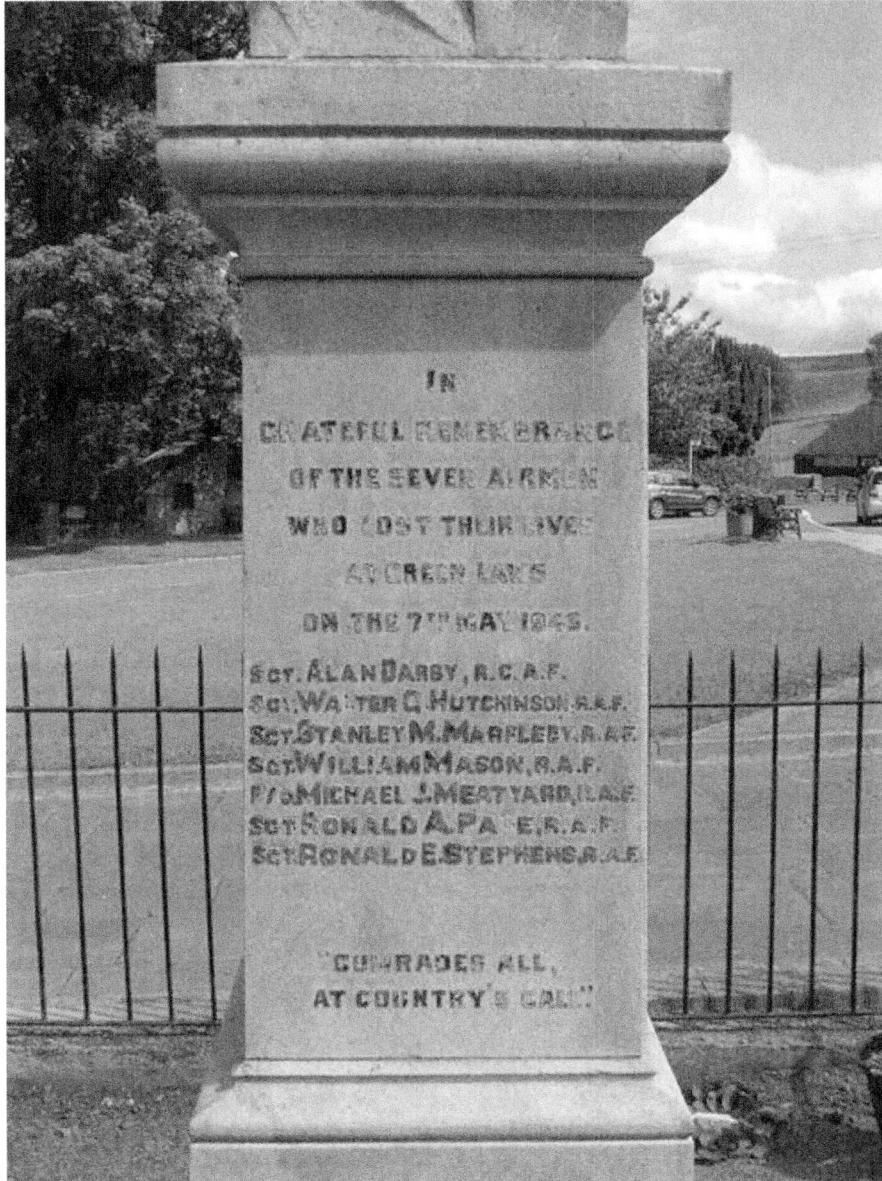

The war memorial at St. John's Chapel in Weardale includes the names of all seven members of the crew of Wellington Mk.III BK441.

An investigation ensued but given the weather conditions that night, the cause was believed to be all too clear. The official conclusion determined that Sergeant Mason became lost in bad weather, and with his Canadian navigator, Flight Sergeant Alan Darby, unable to see any ground features, had elected to descend through cloud in order to pinpoint their position.

The aircraft then struck the hillside whilst doing so. It was a common cause of accidents during the war over the hills of Britain – numerous aircraft had been lost in the same fashion.

The Wellington crashed in this area, a hillside to the south of St. John's Chapel in Upper Weardale. Low cloud can often blanket the hills here and hide high ground lying underneath. This photograph was taken in February 2023. (Author)

Another photo of Sergeant William Mason (centre), one of the crewmembers killed near St. John's Chapel in May 1943. He hailed from Ayr in Scotland.

Wreckage from the Wellington bomber was believed to have been buried in or near an old quarry spoil heap. This spot is located about a mile south of St. John's Chapel. (Author)

Nothing remains at the location of the crash site although sections of wreckage were apparently buried in a quarry spoil heap not far from a farm track near the scene. A more permanent reminder of the incident comes in the form of an inscription that lists the names of the crew on one side of the war memorial in the village of St. John's Chapel. This did however cause a little bit of controversy at the time since some villagers felt that only local names should have been included.

The bodies of the crew were interred at various locations around the country. Sergeant Stanley Marfleet was buried in St. Mary's Churchyard, at Stamfordham in Northumberland. He was just 20 years old at the time of the crash. The pilot, William Mason, was buried in Ayr Cemetery. Walter Gibley's gravestone can be found in Leeds (Harehill) Cemetery. The body of Alan Darby was not repatriated to Canada but was instead interred at Gillingham (St. Mary) Churchyard, Norfolk. Ronald Page was buried in Greenford Park Cemetery, Middlesex, whilst the gravestone for Michael Meatyard, who came from Shoreham-on-Sea, can be found at Henfield Cemetery in Suffolk. Finally, the rear gunner, Ronald Stephens, was buried at Plymouth (Ford Park) Cemetery.

The crash site itself was investigated by aviation archaeologists some years ago and live ammunition was discovered. It is said that some of the engine parts did not tally with the identity of the airframe involved, although no further details regarding this are known.

THE BUNKER HILL WELLINGTON

Vickers Wellington Mk.X PR547 is shown here coming into land. Aircraft such as these were used by training units to instruct new bomber crews how to work as a team in preparation for posting to an operational squadron. A Mk.X from No.20 Operational Training Unit was lost near Consett in May 1944 with the death of four of its seven crewmembers.

Despite their government having surrendered to the Nazis in June 1940, many Frenchmen decided to fight on, travelling to Britain by various routes and then signing up as members of the Free French Forces. In May 1944, the first French RAF bomber unit was formed, namely No.346 ("Guyenne") Squadron, which was based at Elvington in North Yorkshire. However, in order to staff the new squadron, crews had to be formed from personnel newly trained as pilots, flight engineers, navigators, bomb-aimers and air gunners. Crews of seven were then the norm. Bombers such as the Halifax and Lancaster were a great deal larger than the Blenheims, Hampdens and Wellingtons that had equipped most of Bomber Command in the early days of the war. These new crews were trained at Operational Training Units located at bases dotted across the country.

No.20 OTU was based at Lossiemouth, on the Moray Firth just north of Elgin, Scotland. Equipped with Wellingtons, at least one Free French crew was engaged in training there during May 1944. Unfortunately, they were killed in a crash at Bunker Hill, between Leadgate and Shotley Bridge, whilst on a training flight towards the end of that month.

On the evening of 25th May 1944, *Capitaine* Rene Richard's crew was detailed to fly a night cross-country exercise over the North of England. His colleagues on that ill-fated flight were *Lieutenant* Raoul Blot (navigator), *Lieutenant* Jean Vles (navigator), *Sous-lieutenant* Alexander Ponton (bomb-aimer), *Serjent* Jean Fischbach (wireless operator), and *Serjents* Guy Soury-Lavergne and Gilbert Allain (both air gunners).

Serjent Guy Soury-Lavergne is pictured here on the left whilst serving with No.347 ("Tunisie") Squadron at Elvington in late 1944.

Capitaine Richard and his crew took off from Lossiemouth and headed south to carry out the navigation exercise. They were flying in a Wellington Mk.X, serial number MF553, coded "JM-F". Over northern England, they ran into severe icing conditions at 15,000 feet. Ice forming on control surfaces was a dangerous thing – it made manoeuvring difficult, caused aircraft to be out of correct trim and if the build-up was bad enough, pilots could lose control of their machines. De-icing "boots" were fitted to the wing leading edges and control surfaces of bombers, comprising of rubber membranes which, after inflated, would break-up ice formation.

Unfortunately for Rene Richard, either a de-icing system wasn't fitted to his Wellington, or if one was, it couldn't cope with the rapid build-up of ice or had become unserviceable. He elected to descend to 7,000 feet to see whether conditions were better below. Once at that altitude, the icing continued, and the French pilot informed his crew that they should prepare to abandon the aeroplane. He was having difficulty in flying the bomber, so it was prudent to jump safely whilst he still had a modicum of control.

However, before anyone could jump from the iced-up Wellington, it flew into a marginal improvement in the weather. Richard gained more control and decided to put the aircraft down on what he believed to be an airfield in north-western County Durham. The crew were told to prepare for a forced landing in the dark. The pilot descended towards his intended landing site at around 0110 hours on the morning of 26th May 1944.

Rather than landing at an airfield, *Capitaine* Richard had instead touched down in a field on top of Bunker Hill, just south of the Hat and Feather pub, located on the junction of the B6308 and B6309 roads north of Consett. His Wellington bomber crashed through a line of trees and caught fire as it slid to a halt. Rene Richard, Raoul Blot, Jean Fischbach and Alexander Ponton were all killed in the incident. Jean Vles, Guy Soury-Lavergne and Gilbert Allain sustained injuries in the crash, but these were not serious.

Initially, all four of the dead crew were buried at Harrogate Cemetery, a service taking place on 30th May 1944. The bodies of Richard and Blot were later re-buried at Brookwood Military Cemetery in Surrey, where over 240 of their countrymen were finally laid to rest, this taking place after the war was over. The bodies of Fischbach and Ponton were repatriated to France once the fighting was over – the latter had been born on the island of Madagascar, a French colony at that time.

After his recovery, *Lieutenant* Vles joined No.346 "Guyenne" Squadron at Elvington but was shot down and killed on 4th November 1944 whilst on a mission to Dortmund. He had been part of the crew of Halifax NA558, which was lost over Bochum. His father, Frederick, had been a professor at Strasbourg University and was taken to the Dachau concentration camp where he died on 2nd July 1944. *Sergent* Allain survived the war and died in March 1983.

A French-Canadian, *Sergent* Soury-Lavergne also joined a Free French squadron after recovering from injuries sustained in the forced landing near Consett. He eventually joined No.347 ("Tunisie") Squadron at Elvington and served as a rear gunner in a Halifax crew. On the night of 2nd November 1944, his aircraft was shot down near the Belgian/German border. Bailing out, he evaded capture for five days and nights, re-joining his unit on his return to England. Flying another 20 missions before the war ended, he remained in the post-war French air force, first of all flying in former *Luftwaffe* Junkers Ju 52 transports based in Madagascar. He then retrained as a navigator and served in Indochina, flying as part of various B-26 Invader and C-47 Dakota crews. Retiring to Limoges, he became a noted member of the Limousin Aero-Club, based at Limoges-Bellegarde airfield, known as "the man in the white suit and cap". He died in 2010.

For many years after the war, it was possible to work out exactly where Rene Richard's bomber had crashed through the line of trees atop Bunker Hill. Several of the trees were missing their top sections.

STIRLING BREAK-UP OVER SHILDON

A Short Stirling Mk.III bomber, similar to the aircraft that came down near Shildon at the end of May 1944. By that time, the type had all but been withdrawn from front-line service but was still useful for training new bomber crews at what were known as Heavy Conversion Units.

Bombers on training missions that crashed on the County Durham hills were one thing, but when they came down close to towns, it affected a lot of people – witnesses, would-be-rescuers and those charged with the clear up work. People around at the time aged but their memories of the event remained strong. Stories regarding the crash were passed from parents to children, ensuring the incident was never forgotten. The town of Shildon played host to one such event on 31st May 1944.

Valerie Johnson, just five years old at the time, remembered being part of a group of mothers and children returning from Bishop Auckland, where they had been to visit the cinema. They watched in awe and disbelief as a huge bomber aircraft flew over and then crashed nearby:

"We were walking along the old railway line which leads from the King William to Shildon station. Before the Jubilee Estate was built, there was a completely open view towards the Store Farm. My mother and most of the other ladies gazed in fascination at the plane. Then they realised that one lady who lived in London for part of the war had pushed her son onto the ground and was lying on top of him to protect him."

Short Stirling Mk.III LK517 was the aircraft in question. The Stirling was a four-engined machine, a type which had been a mainstay of RAF Bomber Command in the early days of the force's campaigns against German cities and industrial targets. With the advent of more capable designs such as the Halifax and Lancaster, Stirlings had been relegated to second-line duty such as glider towing, para-dropping and bomber crew training. It was the last role that the aircraft lost near Shildon was carrying out that day. LK517 belonged to No.1654 Heavy Conversion Unit, based at RAF Wigsley, near Lincoln. The unit received newly formed crews and taught them how to fly and fight in bigger ("heavier") aircraft, the pilots "converting" to these types after having learnt to fly multi-engined machines on twin-engined planes such as the Airspeed Oxford, Bristol Blenheim or Vickers Wellington.

Pilot Officer Stanley Wilson was detailed to fly a five-hour-long daytime cross-country navigation exercise on 31st May 1944. According to the official records for RAF Wigsley, the training sortie involved the following:

"A Stirling aircraft, LK517, was detailed to complete a short cross-country exercise with Time and Distance runs, this aircraft crashed at Shildon, County Durham, though causes at present unknown."

Stan Wilson's crew consisted of Flying Officer John Brooks (Bomb Aimer), Sergeant Donald Curtis (Flight Engineer), Sergeant Nathaniel Crawford (Navigator), Sergeant Fred Bates (Wireless Operator), Sergeant Walter Lawton (Air Gunner) and Sergeant Thomas Parr (Air Gunner). Lawton's position was in the mid-upper (dorsal) gun turret and Parr's in the tail turret as "Tail-End Charlie".

Before take-off, the crew had been informed that thunder clouds with tops reaching up to 20,000 feet were forming over the Pennine Hills, these expecting to move eastwards. Bad weather was certainly a hazard for all crews, but especially inexperienced ones.

At 1645 hours on the afternoon of the 31st, the Garrison Engineer of a prisoner of war camp near Darlington heard an aircraft flying nearby. From the unusual noise it appeared to be making, the officer believed it to be in difficulty. Shortly afterwards, he heard two muffled explosions, immediately followed by the sound of engines being revved up to full power. He stated that they were *"producing a noise such as I have never heard from any aircraft before."* The witness then watched pieces of airframe falling out of the clouds.

LK517 crashed into fields located between Middridge and Shildon, just off Spout Lane and directly opposite the access lane to East Thickley Farm (now demolished but situated on the opposite side of the railway line from the modern-day Locomotion Museum). The area of the impact was known as "Store Fields". Den Ewbank, who was taken to see the wreckage by his father, said:

"The enquiry put the crash down to pilot error, but the crash report states that there was something stuck in the scavenge pump of one of the engines. These aircraft were notoriously underpowered and so the height from wheels to cockpit was huge to give it extra lift at take-off."

The location of the 31st May 1944 crash: Spout Lane is the road running north from the railway bridge bottom left, and the access from the old East Thickley Farm can be made out, running from a point just south of West Thickley Farm. The Stirling crashed in the "Store Fields" on the other side of Spout Lane from the junction with the access road. Shildon is off to the left of the map and the village of Middridge is just off the map's top right. (OS Six-inch England and Wales, Durham Sheet XLII S.E., Revision of 1914-15 (with additions in 1938), part revision 1939, reproduced with the permission of the National Library of Scotland).

All that remained of the Stirling was its forward fuselage section, with both wings and all four radial engines still attached. However, both wing tips were missing, along with the fuselage aft of the wing trailing edges and the tail section. These had detached prior to impact.

At first, air accident investigators who examined the wreckage could not ascertain which part of the Stirling had failed first, or importantly, why it had done so. The subsequent RAF Board of Inquiry into the incident could not offer much beyond speculation on the cause of the crash:

"Loss of control when flying in cloud in which icing, and extremely bumpy conditions were to be expected... this may have resulted in a steep dive at very high speed in which over-speeding of the motors occurred. A violent pull out of the dive, probably on catching sight of the ground, may have resulted in an initial structural failure, followed by the disintegration of other portions of the airframe."

The crash at the Store Fields did not occur in isolation. It was the third in a series of five such incidents, all involving Stirlings that were lost in similar circumstances.

Each Stirling emerged from a storm cloud in a steep dive, and their pilots had pulled back hard on their control columns, attempting to level out. This action overstressed the airframes to the point where they had completely failed, the aircraft breaking up in the process. An examination of the fifth such crash, involving the loss of LK207 over Bedfordshire, revealed that the aircraft had become inverted at one point. Flight tests showed that a Stirling dived beyond its limiting speed would lead to a progressively nose-heavy tendency building up. This led to an increasing loss of control which, if not corrected, would lead to the aircraft "bunting" over onto its back, and once in this inverted position, the resulting overstress would result in the airframe breaking up.

However, the reasons for the steep dives needed to be explained. It turned out that the pilot's seat harness restricted movement to the point where it was uncomfortable to wear for extended periods. It was soon discovered that pilots tended to only fasten their harnesses during take-offs and landings, but not during the remainder of their flights. Therefore, if a Stirling flew into a storm and turbulence forced it into an unexpected dive, the pilot could easily slide forwards out of his seat, the resulting push on the control column sending the aircraft into an even steeper descent.

The Northern Echo's 2nd June 2013 edition ran a story about plans to establish a permanent memorial for the crash in the town:

"A man who witnessed a Second World War bomber crash which killed seven airmen is seeking support to erect a memorial to the accident ahead of its 70th anniversary.

Craig Allison, 73, hopes to create a tribute to the men killed when an RAF Stirling bomber crashed on the outskirts of Shildon, County Durham.

The four-engined bomber got into difficulties during a training flight from RAF Wigsley, Lincolnshire, and crashed at 5.15 pm on Friday, March 31, 1944. Pilot Officer Stanley Wilson, of Newcastle, and six Canadians were killed.

A plaque was placed at the British Rail Staff Association, on Hackworth Road, but Mr. Allison believes there should be a more prominent memorial. The former Merchant Navy seaman, of Whitby, North Yorkshire, said: 'I lived with my grandparents on All Saints Road, Shildon, during the war. As we were sitting down for tea there was an almighty bang and everyone ran onto the streets. In the distance there was a big pall of black smoke and the windows were still shaking. No-one knew what it was. I saw the wreckage and it was smouldering. It was a horrific site for me as a four-year-old. I wondered about what caused the crash for many years and it would be nice to see a bigger memorial erected in the town to these men.'

Alan Elwood, secretary of Shildon History Recall Society, said: 'We can't support the idea financially, but we will give support in other ways.'

Eye witnesses to the crash claimed that the aircraft passed low over the town, engulfed in flames, before the impact.

The wreckage was scattered over a large area on the Co-operative Farm, near to where Jubilee Estate is now, and people searched for survivors despite exploding ammunition."

A "1944 Bomber Benefit" event was to be held on 4th April 2020, with the funds raised going towards the creation of a suitable memorial, but this had to be cancelled due to the COVID-19 outbreak. There may be no plaque or commemorative stone to the crew of LK517 at Shildon, but memories of the event lingered for many years after the event, and stories have been passed onto subsequent generations. It is unlikely that the crash in May 1944 will ever be entirely forgotten by people who live there.

THE MICKLE FELL STIRLING

Pictured in July 1977, this was the debris that could still be found up on Mickle Fell, County Durham. It was the surviving wreckage from Stirling LK488, which crashed there back in October 1944. During the 1960s it was possibly the most complete high ground aircraft wreck in the country and proved to be something of a mecca for the burgeoning wreckovery movement. Identifiable pieces were removed some time ago. (John Earnshaw, CC BY-SA 2.0)

During the Second World War, high ground located along the western border of County Durham was responsible for claiming the lives of several airmen. The Pennines proved to be a killer, especially in conditions of poor visibility and low cloud. Training flights, often involving newly formed crews with limited experience of cross-country navigation, occasionally came to grief over these hills. One such mission ended in disaster in the early hours of 19th October 1944. Miraculously, however, one member of the doomed crew survived to tell the tale.

No.1651 Heavy Conversion Unit was based at RAF Wratting Common in Cambridgeshire. HCUs were used to convert crews from smaller twin-engined bombers such as the Wellington and Whitley to the "heavies", Lancasters and Halifaxes. Training involved frequent cross-country navigation flights, initially by day and then as crews became proficient on the much larger machines, at night. Flying as a team needed to become second nature before these new crews could be posted to an operational squadron and take part in raids over Germany.

In mid-October 1944, one of the training crews assigned to No.1651 HCU consisted of six New Zealanders and their British flight engineer. 22-year-old pilot Flight Sergeant Peter Young's crew was made up of the following airmen: Flight Sergeant Neil Burgess (Navigator), Sergeant Bertram Davis (Flight Engineer), Flight Sergeant John Slack (Bomb Aimer), Flight Sergeant Rex Furey (Wireless Operator), Flight Sergeant George Child (Air Gunner, Mid-Upper Turret) and Warrant Officer Alan Small (Air Gunner, Tail Turret).

On the evening of 18th October 1944, Young was assigned Stirling Mk.III LK488, coded "QQ-E". He and his crew were briefed to fly a cross-country navigation exercise at low level. It was to be their final flight before they were posted to a front-line squadron. From Wratting Common, they were to fly north towards South Yorkshire and then head for Hexham, on the Tyne Valley, before turning south and turning at Gainsborough for their final leg back to base.

Their time of take-off was 2305 hours. Young headed north-west and as he reached North Yorkshire, fog was encountered sitting over the Vale of York – not an uncommon event but deadly for novice crews. Rather than continue the briefed mission at low level, the pilot climbed to 4,500 feet to find better visibility. However, before long he turned westwards, diverting from their planned direct track towards Hexham. In addition – something that would prove to be a fatal decision – the New Zealander descended to 2,500 feet, an altitude just below the top of one of the Pennine Hills directly ahead of them.

Mickle Fell, pictured from the west. A steep cliff runs along the upper southern flank of the summit plateau and the entire area lies within the Warcop Training Ranges, north-west of the B6276 at Grains o' th' Beck. Access is restricted to a handful of days a year, with permission. (Richard Webb, CC BY-SA 2.0)

Flight Sergeant Peter Dawbarn Young hailed from Auckland, New Zealand. Aged just 22, he met his death on a lonely hilltop in what was Yorkshire, but now lies in County Durham.

Mickle Fell is a 2,585-foot-high top, at that time lying in North Yorkshire (but passed to County Durham for administrative and ceremonial purposes in 1974, thus its inclusion in this book). At around 0100 on the 19th, LK488 flew into the south side of the summit ridge, the impact causing the aircraft to cartwheel over the top which was not much higher up. The Stirling broke up as it did so, large pieces of airframe coming to rest in shake holes on the north side of the ridge.

It seemed that Flight Sergeant Young had hit the fell top one wing high, presumably during a banking turn, possibly to avoid the ridge line at the last minute. Most of one wing, the one lower than the other, was torn off in the impact. The resulting cartwheel saw the bomber fall upside down on the upper northern slopes, an assumption made due to an intact bomb rack being found at the site in the 1960s. If the Stirling had crashed right side up, this piece would likely have been damaged due to the impact.

Most of the crew were sitting in the front section of the bomber, either in the cockpit or just below and behind it. The mid-upper gunner sat in his dorsal turret on top of the fuselage, just aft of the wing-trailing edge. All six died in the impact. However, the rear gun turret was torn off the aircraft as it cartwheeled over the summit, rolling for some distance down the north side of the ridge before coming to rest. The tail gunner, Warrant Officer Small, was thrown about in his turret and received numerous injuries.

Alan Small was lucky to be alive. After checking to see whether any of his colleagues had survived the crash, he sadly found that they had all perished. Despite his own predicament, which included a broken leg and chest injuries, the tail gunner managed to crawl some two miles to the north and found help at Birkdale Farm, on today's Pennine Way just above the Maize Beck, which he would have had crossed in the dark. The alarm was then raised by the farmer, although given Birkdale's isolation at the top of the valley, this took some time. Small was eventually taken to the Friarage Hospital in Northallerton for treatment. He spent five weeks there before being allowed to return to his unit. The warrant officer became a "spare gunner", filling in for missing members of other crews, before training as an instructor, surviving the war. His colleagues were buried at the Commonwealth Cemetery in Harrogate.

Given the remoteness of the crash site, the RAF recovery and clear-up duties were not without their own difficulties. Personnel from Croft-on-Tees aerodrome, south of Darlington, were assigned to retrieve the bodies. The station's Operations Record Book provides the following details:

"Under the direction of the Adjutant, F/Lt. Burgoyne had to hike over boggy ground and then up a sheer, slippery incline. The expedition was carried out successfully in very bad weather, it having rained continuously throughout."

An RAF Maintenance Unit party – possibly from No.83 MU at Woolsington (now Newcastle International Airport) – was also tasked with salvaging any useful and serviceable instruments and other items from the wreckage of the Stirling. This would not have been an easy task. Bad weather finally forced the clean-up work to be abandoned on 6th November 1944.

Sergeant Bertram George Davis was a member of the RAF Volunteer Reserve. At 36 years of age, he was the "old man" of Peter Young's trainee bomber crew. He was one of the six airmen onboard Stirling LK488 to perish when it struck the top of Mickle Fell in October 1944. He is buried at Harrogate, North Yorkshire.

Salvage crews often buried wreckage where possible in order to dispose of it. One reason was to stop other pilots flying over the area reporting a new crash when the pieces they saw came from a known incident. Up on Mickle Fell, this was impossible, so the RAF men improvised. Several small sink holes were located near the impact site. They cut up the larger sections of airframe into smaller chunks and pushed them into the holes, collected the smaller scraps lying around and threw them on top as well. The sink holes – which were also known as "shake holes" - became home to pieces of engine and airframe.

An early mention of the Stirling wreckage appeared in *The Yorkshire Evening Post* on 19th August 1950, and it appeared that the hikers' discovery had sparked an RAF search and rescue operation due to a more recent aircraft disappearance:

"Twelve men from a Royal Air Force Moorland Rescue unit from Topcliffe aerodrome today resumed their search of Mickle Fell, Yorkshire's highest peak, for the wreckage of a plane reported seen by two ramblers

yesterday. The ramblers, who were walking from High Force to Brough, had reported to Kirkby Stephen police that they had seen the wreckage near High Cup Nick.

Footnote: Last January, a Mosquito plane and crew of two disappeared while on a cross-country flight from Coningsby, Lincs. Its route was over the Mickle Fell area. Their plane was never found. It is believed the wreckage seen yesterday is a Stirling bomber which crashed during the war."

High Cup Nick is located a couple of miles to the west across in Cumbria, on the other side of Murton Fell. It was not the area where LK488 had gone --down in 1944.

Before the RAF Maintenance Unit salvage party finally abandoned work on Mickle Fell in early November 1944, they pushed large sections of wreckage from the crashed Stirling into several shake holes close to the impact area. The photo was taken on 12th July 1977, less than two months before RAF helicopters were used to retrieve some of the larger remaining sections of airframe. (John Earnshaw, CC BY-SA 2.0)

Aviation archaeology suddenly became "a thing" during the 1960s, when groups of enthusiasts scoured the hills for crash sites. Back then, most aircraft wrecks were found in the same condition that they had been left in during the Second World War, including the Stirling crash on Mickle Fell. Indeed, this became one of the most visited locations in the country, due to the completeness of the remains, albeit pieces of airframe scattered across several holes in the hillside.

Flight Sergeant Rex Furey was another of the New Zealanders in Young's crew. An air gunner, he had been posted to No.2 Bombing and Gunnery School, RCAF Mossbank, Saskatchewan, in October 1943 for training. He is pictured here with his new Wireless Operator/Air Gunner brevets.

Some of the more identifiable pieces such as propeller blades, guns and Alan Small's turret, which was largely intact, vanished from the site over the years. RAF Puma helicopters were used to retrieve some of the larger sections on 1st September 1977, the plan being to use them in a future Stirling "rebuild" project. In March 2013, the *Northern Echo* published an article describing this exercise. David Thompson was quoted in the piece:

"'The wreckage was removed by the RAF using a Puma helicopter in 1977 – I should know as I was there.' He was among the air cadets from Darlington and Stockton who, under the leadership of Stan Howes, assisted in the operation. 'Unfortunately, a lot of the wreckage was scrapped, but the more significant and larger pieces, such as the fuselage, are now stored in the RAF Museum Reserve collection at RAF Stafford.' The items are not on public display. 'I've been back to the crash site several times and parts still remain on the fell, which is rather nice as there is no memorial, but the remains provide a fitting reminder of what happened nearly 70 years ago.'"

In fact, the task had taken two days, having begun on 31st August 1977. Despite the use of helicopters and numerous air cadets and RAF staff, bits remained on the hillside. There was also a poignant return for the only survivor from the crew. Alan Small returned to the scene of the crash in the 1970s to pay tribute to his former colleagues.

A second proposed retrieval job was scheduled for some time during 2007 but this never transpired. Pieces of wreckage from Stirling LK488 still lie up on Mickle Fell today. Please note that the crash site lies within a Ministry of Defence Training Range and a permit is required to access the area – even on the 12 weekends each year when firing or training does not take place. The area around Mickle Fell is not necessarily used for training by the Army directly but is an "overshoot" area for artillery firing, which explains the official caution that is exercised.

THE TUDHOE V-1

Two views of Heinkel He 111H-22 bombers carrying V-1 flying bombs. The aircraft were adapted to air-launch these weapons in late 1944, due to the original missile launching sites in northern France being overrun by the Allies. The flying bomb's range precluded it being launched from northern Holland, Germany or Denmark against targets in and around London, so air-launching would extend the weapon's range. A V-1 was launched off the Lincolnshire coast at Manchester on Christmas Eve 1944. It flew off course and landed in Tudhoe, County Durham. The top image is of a test aircraft with a V-1, the lower an operational He 111H-22.

Ask anyone who knows something about the V-1 flying bomb and they will almost certainly associate it with attacks on London starting in June 1944. Until the last of the launching sites located along the Pas de Calais on the northern French coast and some in southern Holland were liberated in October 1944, some 9,500 of these unguided, pulse jet powered missiles were fired at the capital. By August, only 20 per cent of the V-1s launched reached their targets, but those that landed and exploded caused a huge number of deaths, together with much damage and destruction.

Even before the first V-1 had been launched operationally, the Germans looked to find methods of boosting the weapon's effective range. One was to launch the missile from the air, using a Heinkel He 111 as a transport. The ageing bomber type had all but been removed from front line *Luftwaffe* service as it was obsolete in the face of new jet powered designs. It was considered useful as a potential missile carrier, however, and tests carried out in early 1944 demonstrated that a single V-1 could be carried under the wing of a He 111 and its engine started in mid-air. Once the pulse jet was working, the weapon would be released from its cradle, fall away below the bomber and head off towards its target. As a delivery system, the Heinkel would certainly increase the V-1's range but accuracy was bound to suffer given that the aircraft was moving during launching.

Mere weeks after V-1s were fired from ground sites in France, the first air-launched weapons were dispatched by He 111s flying over the English Channel at cities such as Southampton, which had previously lain outside the flying bomb's effective range. These attacks began in July 1944 and went onto occur sporadically during the remainder of the summer. The 3rd *Gruppe* of *Kampfgeschwader* 3 (III./KG 3) was equipped with He 111H-22s that had been especially adapted for air-launching purposes. This *Gruppe* was the sole survivor in KG 3 as both I./KG 3 and II./KG 3 had disbanded by autumn 1944. III./KG 3's air launching activities ended in October 1944 due to a lack of aviation fuel for heavier bombers and the lack of perceived success the missions were achieving. However, another bomber unit, *Kampfgeschwader* 53 (KG 53), had converted to He 111H-22s after being withdrawn from the Eastern Front in August 1944, assuming responsibility for the air-launch role from that time.

All available aircraft were gathered for a sortie on Christmas Eve 1944, Manchester being selected as their target. Although the Heinkels would not have to cross the East Coast of England, their planned launching positions over the sea between Hornsea and Mablethorpe left them extremely vulnerable to attack from RAF night-fighters.

A large force of bombers was sent out in the early hours of Christmas Eve 1944. They flew across the North Sea from bases in northern Holland and after reaching their launching points, fired 45 V-1s at Manchester. The mission went awry from the start. Some missiles fell into the sea almost, their guidance systems malfunctioning. Others failed to cross the Pennines and instead exploded where they fell around Buxton and other locations in the hills. Only a few managed to reach the Manchester area, the same overall 20 per cent effectiveness rate the weapon was reduced to in August 1944. One of them would fly off course and land in County Durham.

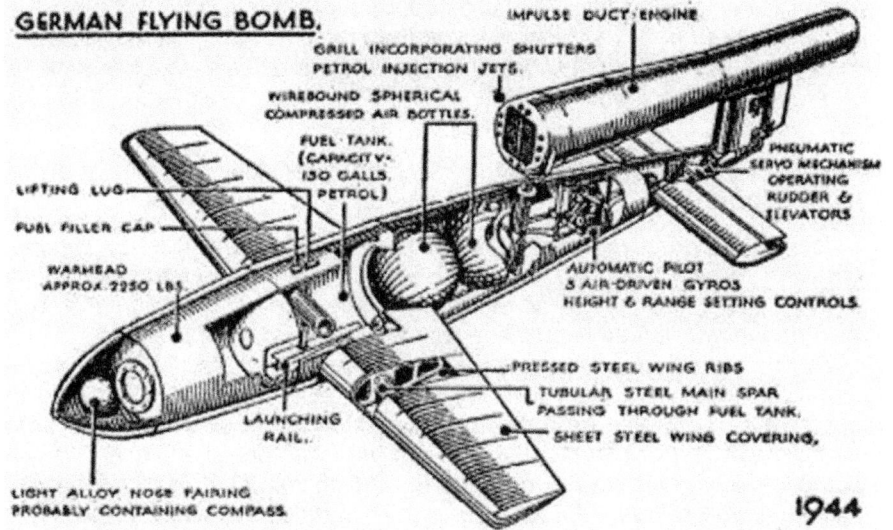

A 1944 schematic of a Fieseler Fi 103 (V-1) flying bomb. It was largely accurate although the weapon did not have tapered wings.

Shortly before 0600 hours on Christmas Eve morning, the Royal Observer Corps posts located on Teesside saw a V-1 crossing the coast. Personnel stationed further inland recorded its passage over the Sedgefield area as it headed north-westwards. One of those watching the missile was an air raid warden whose son was the vicar at Tudhoe, located about a mile north of Spennymoor. He remembered joking with a colleague about the V-1:

"I bet that's bound for Tudhoe."

Little did the man realised that soon, an explosion would badly damage the vicarage and send a door flying over his son's wife and mother-in-law. At 0605 hours, the V-1 exploded just above the cricket pitch at Tudhoe. Detonation had occurred at about roof level, the weapon's nose fairing ending up on the pitch itself, close to where the current clubhouse now stands. Cecil Lowes was six years old at the time of the incident, and lived on Back Row, Tudhoe, close to an ammunition hut. He recalled the events of that morning:

"When the sirens sounded, everybody was advised to go under the stairs, which was always accepted to be the safest place. My mam got us safely under the stairs and then you had to black out, so she went to draw the curtains, and as she did the window blew and the glass came in, then the front door blew open and she suddenly remembered our Trevor. He was only about one year old and had been left in one of our two bedrooms. She went upstairs to find the ceiling had come down on top of the bed, and Trevor was laid underneath it, blackened by soot, but otherwise unharmed.

It was mayhem outside. Most of the people wanted to see what had happened. We lived about 500 yards away from where it had landed, so we ran across the cricket field to see it. It was fantastic for a six-year-old. It was sitting on top of the grass tennis courts that used to be in the corner of the cricket field near the vicarage, but the crater was only one or two feet deep, very black all round, but only about the size of a snooker table. It seemed a bit disappointing, but I don't know what we'd expected it to look like."

Another child who lived near to the scene of the explosion at that time was Sandra Chaytors:

"I was a four-and-a-half-year-old blonde girl living in Front Street, Tudhoe, and went to bed that night wearing a white winceyette nightdress. I woke up with glass from the window covering the bed. I looked in the long wardrobe mirror and all I could see was a little girl covered in soot.

Downstairs in the sitting room, which was kept only for best, we had a large Christmas tree, right in front of the window. It was decorated with miniature crackers and delicate baubles. On top of the piano and along the mantelshelf were Christmas cards. When the flying bomb exploded, it blew all the windows and doors out, and all the Christmas cards down, yet the delicate baubles and miniature crackers still hung on the tree."

Despite the V-1 falling near houses, no-one was killed, although three were injured. Damage to nearby properties was however rather extensive, with hundreds of windows and doors being blown out. Roofs lost their tiles; chimney stacks came down and the locality was a scene of devastation over what should have been a festive period.

Mrs. Flemming and her daughter lived near the cricket pitch. The roof of their house was lifted by the explosion and all of the ceilings apart from one – the one in the kitchen – came down. Her son Robert was a Spitfire pilot based at Biggin Hill. He heard news of an attack in the North-East but didn't suspect Tudhoe had been hit until he heard from his mother:

"I heard on the radio news that one had dropped in the North-East but I never thought it would be Tudhoe. Then I got a heavily censored telegram from my mother about the bomb. But when I phoned up, I could not get through because all the telephone wires were down. I had to wait for a letter telling me all that had happened and then got leave to go home.

Everyone had heard of them [V-1s] falling on London. People found it hard to understand why one had landed on Tudhoe. Censorship meant even the village was not named as being bombed and it was only after the war that the facts of how it came to land on Tudhoe emerged. Probably no-one in the village heard it until it exploded. Before it dived to earth the rocket system [sic] cut out and there was a long silence before it glided down to earth and exploded."

The *Luftwaffe* did not – and could not – mount such an attack on that scale again. KG 53 suspended its air-launching operations on 25th January 1945 when almost the entire German piston-engined bomber fleet was grounded due to a lack of fuel. No further missions of that nature were carried out. No doubt if news of this had reached England, it would have been of little comfort to the residents of Tudhoe whose quiet life in County Durham had been temporarily shattered by a flying bomb that had flown well off course in the early hours of Christmas Eve 1944. However, at the time, it was not known whether there would be future raids of that nature. The Scottish *Daily Record* published the following commentary in their Christmas Day 1944 edition:

"It seems fairly certain that the Germans gambled on surprising our defences in the first V-bomb attack on Northern England recently, writes an air correspondent.

The new tactics may be taken as an admission by the enemy of the great difficulties they experience in piercing our intercepting 'shield' in the South and as a tribute to the strength of our defences in that part of the country.

It may well be that this blow at the North was merely an attempt to compel us to redistribute our intercepting forces so as to make an attack on London easier.

It is unlikely that the range of the V bombs has been increased. If these bombs were launched from 'parent' planes it is probable that the bomb-carrying aircraft ventured farther out to sea, hoping that on this new route they would escape detection and destruction."

Reports of the damage were kept deliberately vague due to censorship:

"One of the bombs launched against Northern England for the first time exploded in a field on the borders of a town, causing superficial damage to houses. The only casualties were caused by flying glass.

Some persons were killed and a number injured when a bomb fell on a residential district in Northern England. A number of houses were wrecked or damaged. Among the dead were a number of children. Workers dug among the debris throughout the following day.

V-bombs fell in Northern England early one morning recently. One fell in a field near an old market town mentioned in the Domesday book. Several bombs fell near other Northern towns.

A Heinkel pick-a-belly plane was destroyed during Saturday night."

The *Newcastle Journal* newspaper carried more of the same vague details in its 27th December 1944 edition:

"V-bombs fell in Northern England for the first time recently, it is disclosed in messages from correspondents, released on Sunday [Christmas Eve].

The phrase 'Northern England' was used in Sunday's 7 am official statement on enemy air activity during the previous 24 hours – the first such mention since the statements have been issued in their present form.

Sunday's German communique said that 'Manchester, as well as London and Antwerp, were shelled by our long-range weapons.'

If pick-a-back bombs are being used, their range would not be less than 300 miles. If the V-bombs come from Germany or Jutland, their range would be some 400-500 miles.

In one area in the North, a recent V-bomb killed some persons and injured a number of others, and a number of houses were wrecked."

Used to illustrate an article about the raid on a North-East pit village, due to wartime censorship this photograph of a row of houses at Tudhoe did not carry the name of the street involved.

The wartime photo was taken on St. Charles Road This is a comparison image taken in August 2022. Tudhoe Cricket Club is located on the opposite side of the road from this row of semi-detached houses.

Despite the censorship, the *Journal* managed to include an article entitled "V-Bomb Lands in North Pit Village Cricket Field":

"The North-East had a V-bomb recently. Believed to have been launched from a plane over the North Sea, the bomb landed in a cricket field in the centre of a mining community in the early hours.

Although considerable damage was done to house property over a fairly extensive area, only two families had to obtain alternative accommodation, and casualties were limited to a few people who were treated for cuts caused by flying glass.

A Catholic boys' orphanage stands near where the bomb fell, but not one of the 160 children suffered any ill effects.

'There was no panic,' the Sister told a Newcastle Journal representative. 'All the children were in bed at the time, and although a few of the babies cried after the explosion they soon calmed down. The older boys and sisters soon cleared away the glass blown out of the windows. They have treated it as an adventure.'

Damage in the main consisted of broken windows and doors, and tiles blown off roofs, and a flying column of workmen were soon on the scene to effect temporary repairs. Many of the householders, however, immediately began on emergency repairs, and soon one road, the scene of the most intensive damage, was busy with furniture vans and repair wagons.

Considerable damage was done to a vicarage standing near. All the windows and doors at the front of this substantial, stone-built dwelling had been blown in. Inside, there was considerable damage, and the Vicar and his wife were clearing up while workmen were busy with the repairs.

Broom in hand, the Vicar's wife told a reporter: 'I was sitting up with my mother, who is seriously ill, when we heard the explosion, and my husband who had come into the room with our four-year-old son Peter, was thrown to the ground. My husband received a blow on the head, and Peter's arm was cut. Mother suffered from shock, but otherwise we are all right.' Mrs. Hutchinson, of Clayton Park Square, Newcastle, a friend who was visiting the vicarage, also escaped unhurt.

Jack Rivers, an ARP first-aid man, who arrived at the vicarage within a few minutes of the incident, said: 'When I arrived, the Vicar was already on the job. Although he was still in his night attire, he was running about rescuing members of his family and other inmates.'

James Ball, a native of Sunderland, who lives at the vicarage where he is employed as a handyman, had to be treated for a cut arm. 'I was in bed, and the first I knew was when something fell on me,' he said.

Mr. J. W. Harris, who lives in a road which runs alongside the cricket field, had a small house party, but no one was injured, though the house was rendered uninhabitable. The village schoolmaster was slightly injured.

Blast played some curious tricks. In a neighbouring village, the windows were blown out of a shop, but not another window was damaged in the vicinity. A similar incident occurred in a village a mile on the other side of where the bomb fell. Various Regional officials, including the Deputy Controller, inspected the scene during the course of the morning."

Due to wartime constraints, little information was provided regarding the extent of the attack, its accuracy or what locations had been hit. However, post-war analysis shows that 14 of the 45 V-1s had indeed crashed into the sea just after they were launched from their parent aircraft. Out of the 31 missiles that made the coast, just seven fell in what is now the Greater Manchester area, and of those, only a single flying bomb landed within the Civil Defence Area for the city. It landed at Didsbury. Three of the missiles wandered off course – apart from the one which ended up in Tudhoe, a second flew across and landed in Cheshire, whilst a third fell in

Northamptonshire. In total, 42 were killed and just over 100 injured, half of them seriously. The *Luftwaffe* lost one Heinkel to a Mosquito night-fighter off the East Coast, whilst another was damaged to such an extent that it crash-landed on its return to base, killing one of its crew.

Looking back on the mission, the amount of effort expended for what were minimal results, deaths and injuries notwithstanding, hardly seemed worth it. Christmas 1944 saw the Germans losing on all fronts, with their offensive in the Ardennes stalling through lack of fuel and firepower and the Russians only a few months away from the gates of Berlin. At this stage in the conflict, firing nearly 50 V-1s against one of Britain's northern cities appeared to be a rather futile gesture.

A DEADLY MOCK ATTACK

A Vickers Warwick ASR Mk.I air-sea-rescue aircraft pictured in flight during the Second World War. When the type finally entered squadron service after a rather long time in development, it was relegated to transport, maritime reconnaissance and air-sea-rescue roles. One of these aircraft crashed at Dinsdale, south-east of Darlington, in January 1945. (Copyright expired)

The Vickers Warwick had been designed in parallel with the company's successful Wellington bomber in the mid-1930s. Due to a lack of suitable, high-powered engines, development was protracted. Once these problems had been resolved, the design was obsolete due to the introduction of new four-engined types. Warwick aircraft coming off the production line were relegated to second-line duties such as air-sea-rescue and transport.

No.279 Squadron based at Thornaby near Stockton-on-Tees received Warwicks in October 1944 when the unit moved to the aerodrome. Its job was to support maritime patrol and strike squadrons operating from various airfields in North-East England and Eastern Scotland. Small detachments of Warwicks therefore operated from a number of different sites. However, the unit would lose one of its converted Mk.I air-sea-rescue machines in tragic circumstances near what is now Teesside International Airport at the beginning of January 1945.

BV233 served with No.279 Squadron and was coded "RL-J". It had been delivered to Thornaby on 14th October, the day the unit arrived there. On 7th January 1945 it was selected for a radio navigation and flare dropping exercise somewhere over County Durham. Flight Lieutenant Harvey Luck was assigned to fly the training sortie, his crew consisting of Flight Lieutenant Ronald Cooper (Navigator) and no less than four Wireless Operator/Air Gunners, Flying Officers Desmond Holland, Frederick Ritchie and Robert Woolfield, plus Sergeant James Wiles. Holland, Ritchie and Woolfield were from New Zealand, whilst Harvey Luck was a Canadian.

Flight Lieutenant Luck had acted as navigator in Warwick "L" of No.279 Squadron on a mission just five days before his death. None of the airmen who died with him were part of the crew on 2nd January 1945 when he was part of a search that originated in North-East Scotland and ended down at Thornaby, as the official logs for the squadron show. The following gives some idea of the type of missions that Luck and his colleagues carried out:

"Warwick 'L' was airborne from Fraserburgh and a search for the dinghy with survivor in position 5754N 0321E which had been lost and so far not relocated.

At 1544 in position 5755N 0350E an empty Lindholme dinghy was sighted. A message was received from control instructing 'L' to sink the dinghy by gun fire but it was lost in circling and could not be located again.

A message on VHF was intercepted from a Mosquito (KYU88) that it was over a dinghy in position 5756N 0427E. Course was set for this position and the area circled but nothing was found. On completion of the sortie the aircraft landed at Thornaby."

Flight Lieutenant Luck does not appear to have participated in any other operational sorties after that date, although training missions were not routinely listed in the Operations Record Book.

The tragic loss of this crew occurred on their return flight to Thornaby. BV233 was approaching Dinsdale, just a mile or so west of what was RAF Middleton-St.-George (now Teesside International Airport), at an altitude of about 500 feet when two Hurricanes suddenly came out of the blue. Their pilots carried out an unauthorised "dummy attack" on Luck's Warwick. To evade the fighters, the Canadian pilot hauled back on his control column, sending the air-sea-rescue machine into a steep climb.

As the Warwick ascended abruptly, Harvey Luck somehow lost control of the aircraft and it dived into a nearby field. He had no time to correct the machine's fatal descent. All six onboard were killed in the impact. The crew were buried at the Commonwealth Cemetery at Harrogate.

The Royal Canadian Air Force's official Casualty Notification sent out on 6th March 1945 read as follows:

"Previously reported 'Missing Believed Killed' 7-Jan-45 as a result of a flying accident (overseas) (approximately two miles southeast of Middleton St. George, Durham County, England). Now reported 'Killed' 7-Jan-45 (body recovered)"

Flight Lieutenant Harvey Samuel Luck belonged to No.279 Squadron based at RAF Thornaby, near Stockon-on-Tees.

An obituary for Flight Lieutenant Luck was later published in his home town newspaper:

"F.O. Harvey Samuel Luck, 32, pilot, and attached to an air-sea-rescue unit, was killed Jan. 7 when his plane crashed. Burial took place in the RAF regional cemetery, Harrogate, Yorkshire, Jan. 15. He enlisted in October 1939, at Fort William and was a member of the first class to graduate from St. Thomas T.T.S. in April 1940. After serving in ground crew, he remustered to aircrew in March 1942 and won his wings and commission at Brandon, Dec. 17, 1942.

After an astral navigation course at Summerside, P.E.I., he proceeded overseas in March 1943, and served for a time in the Middle East on torpedo bombers.

F.O. Luck is survived by his widow, Min Cathcart Luck, whom he married in April 1940; a two-year-old son, Harvey George; his father, H. M. Luck., Montreal, and a sister, Mrs. Perc. Leahey, Detroit. Three brothers-in-law are in the forces, Captain Robert B. Cathcart, Camp Borden, Private George Cathcart, Italy, and Leading Aircraftsman William Cathcart, RCAF."

The RAF Board of Inquiry held regarding the incident concurred that Flying Officer Luck had put Warwick BV233 into a stall, causing the aircraft to dive into the ground and explode. This had been carried out by means of *"excessive evasive action"* at 500 feet. The two Hurricane pilots that had carried out the unauthorised "bounce" on the air-sea-rescue Warwick, both New Zealanders, were acquitted.

MOSQUITO CRASH AT OLD THORNLEY

De Haviland Mosquito Mk.III ZK-FHC is finished in the markings of NZ2337. When originally built in 1945, it was allocated the serial number TV959. Used in the film "633 Squadron", it was then displayed in London's Imperial War Museum before moving to Duxford for restoration before moving to New Zealand in 2011 and work on bringing it back to flying condition being carried out there. A similar aircraft to this one was lost in a crash near Wingate, County Durham, in May 1946.

Even though the Second World War in Europe had ended just over a year previously, aircraft accidents were still occurring over County Durham in May 1946. There were plenty of air force stations located in the region and the numbers of training flights, though obviously reduced due to the end of hostilities, were still enough to see a small proportion of missions ending in disaster for the participating crews.

Mosquito T. Mk.III LR565 was built at de Havilland's Leavesden plant in early 1945. It served with No.13 Operational Training Unit at Middleton St. George (now Teesside International Airport). On 11th May 1946, Flight Lieutenant George Williams and Warrant Officer Ernest Goodman took off from the aerodrome on a routine training flight, the purpose of which was to have the pupil pilot (Goodman) practicing flying on instruments only at low level. Shortly after take-off, the Mosquito was seen spinning out of control above Bankdam Farm, Thornley, County Durham. The aircraft crashed into the ground between there and Thornley Hall Farm, with both airmen being killed outright as the machine exploded on impact. The *Sunderland Echo* reported the crash in its 11th May 1946 edition:

"Mr David Griffiths, a miner of Thornlaw South, Thornley, told a Sunderland Echo representative: 'I was walking along the road towards Thornley when I noticed the plane which was making an unusual noise. It was foggy at the time. Then I saw that the plane was on fire. The machine crashed in a field

on Thornley Hall Farm, a few yards from the hedge. There was a loud explosion and parts of the plane flew all over the field. The flames were so fierce that I could not get anywhere near the spot nor could anyone else.'

Mr. Albert Robinson, farmer of Thornley Hall Farm, said: 'I was in the house when I heard a plane and a big bang. I ran outside and found that the debris was burning furiously. There was no chance to do anything. The plane was in pieces and on fire and all that could be done was to summon the police and the National Fire Service.'

Sunderland N.F.S. attended along with other units."

One of the engines from LR565 was put on display at the Bamburgh Castle Aviation Artefacts Museum, Northumberland.

The Exactly a week later, the *Echo* carried a story about what had been said at the inquest:

"'Accidentally killed while on duty with the RAF,' was the verdict of Coroner T.V. Devey at an inquest at the Police Station, Thornley, last night, on the two aircrew who were killed in the plane crash near Thornley last Saturday. The men were Flt-Lieut. Arthur George Williams, of Skewen, Glamorgan, and Warrant Officer Ernest Christopher Goodman, of Kenton, near Fakenham, Norfolk. It was a rather bad day for flying, with mist and low clouds.

David Thomas Griffiths, of Thornlaw, Thornley, a miner, said he was walking along the road from Trimdon to Thornley, and heard an aeroplane.

As the sound of the plane came nearer, the engine seemed to be missing fire. He next saw the plane coming down in a nose dive. It plunged nose first into a field about 50 yards from where he was standing, and on striking the ground, exploded and burst into flames."

The Belfast Telegraph's 11th May 1946 edition carried the following story:

"The crew of two, believed to be a flight lieutenant and a warrant officer, were killed when a Mosquito aircraft of the RAF crashed in flames between Thornley and Trimdon (Durham) today. As the plane struck the ground there was a violent explosion which threw debris over a wide area.

The aircraft, which came from Middleton St. George RAF Station, Durham, was on an exercise flight.

Because of fierce heat and flames, no-one could approach the wrecked pieces in the explosion, but from papers found on their remains it is believed they were Flight Lieutenant Williams and Warrant Officer Goodman."

The second engine from LR565 can be seen at the North East Land, Sea and Air Museum at Sunderland (Author)

Ernest Goodman was buried at Fakenham Cemetery, Norfolk, whilst Arthur Williams was buried at Coedffranc Cemetery in Gloucestershire. The following appears on a website devoted to the history of Wheatley Hill:

"The Hospital Farm was at one time the Smallpox Isolation Hospital and the wood adjacent to the farm was called Hospital Farm Wood. There are some brick ruins in the wood and according to the maps may have been

limekilns. There were lots of high trees to climb and lots of places to play. My father told me at one time that after the war a plane crashed producing the crater next to the wood. The aircraft was a De Havilland Mosquito, serial number LR565."

The RAF salvage team apparently buried both engines in Hospital Farm Wood and these were recovered in October 1979. One was put on display at the Bamburgh Castle Aviation Artefacts Museum, Northumberland. The other one can be seen at the North East Land, Sea and Air Museum at Sunderland. Hospital Farm Woods itself has partially disappeared due to work carried out in constructing the A181 Wheatley Hill bypass, just east of the roundabout at Old Thornley.

AIRSHOW HORROR AT TEESSIDE AIRPORT

An artist's impression of Wellington T Mk.X LP597, which belonged to No.5 Air Navigation School, which was based at RAF Topcliffe, North Yorkshire, in the late 1940s. An identical aircraft, NC430, served with No.2 ANS based at Middleton St. George and was lost in a crash during an air display held there in September 1949.

The September 1949 Battle of Britain "At Home" Day Air Display held at RAF Middleton St. George was only the second such event held at the aerodrome, one of 82 such airshows to be held at stations the length and breadth of the country. These proved to be extremely popular events with the civilian population, who were only too happy to travel to their nearest RAF base to see the service's latest jet fighters, together with more familiar piston-engined types that had seen service during the Second World War, be put through their paces in a series of displays and mock exercises.

Some 7,000 visitors were recorded arriving at the 1949 display held at Middleton St. George. The day's events went without incident, at least until the final one of the day. A squadron of tanks carried out a mock attack on the aerodrome's control tower. Six Wellington Mk.X aircraft from No.2 Air Navigation School, which was based at the airfield, were scheduled to drop dummy parachutists and supply canisters in support of them. The *Sunday Sun* (Newcastle) newspaper's edition of 18th September 1949 provided details of what happened during this last display at the show:

"Crowd See Six Die in North Bomber Crash – More than 764,000 people throughout Britain, guests at 82 RAF stations' 'at homes' – saw spectacular displays by the nation's latest machines. And many saw the crashes.

As they watched fighters screaming through the air and bombers roaring overhead, they remembered the grim Battle of Britain nine years ago, when a handful of fighter pilots, with their Spitfires and Hurricanes, triumphed in a tireless fight against hundreds of Nazi bombers to save Britain from invasion.

One of the worst tragedies of the day occurred when one of a squadron of Wellingtons engaged in a combined air-land exercise at the end of the display at Middleton St. George aerodrome, near Darlington, flew straight into the ground and burst into flames.

As light tanks were engaged in a mock sortie on the control tower of the aerodrome in the last event of the day, the squadron of Wellingtons flew over in support, dropping supply parachutes from about 200 or 300 feet.

An eye witness said: 'It seemed as if one of the parachutes caught in the machine's elevators, and it crashed straight into the ground and exploded before hundreds of spectators.'

The 'plane burnt out in a matter of seconds and though fire tenders, ambulances and rescue squads were on the scene in a few seconds, there was no hope for the men trapped in the blazing plane.

Only a twisted mass of wreckage remained on the airfield about 300 or 400 yards from the nearest spectators.

Another eyewitness said: 'I never want to see that again. The crew must have had no chance. It was all over in a matter of seconds. The plane seemed to dive straight into the ground while it was banking. It slithered for a few yards and then it was all over in no time at all.'

At the time of the crash there were also powered model aeroplanes in the sky which were attracting the attention of many of the spectators.

An Air Ministry spokesman in London last night said there were six RAF men in the Wellington at the time of the crash. The names of the dead were given as: Flying Officer J. H. A. Macpherson, captain of the aircraft; Flt.-Lieut. H. B. Tatham, Flt.-Lieut. R. V. Wilson, Signaller (1) H. Chapman, Officer Cadet D. Hall and Officer Cadet R. H. Munday."

Memories of the disaster appeared in the Newcastle *Evening Chronicle's* 8th August 2017 edition:

"Thousands of spectators gathered for a North East air display almost 70 years ago to commemorate the Battle of Britain. But during the grand finale, the 7,000 County Durham crowd watched in horror as one of the aircraft plunged to the ground, killing all six crew members.

The forgotten disaster will be recalled on Wednesday when memorabilia relating to two of the crew, Flight Lieutenant Herbert Barrett Tatham and Flight Lieutenant Robert Wilson, will feature in a sale by Tennants auctioneers in Leyburn, North Yorkshire.

Newspaper reports among the items tell how the display was held at RAF Middleton St George in 1949. The wives of Flt. Lieut. Tatham, 27, and Flt. Lieut. Wilson, 25, were among the crowd. The finale had involved tanks staging a mock attack on the aerodrome's control tower, while a squadron of Wellington bombers flew in at 200-300 feet to drop dummy parachutists. As one of the aircraft banked, it fell to the ground, crashing 300-400 feet from spectators.

Opening and adjourning an inquest, deputy coroner F. Pacey said: 'It is a melancholy fact that what should have been a joyful public recollection of the Battle of Britain ended in this unhappy accident. It was a very great loss of six young lives.'

Another newspaper report is of a court martial of a squadron leader held at the airfield. It was alleged that the method used for fixing the dummy parachutists in the bomber was 'unorthodox, with an element of danger.' The hearing was told that the dummies had been secured in the aircraft's bomb bay by a light cord. The parachute cord had caught in the Wellington's elevators [the aircraft tail plane's control surfaces], preventing them from working properly.

Flt. Lieut. Tatham had joined the RAF at 16 and had served in Coastal Command during the Second World War, earning the Distinguished Flying Cross. Flt. Lieut. Wilson had enlisted in the RAF in 1940 and had served for three years in India.

The memorabilia include portrait photographs, a picture of the funeral cortege, a navigator's log book, cap badge, a copper flask and binoculars."

Thought to be part of the bomb bay of Wellington NC430, this section of geodetic structure was photographed at Teesside International Airport in 2012. (Stuart Reid)

Whilst the official cause of the accident was that a parachute had fouled one of the Wellington's elevators, the billowing 'chutes had in fact disturbed the airflow over the tailplane. This had immediately led to a loss of control and the resulting crash. One of those onboard was from Redcar, a former pupil at Coatham Grammar School.

Wreckage from the Wellington remained at Teesside Airport for more than 60 years following the incident. Pieces of airframe described as *"crashed remains of a resident aircraft from the RAF days"* were housed in Hangar 2 after initially being recovered from the crash site *"before being returned to their original location"*. However, by the end of 2012, these had been moved somewhere else (possibly off the airport site) and their current whereabouts are unknown.

The aircraft had apparently crashed into what had been the bomb dump area at Middleton St. George during the Second World War, when several heavy bomber squadrons were based at the airfield. Although cleared after the end of hostilities, this area was left undeveloped when Teesside Airport was built. Around the turn of the 21st Century, Defence of Britain, part of the Council for British Archaeology, conducted a survey of the entire south side of the airport and plans were drawn up to recover the remains of NC430, the intention being to display them at a suitable location.

However, in order to do this, a Notice to Airmen (NOTAM) would have had to been issued to warn pilots using the airport that work was going on just off the main runway. It was thought by some that mention of the word "bomb" caused the airport authorities to quickly develop a case of cold feet about the whole plan. Whatever the reason, work to recover the remains of the Wellington never went ahead. However, at least one piece was in good enough condition and visible, as shown by the accompanying photo. Who knows what lies just under the surface at the crash site?

A SHOWER OF METEORS

Gloster Meteor F Mk.IV VT340 was part of the same construction batch as VT324, which crashed at South Moor, Stanley, on 25th September 1951.

Nine incidents involving Gloster Meteors from No.205 Advanced Flying School at Middleton St. George took place over County Durham between September 1951 and January 1953. Six airmen would lose their lives in these crashes. The attrition rate for airframes and aircrew was considered high but still within tolerances at a time when British forces were engaged in Korea and keeping an eye on Warsaw Pact intentions closer to home.

New jet fighter types entering service during the last year of the Second World War were not without their own teething troubles. One of these was the Gloster Meteor, the first production examples of which were delivered to RAF squadrons in July 1944, just in time to be used against V-1 flying bombs. Compared with the contemporary German Messerschmitt Me 262 jet fighter, the Meteor's Rolls Royce Derwent engines were much more reliable and were capable of rougher handling by trainee or inexperienced pilots. However, despite being better than the wartime German jet engines, the Mk.IV's powerplants were not infallible. Occasionally, they failed – and if this occurred during a flight, the results could and often were spectacular.

Meteor F Mk.IV VT324 was delivered to the RAF on 17th November 1948. It was allocated to No.205 Advanced Flying School (AFS), which in 1951 was based at Middleton St. George. The unit had several two-seater Mk.7s on its books, but once trainee pilots were ready, they progressed to the single-seater Mk.IV.

Flying Officer Michael Rogers was one of the pilots undergoing training on Meteors with No.205 AFS. On 25th September 1951, he took off from Middleton St. George in VT324 on a routine training flight in conjunction with another machine from the unit. Their sortie would take them north-west of Durham. What should have been a normal, uneventful trip turned into disaster over Stanley. The *Yorkshire Observer* described the events which happened over the town in its 26th September 1951 edition:

"Main street shoppers in Stanley, County Durham, raced for shelter yesterday when an RAF Meteor IV jet almost skimmed the rooftops before crashing and killing the pilot on the South Moor golf course, about a mile away.

Crowds heard a thud as, according to eyewitnesses, an engine exploded in mid-air.

Wreckage was scattered over a radius of 50 yards, and it was three hours later that the pilot's body, embedded some 15 feet in the ground, was recovered.

It is understood that the 'plane took off from Middleton St. George RAF Station, near Darlington. The pilot was Pilot Officer M. F. Rogers, of Northwood, Middlesex."

The Meteor had crashed at The Middles, located a mile south of Stanley town centre. The site lay between South Moor and Craghead. It had been seen emerging from cloud in an inverted state, the nose dropping before the machine dived straight into the ground. More details were given by *The Journal* (Newcastle) in its 26th September 1951 edition:

"The pilot of a twin-jet RAF Meteor fighter was killed yesterday when his aircraft, after skimming over Stanley's main shopping centre, exploded and crashed seconds later about a mile away on South Moor golf course. The engines and fuselage were buried in a crater more than 15 feet deep.

Units of Durham County Fire Service from Consett and Stanley, and police and ambulances arrived on the scene and were followed by a rescue team from the nearby Louisa Colliery. A tractor was used to drag pieces of the plane from the crater. The plane fell about 300 yards from the clubhouse and wreckage and soil were scattered for more than 100 feet.

Among the first to arrive at the crash was Senior Aircraftsman J. Frost, who is spending leave with relations at Hollyhill Gardens, Stanley: 'I was standing near the golf course when I heard two planes whistle over quite normally,' he said. 'Suddenly, one began to make a noise like a motorcycle engine exploded and fell vertically from the clouds.'"

The townspeople of Stanley had a lucky escape that day. If engine failure had occurred a minute or so earlier, it is possible that the jet could have come down in the middle of a busy shopping street, with the resulting large loss of life. It is possible that Flying Officer Rogers somehow managed to steer his stricken Meteor away from the town when the engine exploded, saving lives on the ground, although from the description eyewitnesses gave to the newspapers, it appears that he had very little time to react before his jet slammed into the golf course. A local resident at the time remembered the incident well:

"I lived in Quaking Houses, right next to South Moor when the plane crashed on the golf course. My pals and I – I was 7 at the time – were

playing in and around the old air raid shelters when it came down and were among the first on the scene. To this day I remember the huge crater it made and the bits of debris lying around."

Gloster Meteor T Mk.7 WA591 (G-BWMF) is pictured here at Fairford in July 2012. This tandem-seat version of the first jet fighter to enter service with the RAF proved to be extremely useful in training pilots to fly Meteors, Vampires and Venoms. The attrition rate for these aircraft – and the single seaters – were somewhat high. One of No.205 Advanced Flying School's trainers was lost near Barnard Castle in November 1951. (Aldo Bidini, via Creative Commons)

The second accident to occur over County Durham involving Meteors from No.205 Advanced Flying School took place in November 1951 close to Barnard Castle. A two-seat training version, the T Mk.7, was lost when the aircraft entered an unrecoverable spin and crashed.

WA720 was delivered to the RAF on 26th October 1950 and assigned to the training unit at Middleton St. George. On 20th November 1951, one of No.205 AFS's instructors, Flying Officer H. Williams, was scheduled to fly with a student, Pilot Officer Peter Poppe, in order to practice aerobatics. The flight would take them westwards, beyond Darlington and across in the direction of Barnard Castle.

Peter Poppe was in control of the Meteor when he performed a loop and then tried to roll out of the top into straight and level flight. However, he did not have enough airspeed to accomplish this manoeuvre. The aircraft stalled in mid-air and entered an inverted spin. Flying Officer Williams took control of the jet in order to try and recover but it was no use. The spin was unrecoverable, and he ordered his student to bail out. Both airmen exited the doomed Meteor trainer, which crashed near Barnard Castle.

News of the accident was published in numerous newspapers across the UK. The *Coventry Evening Telegraph's* 20th November 1951 edition provided a brief summary, details echoed by the other publications:

"A pilot and a trainee baled out of a twin-jet Meteor near Barnard Castle, Co. Durham, seconds before the 'plane crashed into a field and

disintegrated after an explosion. The aircraft left Middleton St George RAF Station on a training flight with Flying Officer Williams and a student pilot. Williams landed safely two or three miles from the 'plane and was treated for a broken arm. The student also landed safely and telephoned back to base."

Together with his brother, Tony Crooks was walking to school in Barnard Castle from Startforth when they heard the Meteor approaching:

"We heard a jet flying over the town and saw two white parachutes drifting to the east. The aircraft circled to the west and disappeared. We heard at school that it had crashed at Cross Lanes, near the A66, so we set off after school to go and find it. We walked miles up the road towards Cross Lanes and found it in a crater in a field, which is now under the new A66 junction."

On this occasion, there were no deaths, although the instructor was laid off flying for a while with his broken arm. However, whilst Peter Poppe may have considered himself lucky, his luck ran out nearly 14 years later. He was killed in November 1965 when Gloster Javelin FAW.9 XH959 crashed into the sea during a search mission for downed colleagues off Changi, Singapore. His aircraft came down a few hundred yards from where the other Javelin had gone into the sea. Poppe's navigator survived but the pilot drowned.

Numerous accidents occurred at Middleton St. George, involving jets on take-off or coming into land. A fatal accident took place on 24th November 1951, just four days after the crash near Barnard Castle. Flying Officer Raymond Norman was assigned to fly asymmetric (one engine switched off) approaches to the station's runway, using Meteor F Mk.4 VW297.

Flying Officer Norman landed safely on only one engine, allowed the aircraft to roll along the main runway and then attempted to take off again, still with only one of the Rolls-Royce Derwents running. However, this caused the aircraft to slew to starboard as it became airborne. VW297 flew into the west wing of the Officers' Mess building. Despite this, the pilot was uninjured and attempted to extricate himself from the cockpit. However, as he did so, he was struck on the head by falling brickwork that had been dislodged by the Meteor's impact. He died from head injuries sustained at that point.

The way the Meteor had hit the Officers' Mess soon led to the creation of a legend at RAF Middleton St. George. It was suggested that Raymond Norman's jet had initially struck his own car, which just happened to be parked outside the building, then had come to rest inside his own room. It sounds too good to be true and probably is. Another persistent tale is that one can see the repaired brickwork outside Rooms 51 and 52 at what later became the St. George Hotel at Teesside Airport (which itself closed in the summer of 2019). However, all that can be seen today are bricked-up windows, evidence of later remodelling when the rooms were combined to make a larger bedroom fitted with an en-suite bathroom.

Another legend that has been built up around the sorry tale of Flying Officer's death is that his ghost is said to haunt the St. George Hotel. There have been several sightings reported over the years, including ones from British Midland Airways flight crew staying at the hotel. It is claimed that airline stewardesses overnighting at Teesside Airport would refuse to accept reservations for rooms at that end of the building. Ground staff working in and around Hangars 1 and 2 have also apparently witnessed apparitions. Flying Officer Raymond Norman was buried at Darlington West Cemetery but if you believe the stories, his ghost has wandered the corridors at the former Officers' Mess and its surroundings for years after his death!

Three further crashes occurred within four weeks of each other during March and April 1952, two of the incidents happening in roughly the same location. The first loss happened on 28th March and involved another two-seater, VZ632. A trainee was conducting supervised asymmetric landing overshoots at Middleton St. George, flying with the aircraft's port Derwent engine running only.

On the downwind leg to the runway in use, the engine in use suddenly cut out and the instructor immediately took control, trying to relight the starboard motor. His attempts failed and given the low altitude the aircraft was flying at, there was no option but to force land the jet. The instructor put the stricken Meteor down into a field next to the road between Darlington and Yarm, opposite the Old Farmhouse Inn. Both he and his trainee pilot were unhurt in the force-landing but VZ632 was written off. News of the incident made the same day's *Evening Despatch* newspaper:

"Two occupants were only slightly cut when a Meteor jet plane crashed this afternoon in the grounds of Morton Palms Farm, near Darlington.

According to eyewitnesses, the plane flew very low with its engines off. It then dived between two trees, hit the ground, bounced over a hedge and long a ploughed field. The pupil and a flight lieutenant climbed out."

T Mk.7 WF878 was also lost on 17th April 1952 when it skidded on landing at Middleton St. George, causing the undercarriage to collapse. The pilot was uninjured, but the jet was severely damaged and after an inspection, considered to be a write-off.

Morton Palms Farm saw another accident, this time a fatal one, on 24th April 1952. An instructor from No.205 AFS, Flying Officer Hugh Williams, was supervising Flight Lieutenant Arthur Lockyer. They took off from Middleton St. George at 0655 hours in Meteor T Mk.7 WA665. Solid overcast lay at 3,500 feet and the tops of the cloud were at 10,000 feet. Visibility was said to be around eight miles.

During the initial climb out from the aerodrome, WA665 entered cloud soon after take-off. About two and a half minutes later, the jet was seen to plunge out of the cloud bank at a steep angle, breaking up as it did so. The aircraft was thought to have disintegrated due to high "G" loading during the descent, possibly caused by the pilot trying to recover from the dive. It was never established why the pilot was flying at such a steep angle in the first place.

Pieces from what once was Meteor T Mk.7 WA665 were photographed adorning a tree at Morton Palms Farm after the jet exploded in mid-air in April 1952.

Wreckage from WA665 came down in fields at Morton Palms. The farmer had a very lucky escape, as reported by the *Newcastle Evening Chronicle* in their 24th April 1952 edition:

"Within a few minutes of taking off from Middleton St. George RAF Station, near Darlington, today, a Meteor jet plane blew up in mid-air at Morton Palms, only a few miles from the airfield, killing its two occupants, two flying instructors.

Owen A. G. Robson, of Morton Palms, on whose land the wreckage fell, was struck and knocked down by a flying piece of tail plane as he ran to see if he could help the occupants. He recovered and went on but found that there was nothing he could do.

Mr. Robson told a reporter: 'I heard the engine falter, then came the explosion and the plane simply disintegrated.' The victims were Flt. Lieut.

A. D. Lockyer and P.O. M. Williams. Both were married and lived in married quarters at Middleton St. George aerodrome."

Further details were given in a piece published in the *Hartlepool Northern Daily Mail* on the same day:

"Wreckage was spread over about a mile when a Meteor jet aircraft disintegrated in mid-air near Darlington today. The plane was from the nearby Middleton St. George RAF Station, and it is understood that both members of the crew, who were killed, were instructors.

A farm sale was to be held today at the farm where the accident took place, and parts of the aircraft were lying among the farm implements spread out in one of the fields for inspection.

The farmer, Councillor Angus Robson, said that he heard the engine falter and there was a terrific explosion. 'As I looked, the machine disintegrated in the air,' he said. As the machine exploded, a piece of wreckage struck him on the shoulder and knocked him down, but apart from bruises, he was unhurt."

The *Evening Despatch's* 24th April 1952 edition carried a poignant section dealing with how the wife of one of the pilots heard the jet come apart :

"While on her way to Darlington, Mrs. Williams heard an explosion. She thought it sounded like an aircraft, and as she knew her husband would be flying, she telephoned the RAF station."

Geoff Craggs, who was in his early teens at the time, did not witness the crash but after hearing about the incident, decided to cycle out to the site in order to see if any pieces could be salvaged. Instead, he was privy to a chilling sight:

"It had nose-dived straight into the ground. It had made a big hole in the ground and the RAF men were digging it out when I arrived. I was looking for Perspex that I could make rings out of.
They'd covered the plane with a tarpaulin, and I turned it back and there was the body of the pilot underneath – there was a pair of flying boots and his legs had been cut off but were still in the boots."

Denis Ralphs also remembered the events of that day. He was stationed at Middleton St. George at the time and was assigned to watch over the wreck at Morton Palms Farm:

"I was tasked as a crash guard, and I was there for about three days. We were sent with a hessian sack and a stick to pick up human remains before the foxes got them, and then we had to collect the other debris."

Peter Caygill, an aviation historian, provided the *Northern Echo* with more details about the incident for a piece published in 2020:

"It [the Meteor] was seen by a ground witness who reported that there was a considerable time lag between the break-up and the impact of the forward fuselage. It was also his impression that the larger pieces of the aircraft gained height after the breakup before falling to the ground."

Another picture of the devastation wreaked at Morton Palms Farm in the wake of the Meteor crash in April 1952.

Just five days later, No.205 AFS lost another two Meteors and their pilots in a mid-air collision close to RAF Middleton St. George. On this occasion the aircraft involved were RA480 and VW298, two of the single-seater fighter variants allocated to the unit. Pilot Officer Ian Gerrey was in RA480, and Pilot Officer Malcolm Goddard was flying VW298. They were both engaged in separate night flying training, the collision occurring in the early hours of the morning, shortly before 0300 hours.

Goddard overshot his landing at Middleton St. George and instead of continuing in the circuit to carry out a second attempt, elected to orbit the airfield instead. This put him on a collision course with Ian Gerry in RA480, and the two Meteors struck each other in the vicinity of the base. The latter jet came down at Low Dinsdale, about a mile south-west of the RAF base, whilst VW298 crashed between Sockburn and Neasham, less than a mile to the south. Both pilots were killed in the respective crashes. Ian Gerrey, who was just 19 years of age, hailed from Bournemouth, whilst 21-year-old Malcolm Goddard was from Bedfont, Middlesex.

More details regarding the crashes were given by the *Yorkshire Evening Post* in their 29th April 1952 edition:

"The two other planes were operating from the RAF station at Middleton St. George, neat Darlington. One of the aircraft crashed on open land at Low Dinsdale, a small village of a few scattered houses 1½ miles south-east of Darlington. The other came down about half a mile away.

In crashing, one of the planes brought down an overhead electricity line, cutting off supplies to farms in the locality. One Meteor dived nearly 6 feet into the earth and burst into flames that lit up the countryside for miles. The other plane apparently broke up in mid-air, for small fragments littered an area of about 10,000 square yards."

Further information was imparted by *The Shields News* on the same day:

"The planes were among a number taking part in night flying exercises. They crashed at about 2.45 am. Firemen from Darlington and Stockton, called out at 4 am, stood by the wreckage.

One aircraft crashed on open land at Low Dinsdale. Police and firemen recovered the pilot's body. The other plane landed at Sockburn, a hamlet four and a half miles from Low Dinsdale [as measured by road]. The pilot's body was not recovered until 9.30 am.

A report reaching Durham County Police headquarters stated that both planes crashed in open country and that no other persons or property had been damaged. Firemen and policemen who located the crashed plane at Low Dinsdale had difficulty in finding it in the darkness."

Concern at the number of recent crashes also made the newspapers. The *Yorkshire Post and Leeds Intelligencer's* 30th April 1952 carried the following story:

"There is much concern in the Royal Air Force at the steadily mounting number of crashes of pilots flying jet aircraft while under training.

Many senior officers ascribe the high incidence of accidents to the fact that the Service lacks adequate training aircraft in which pilots may learn to fly jet-propelled machines in relative safety.

Three jet 'planes crashed yesterday over the North of England; two collided near Darlington and a third crashed outside Hull. These raise the number of reported accidents to jet aircraft to at least 29 since the beginning of the year.

At present all conversion to flying jet aircraft is carried out on Meteor VII machines fitted with two seats. Last July, the then Secretary of State for Air (Mr. Arthur Henderson) promised that a new trainer jet aircraft would be in service with the RAF by this year.

This is a two-seater De Havilland Vampire, an operational machine adapted for training purposes. It does not meet all the requirements of the Service. Experienced pilots maintain that its speed will be too high for safe training. Even so, it is not yet supplied to the RAF.

Many pilots favour the latest Dutch training machine, produced by the famous firm of Fokker, and specifically designed for training aircrew in the ways of high-speed jet machines.

It is maintained that the policies of the late Socialist Government left the Royal Air Force with inadequate front-line jet aircraft and without any suitable machine in which to train operational pilots. By July last year, accidents were officially stated to have increased fourfold since 1949. I understand that this rate of increase, including published and non-published incidents, has been surpassed in the last 12 months.

The matter has engaged the rigorous attention of Mr. Donald Kaberry, the Leeds M.P. who, in the House of Commons, asked the former Secretary of State for Air a number of questions on the subject."

JET "DIVED OUT OF LOW CLOUDS"
Crash in Field Near Stockton

BY A "MAIL" REPORTER

THE pilot was killed when a Meteor jet plane from Middleton St. George crashed at Great Stainton, near Stockton, this morning. The plane came down in a barley field on the Town Farm, belonging to a Mr. Kitchen, at Great Stainton. It was only a few yards from the main road from Bishopton to Aycliffe.

As the plane crashed, it exploded and burst into flames. The pilot was killed instantly, and wreckage was scattered over a wide area.

CABINET AND OIL Part of the wreckage cut through an overhead electric cable, and other burning fragments set fire to a haystack 100 yards away on the other side of the road.

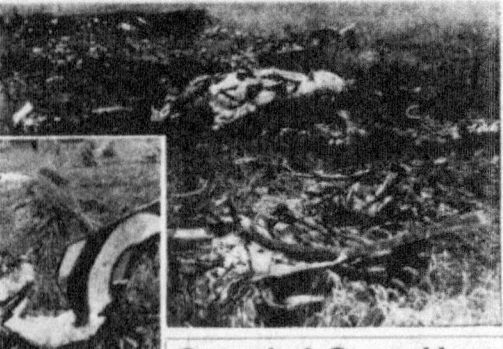

Crowded Court Hears

The headline in the 20th September 1952 edition of the Hartlepool Northern Daily Mail concerned the No.205 Advanced Flying School Meteor that crashed at Great Stainton with the loss of its pilot.

As far as County Durham and the Meteors of No.205 AFS were concerned, things on the crash front went a bit quiet until August 1952. On the 20th of that month, F Mk.4 RA429 was lost over Great Stainton, a village located a few miles to the north of Middleton St. George. The *Hartlepool Northern Daily Mail* ran the story as its headline in that evening's edition:

"*The pilot was killed when a Meteor jet plane from Middleton St. George crashed at Great Stainton, near Stockton, this morning. The plane came down in a barley field on the Town Farm, belonging to a Mr. Kitchen, at Great Stainton. It was only a few yards from the main road from Bishopton to Aycliffe. As the plane crashed, it exploded and burst into flames. The pilot was killed instantly, and wreckage was scattered over a wide area.*

 Part of the wreckage cut through an overhead electric cable, and other burning fragments set fire to a haystack 100 yards away on the other side of the road.

 Several farm workers saw the plane come down. One said: 'It seemed to dive out of the low clouds, and then could not straighten out. I don't think the pilot could have realised how low he was. He certainly made an effort to level off, but he could not have been higher than 700 feet when he came out of the cloud and just couldn't make it.'

 At the time of the crash – 8.50 this morning – a bus of the Durham and District Road Services, on the Sunderland to Darlington route, was on the road. Although the bus was some distance from the actual point of impact, the crash was visible to the driver and passengers, who were among the first on the scene. It is believed the first calls for fire and police services came from the driver, Robert Smith, of Sunderland.

 Within ten minutes, the first police were on the scene – a radio patrol car from Aycliffe. This car called more fire engines and ambulances from the surrounding towns, and the first fire engine – from Stockton – arrived within ten minutes of the call going out.

Firemen who manned this engine said they were not sure of the exact location of the crash but were guided to it partly by another jet plane. This plane, believed to be another from Middleton St. George, circled over the wreckage until the fire engine arrived.

The RAF authorities have not yet announced the name of the plane's pilot, but an inquest has been fixed for Friday morning. It will be conducted by the Stockton Coroner, Mr. F.W. B. Pacey, at Middleton St. George Aerodrome."

The same article also mentioned an incident near Stanhope in the early hours of the previous day. This involved a mid-air collision between two Meteors from a training unit based in North Yorkshire, and the story of this event will be described in the following chapter. The same newspaper, in its 22nd September 1952 edition, carried news of the inquest mentioned in their earlier report on the Great Stainton accident:

"Wing Commander E. G. Downey, station commander at Middleton St. George RAF Station, near Darlington, said at an inquest today: 'There is a belief among the public that the Meteor jet aircraft crash and burst into flames for no apparent reason. This is not so. There are only two reasons why an aircraft bursts into flames – either because it hits the ground very hard or because it has been strained beyond the limits of its endurance while in the air.'

The inquest was on Pilot Officer Thomas James Burrows (19), killed when his jet crashed at Great Stainton, near Stockton, on Wednesday.

The Deputy Coroner adjourned the hearing until this evening, because he said he felt that the pilot's parents, Mr. and Mrs. J. T. Burrows, of Cardiff, had not been satisfied with the evidence. Although Mr. and Mrs. Burrows then agreed to accept the evidence, the Coroner said the police would call further witnesses.

One witness said that the plane burst into flames before hitting the ground, but Wing Commander Downey said there was no sign of fire damage to the plane except near the crater it made."

It was established that during the flight, Pilot Officer Burrows had contacted Air Traffic Control at Middleton St. George by radio. This initial call was then followed up by a second, unintelligible one, with the only sound being heavy breathing. Burrows appeared to be pressing down on the "transmit" button continuously and therefore control tower staff could not contact him.

The subsequent Board of Inquiry could not establish a definite cause for the crash. However, it was felt that the pilot's heavy breathing and lack of response to his aircraft's terminal dive strongly suggested that he had passed out due to anoxia (lack of oxygen) or carbon monoxide poisoning.

September 1952 saw yet another Meteor loss for No.205 AFS, this time off the coast at Seaham. Early on the morning of the 26th, Pilot Officer John Caistor took off in Meteor F Mk.4 EE528 from Middleton St. George on an aerobatics practice sortie. The flight took him over the North Sea, and he began to perform various manoeuvres three miles off Seaham Harbour. However, witnesses on a tanker vessel spotted the jet failing to recover from a spiral dive. The aircraft was then seen to crash into the sea. Later that day, the *Hartlepool Northern Daily Mail* carried a story about the incident on its front page:

"Following a report by the tanker Diloma, that an aircraft had crashed into the sea three miles south of Seaham Harbour lighthouse, at 9 o'clock this morning. Seaham Harbour lifeboat put to sea immediately to search the area.

In the meantime, the Diloma continued searching along with a drifter, and shortly after 10 o'clock an RAF air-sea-rescue launch joined in. The lifeboat later reported a large patch of oil on the sea, and all vessels, and also an aircraft, were continuing to make a wide search. So far, no actual trace of the crew or wreckage of the aircraft have been found.

After a four-hour search, Seaham Harbour lifeboat returned to port without having found any trace of the plane. The aircraft, a Meteor twin-engined jet, was believed to have been stationed at Middleton-St.-George. A plane was reported overdue there."

Gloster Meteor F Mk.4 EE521 was built shortly before EE528, the aircraft which crashed into the sea off Seaham in September 1952.

More details regarding the search were provided by the *Newcastle Evening Chronicle*, also on 26th September 1952:

"The search began shortly after nine o'clock this morning when the oil tanker Diloma reported that an aircraft had been seen to crash into the sea. The tanker began searching the area and Seaham Lifeboat immediately put to sea. Together with the tanker and other vessels, including an RAF high-speed launch from Amble, the lifeboat covered a wide area.

Shortly before noon, the Diloma and the Sunderland tugs 'Hendon' and 'Ryhope', which had also taken part, abandoned the search. The tugs returned to the Wear and the tanker was due to enter the Tyne this afternoon. When the lifeboat returned, the coxswain, Mr. J. Tate, said they searched for two hours south of Seaham and for an hour south of Roker. The only indication of the position where the aircraft had crashed was a large patch of oil south-east of Seaham.

Aircraft continued to patrol the area. About 10 am, the lifeboat reported by radio that a large patch of oil had been found in the sea. A very choppy sea with a heavy swell was running over the scene of the rescue operations, which were hampered by a North-East wind nearing gale force. Sunderland and Hartlepool lifeboats had been ordered to stand by.

An RAF spokesman at Middleton St. George RAF Station said that an aircraft had been overdue from the station since 8.40 this morning. It is a Meteor Mark IV single-seater jet plane."

The aircraft Pilot Officer Caistor was flying that day had been involved in an accident on the day it was delivered to Middleton St. George back in September 1950. Whilst EE528 was being ferried north, the throttle jammed in the open position, so the pilot elected to attempt a single-engined landing at the RAF station. However, he overshot the runway and ran onto the soft grass. The aircraft's port undercarriage was torn off as it dug in. However, the damage was assessed as repairable and it eventually returned to RAF service and once again was delivered to No.205 AFS at Middleton St. George, this time without incident. No pieces of wreckage from the jet were ever discovered after it was lost in the North Sea. John Caistor's body was never found.

A photo of three Meteor T Mk.7s belonging to No.205 Advanced Flying School at Middleton St. George. WA715/B, the aircraft which was overstressed in flight whilst performing practice aerobatics in January 1953, is on the right.

The damage sustained in the final loss did not really occur over County Durham, although the Meteor involved was written off at Middleton St. George. On 19th January 1953, T MK.7 WA715 (coded "B") was being used to practice aerobatics over Croft-on-Tees, an aerodrome a few miles to the south of No.205 AFS's home base. At some point during the flight, the pilot lost control of the trainer. After managing to regain control, he landed safely back at Middleton St. George. However, an examination of the airframe showed that it had been overstressed during the sortie. WA715 was classed as "damaged beyond repair" and later struck from

RAF charge. It was further categorised as a flying accident since the damaged had been sustained during the aerobatic sortie.

No.205 AFS was renamed No.4 Flying Training School in August 1954, and the unit re-equipped with de Havilland Vampire FB Mk.5 single-seaters and T Mk.11 twin-seat trainers in January 1955.

The incidents mentioned in this chapter were not the only ones suffered by No.205 AFS between September 1951 and January 1953. A mid-air collision on 12th October 1952 between Meteors VW259 and WA707 saw both aircraft and their crews landing safely. Another jet, VW271, struck a telegraph pole on approach to Croft-on-Tees on 27th November that year, the airfield being used as a satellite for Middleton St. George. Yet another Meteor was damaged after it landed wheels-up on 18th December 1951. The pilot of T Mk.7 WG975 crashed on his first solo flight, which took place on 21st January 1952. A similar trainer, WG995, landed short at Croft-on-Tees and struck an electrical junction box on 7th April 1952, just a few weeks before the mid-air collision over Dinsdale described earlier in this chapter. Another trainer, WH227, was destroyed by fire during a refuelling accident at Middleton St. George on 23rd May 1952.

The pilots assigned to No.205 Advanced Flying School certainly seemed to be training at a time when there were lots of incidents, some of them fatal. This loss rate would not be tolerated in today's Royal Air Force.

METEOR MID-AIR NEAR STANHOPE

Gloster Meteor NF.11 WD597 was identical to the two all-weather fighters that were lost due to a mid-air collision near Stanhope in the early hours of 19th August 1952.

No.205 Advanced Flying School wasn't the only unit to lose Gloster Meteor jets over County Durham in 1952. In August of that year, two all-weather NF.11s belonging to No.228 Operational Conversion Unit at RAF Leeming, North Yorkshire, crashed near Stanhope in Upper Weardale after they hit each other near the town. The two Meteor crews were engaged in night interception sorties, using each other as practice targets.

Meteor NF.11s WD714 and WD772 had been allocated to the exercises over the northern Pennine hills. The pilot of WD714 was Pilot Officer Peter Hudson, and his navigator, sitting behind him in the tandem cockpit of the Meteor, was Pilot Officer David Crowther. In WD772, Pilot Officer William Hesketh was the pilot and Pilot Officer Frank Pinckard was his navigator.

Both jets took off from Leeming and climbed into the darkened skies, heading north-westwards towards their assigned exercise area, climbing to the pre-planned level of 17,500 feet. This was well above the Pennines so there would be no risk of crashing into the hilltops below. Hudson and Crowther's WD714 was to act as the "aggressor" aircraft, making a series of head-on attacks on Hesketh and Pinckard in WD772.

The first three mock attacks were performed without incident. However, on the fourth, a collision occurred. Both jets immediately went out of control and dived into the ground two-and-a-half miles north-east of Stanhope. As the aircraft fell out of the sky, Hudson and Crowther managed to bale out of their stricken jet. Hesketh and Pinckard were not so fortunate. For some reason, whether due to being incapacitated or through damage to their aircraft, they were unable to do the same. Both airmen were killed when WD772 crashed into the hills above Stanhope.

Details of the incident were reported in the *Hartlepool Northern Daily Mail* edition dated 19th September 1952:

"Two airmen died and two parachuted to safety when their planes – Meteor Elevens – collided about four miles beyond Stanhope (County Durham) while on night exercises early today.

One machine caught fire. Flames could be seen for miles around and wreckage was scattered over the fells. Search parties of farmers and police found the bodies about 200 yards from the main wreckage of one of the planes. They took them to Stanhope.

The aircraft, each carrying two men, were from the RAF Station, Leeming (Yorks.). The Air Ministry stated that the two men who had parachuted to safety were the crew of one of the Meteors. The body of one of the dead men was buried three feet in the ground when found by the police.

The dead are Pilot Officer F. R. Pickard [sic] and Navigator W. Hesketh. The two who parachuted to safety were Pilot Officer P. D. Hudson and Navigator D. H. Crowther."

A quarry office near Frosterley was used as a makeshift headquarters for the rescue and recovery efforts in the aftermath of the mid-air collision. At least one local resident, George Oliver, recalled seeing large pieces of debris, possibly from a wing belonging to one of the two Meteors, visible just above Crawleyside. These pieces were lying east of the B6278, just south of where the former Rookhope rail line crossed the main road. Mr. Oliver also remembered hearing a story that the surviving pilot had found himself walking along a quarry edge after he had parachuted from his stricken jet. Another resident heard stories suggesting that the two crewmembers who landed on the hills above Stanhope saw the lights of the fluorspar works below and went there to seek help.

It appears that the story itself disappeared from the newspapers almost as soon as the news had been published, as no follow up articles appear to have been published in local journals.

MID-AIR COLLISON OFF HARTLEPOOL

XA832/S is the nearest of these two Gloster Javelin FAW.6 interceptors. The type received the nickname "Flat Iron" due to the shape of its wings and huge tail fin.

The Newcastle *Sunday Sun's* 22nd May 1960 headline screamed *"Escape – Eight Miles Up"*, with the subtitle *"Three leap from plummeting Javelins, but one pilot hero clings on to save Hartlepool housing estate"*. The story itself told of a mid-air collision near the town, which could well have been a tragedy on the ground but for the bravery of one of the jet pilots involved:

"Two hurtling RAF jet fighters collided in mid-air eight miles above the North-East coast yesterday – and the four men in them lived. Two parachuted into the sea 30 miles off Whitby and the others landed near Castle Eden. All were picked up by RAF helicopters.

And later, the people of Hartlepool talked of the bravery of one pilot who wrestled with the controls of his turbo-jet Javelin to haul it away from a housing estate and crash it in open country.

'He deserved a medal,' said one man. 'The jet just managed to skim the housetops before blowing up in a meadow a mile away.'

Said Mr. John Bird, of Naisberry Farm, Elwick, owner of the meadow: 'I saw two planes climbing up and down. I thought they were doing aerobatics. They seemed to be about to loop the loop. They disappeared into clouds and then a few moments later I saw one of them coming back over Hartlepool towards me at rooftop level. It hit a hedge, bounced over the top, and disintegrated in a 400-yard track of flame about a quarter of a mile away from me.'

Another eyewitness, Mr. George Tweddle, of West View, Hartlepool, said: 'The plane came in low over the West View estate. It seemed to climb a few hundred feet over higher ground in the west, then it plummeted into the ground, bursting into flames and sending up black smoke.'

The aircraft – both all-weather Javelins from RAF Station Leuchars, Scotland – were taking part in Fighter Command's annual defence exercise 'Yeoman'. They were on their way to attack the flank of a heavy stream of bombers coming from Denmark to attack East Anglia.

The two-man crew of the Javelin that crashed into the sea 30 miles off Whitby were rescued from their dinghies by RAF helicopters from Acklington [Northumberland] and Leconfield [East Yorkshire]. The other two airmen baled out and landed close together in fields at Castle Eden. They were later picked up by the Acklington helicopter and taken to RAF station Middleton St. George.

Late last night, the Air Ministry named the airmen as: Flt. Lieut. D. J. Wyborn, of Yapton, Sussex (pilot), and Flt Lieut. D. S. J. Clark, of Woolaston, Gloucestershire (navigator), who landed near Blackhall, and Flt. Lieut. J. B. Wilson, of Portobello, Midlothian (pilot), and Flying Officer E. Wood, of Guildford, Surrey (navigator), who landed in the sea. Flt. Lieut. Wilson and Flying Officer Wood hurt their backs when ejecting from their Javelin.

Mr. Harry Gammon, a builder and contractor of High Hesleden, near Blackhall Rocks, was working on the front garden of his bungalow when Flt. Lieut. Clark came running up the path, flying helmet in hand. 'I got the shock of my life,' said Mr. Gammon. 'He said he had just baled out of a jet aircraft and wanted to telephone both the police and the RAF at Middleton. He was the navigator, and his one concern was whether the pilot was safe. He thought he might have dropped into the sea.'

Mr. Gammon took the airman by car to Blackhall Rocks where they learned that the pilot had been taken by a farmer to the police office at Blackhall Colliery. 'I took the navigator there and there was a joyful reunion when he saw his pilot was safe and sound,' said Mr. Gammon.

At the police office, Constable George Langley made tea for the airmen, who were then driven back to a field at High Hesleden where a helicopter whisked them off to Middleton St. George. The helicopter crew included a South Shields signaller, Sergeant Bill Boundy. He was the winchman who hoisted the men aboard. Other members of the crew were Master Pilot Stanley Bousher (37), of Brixton, and Flight Sergeant George Nicholas, of Hackenthorpe, Sheffield.

Soon after the aircraft crashed into the meadow, hundreds of sightseers in cars and on bicycles flocked to the scene. At one time the country lane adjoining the meadow was blocked by cars. Among the first on the scene were nurses from Hartlepool General Hospital and firemen from the West Hartlepool brigade, who put out the flames.

Police, headed by Chief Inspector Harold Coyne, who was playing golf half a mile away at the time of the crash, kept souvenir hunters at bay. There was a danger of ammunition exploding. 'I heard at least one live round in the wreckage go off', said Mr. Bird.

Later, an RAF officer directed a squad of airmen to collect live ammunition. The squad then mounted guard over the wreckage."

Wreckage from what had been Javelin FAW.6 XA835 was scattered across a field just a few miles to the north-west of Hartlepool.

Flight Lieutenant Wyborn had been trying to reach Middleton St. George to carry out an emergency landing following the collision, but as he overflew the Hartlepool area, he realised that the jet was not going to make it. He and his navigator ejected at 14,000 feet, their Javelin flying onwards and eventually crashing into the meadow just to the west of High Throston.

Obviously, this was in complete contrast to the *Sunday Sun's* headline from the previous day, which suggested that the pilot of XA835 had stayed at his controls to avert what could have been a huge tragedy on the ground. The London *Daily News* of 23rd May 1960 printed Flight Lieutenant Wyborn's recollections of the incident:

"Two of the four airmen who escaped when two Javelin jets collided eight miles up on Saturday, talked yesterday about their double brush with death. After they jumped unhurt from their wrecked fighter, the Javelin swerved round and flashed between them. It buzzed madly round them before skimming rooftops in West Hartlepool, Durham, and crashing on open land a mile from the town.

The story was told in the sick bay at Middleton-St.-George, Durham, where Flight Lieutenants David Wyborn, 28, and Derek Clark, 37, were recovering from slight shock. The collision happened during an RAF exercise 50 miles from the Durham coast. Officers watching the mock battle on radar saw the two dots marking the Javelins fuse and then disintegrate.

Wyborn and Clark landed safely near Castle Eden, Durham. The other Javelin's crew, Flight Lieutenant James Wilson, of Portobello, Midlothian, and Flying Officer Evelyn Wood, of Guildford, Surrey, parachuted eight miles down into the sea. They were picked up in their dinghies by air-sea-rescue helicopters and are suffering from shock and back injuries. Both crews are stationed at Leuchars, Fife.

Lieutenant Wyborn, a married man, told his story: 'At the time of the crash, we were about eight miles up and well over the sea, so we struggled gently down towards the coast.

Just over the land we got out in our ejector seats after steering the aircraft so it would head out to sea. It suddenly turned and did some very peculiar things. It even passed between us. Were we worried it would hit us? I think we were more indignant than anything else that our aircraft would behave that way towards us. I've baled out before, and strangely enough, my aircraft behaved just the same then."

Gloster Javelin FAW.9 XH764 is pictured at Manston in June 1971 wearing the markings of No.29 Squadron. (RuthAS, CC BY 3.0)

As mentioned in the newspaper reports, the two jets were from Leuchars, an RAF station located just north of St. Andrews in Fife. They and their crews belonged to No.29 Squadron. XA823 and XA835 were the two Gloster Javelin FAW.6s involved, with "FAW" standing for "Fighter, All-Weather", the designation for an interceptor aircraft that could operated at night and in conditions of poor visibility. Wyborn and Clark had been flying XA835 which crashed into the meadow near High Throston. Both aircraft had intiially collided at 40,000 feet above the North Sea, well off the coast.

However, more information came from Flight Lieutenant D. Freeston, a No.33 Squadron pilot who was also flying his Javelin in the same area. He watched as Wilson and Wood descended by parachute, the abandonment of their own jet being necessary as its tail section had been destroyed in the collision, which occurred at around 1415 hours. A Shackleton maritime patrol bomber, flown by Flight Lieutenant Letchford, was some 30 to 40 miles away when it was ordered to the area ten minutes later.

Letchford and his crew began an air search on arriving at the scene, and it was not before signals from the crew's emergency homing beacons were detected. The Shackleton, which belonged to No.42 Squadron based at RAF St. Mawgan in Cornwall, dropped two sets of Lindholme survival gear into the sea for the downed aircrew. These consisted of five containers which were joined together by floating rope. The centre container housed a dinghy capable of carrying nine men, whilst the other four were stocked with rations and warm clothing.

Although Wilson and Wood were located in their respective dinghies at 1511 hours, it took a while to effect their rescue. Whirlwind helicopters from No.228 Squadron at Leconfield in East Yorkshire were scrambled to pick the airmen from the sea. The unit's detachment at Acklington in Northumberland also dispatched one of their Whirlwinds. Helicopters flown by Master Pilot Bousher and Flight Lieutenant Sparkes carried out the North Sea pick-ups, the former also being involved in the retrieval of both Wyborn and Clark from High Hesleden later in the day. Given the distance to the scene from the helicopter bases and the relatively slow speeds of the machines involved, the Javelin crewmembers spent about two and a half hours each in the water before being winched to safety. However, the main thing was that they were both safe, thanks to their ejection seats and the professionalism of the Shackleton and helicopter crews, plus the No.33 Squadron pilot who had taken note of their position.

Wyborn must have had an enormous struggle to bring his stricken jet to the coastline over Hartlepool. During the mid-air collision, XA835's nose section had been completely torn off, yet the pilot managed to exercise enough control over the aircraft to reach land and steer it back out to sea again before ejecting. It is likely that the damage resulted in the machine turning and flying over the roof tops before crashing.

Neither aircraft had been flying for very long. XA823 was delivered to the RAF in November 1957 and had spent time with No.85 Squadron before being transferred to No.29 Squadon in 1959. It was assigned the individial aircraft letter "P" with that unit. XA835 was delivered in October 1957 and wore the letter "Z" whilst at Leuchars.

IT CAME IN THROUGH THE ROOF

Slingsby T.31 Cadet XA310 (BGA 4963) is pretty much identical to the glider that crashed into a house in Helmsley Road, South Shields, on the afternoon of 26th June 1964. (Alan Wilson, via CC BY-SA 2.0 licence)

Glider crashes have been uncommon events in County Durham, but one notable event occurred in June 1964 when one crashed into the roof of a house in South Shields. Thankfully, neither of the two occupants onboard were killed although one of them was taken to hospital for an emergency operation. The incident occurred on Friday 26th of that month, featuring Slingsby T.31 Cadet glider BGA 1062, which belonged to the Northumbrian Gliding Club. That evening's Newcastle *Evening Chronicle* provided details of the crash:

"*The pilot and his girl passenger were trapped when a glider spun out of control and crashed into the roof of a semi-detached house in Helmsley Road, South Shields, this afternoon.*

Three fire engines, ambulances and police cars went to the scene after the owner of the house, 29-year-old Mrs. Norma Harrogate, raised the alarm.

Firemen were fighting frantically to free the girl trapped by the legs. Mrs. Harrogate and her two-year-old baby Cheryl were in the dining room when they heard a terrific crash. Clutching her baby, Mrs. Harrogate ran into the hall as plaster, bricks and wood crashed in from the roof.

Dozens of people who saw the glider dive out of control into the house rushed to the spot. Mr. John Robson was waiting to go up for a flight when he saw the drama over South Shields. He told the Evening Chronicle: 'The glider took off with a girl in the front passenger seat. She was about 20. I saw the glider spin out of control and the pilot seemed to be heading for a grassy stretch opposite Helmsley Road.'

Hundreds of people were watching the battle to free the couple. During the past few days, the glider has been one of the chief attractions in South Shields Sports Week, taking passengers on seven-minute flights over the town and landing near the coast."

The glider had taken off from nearby Marsden Lea, being winch launched instead of being towed into the air by a tug aircraft. It was being used to give short pleasure flights at South Shields. In a strange twist of fate, the 32-year-old passenger, Edith MacDonald, was the next-door neighbour of Norma Harrogate on Hemsley Road. It is likely that the glider pilot, 30-year-old Brian Watson, had attempted some sort of manoeuvre over Mrs. MacDonald's house, one that had gone wrong and led to the crash landing.

Watson was extricated from the crumpled cockpit of the T.31 Cadet by firemen, having sustained a broken leg in the incident. However, the rescuers took more than 15 minutes to free Edith McDonald, and she was then immediately taken to hospital, as the following day's Newcastle *Journal* newspaper stated:

"A woman passenger was critically ill last night after the glider in which she was flying crashed next to her home yesterday. It rammed the roof of her next-door neighbour's home in Helmsley Road, South Shields.

The woman on the pleasure flight, Mrs. Edith Margaret MacDonald, aged 32, is in the town's Ingham Infirmary with head and back injuries. The pilot, Brian Watson, of Sunniside, Whickham, was also detained with a broken leg.

Mrs. MacDonald had paid 8s to take a trip in the glider, which was carrying passengers on 'seven-minute hops' over the town as part of the Sports Week programme.

As the glider – there were no other passengers – swooped over the street, it suddenly turned and spiralled into the neighbour's house, burying its nose in the roof.

Mrs. Marina Harrogate was in the dining room with her two-year-old daughter Cheryl when it happened. 'I was just about to go upstairs when I heard a terrific crash,' said 29-year-old Mrs. Harrogate. 'I ran into the street with Cheryl in my arms just as plaster and rubble started to fall down the stairs into the hall. I saw the glider's tail sticking out of the roof.'

Many people in the area heard the crash and rushed into the street. Police, firemen and ambulances were called. Firemen crawled over the rafters into the loft to find the glider's cabin a twisted mass. Mrs. MacDonald was trapped in the front passenger's seat. She took the full force of the impact.

Mr. Watson was carried through the loft and down the stairs by two firemen and Mrs. MacDonald was brought out the same way. The glider was cut into pieces and lowered from the roof by ropes."

NORTH WOMAN CRITICAL AFTER GLIDER CRASH

The scene on Helmsley Road was captured by a press photographer. The wing of the Slingsby Cadet is immediately to the left of the fireman's ladder, bent forward by the impact with the roof.

Unfortunately for those would-be passengers who may have been unafraid to fly in a replacement glider after this incident occurred, a decision was taken to ban gliding at the event, as reported by the Newcastle *Evening Chronicle* in their 27th June 1964 edition:

"Gliding from Marsden Lea, South Shields, has been cancelled after the accident yesterday in which a 32-year-old woman was seriously injured.

Mrs. Edith Margaret MacDonald, aged 33, of Helmsley Road, South Shields, was 'very, very ill' in the town's Ingham Infirmary, with head and back injuries. The glider pilot, Mr. Brian Watson, of Sunniside, Whickham, who has a broken leg, was 'quite comfortable'.

Mrs. Watson [sic – should have been Mrs. MacDonald] had paid 8s to take a trip in the glider as part of the council's Sports Week programme. The plane was flying over her own home in Hemsley Road when it suddenly spiralled into the house next door, embedding its nose in the roof.

Mr. Len Hay, the town's entertainments manager, said today: 'The gliding has been cancelled. This is all we can do after this tragic incident. It is a big blow to the Sports Week, but I don't think it will spoil it altogether.'

Another view of T.31 Cadet XA310 (BGA 4963), showing the flimsy nature of the machine and the open two-seater tandem cockpit. Although of strong construction in terms of stability and airworthiness, impacting a house roof was never among the risks that the type's designer would have had to consider. (Alan Wilson, CC BY-SA 2.0 licence)

SECONDS FROM DISASTER

Avro Vulcan B.2 XM610 crashed at Wingate in January 1971, narrowly missing the local school and numerous houses. Apart from being a lucky escape for the village, it was also a lucky day for the entire crew of the aircraft, who survived the incident. Crews did not always survive Vulcan engine fires in their entirety. (Photo copyright Ad Vercruijsse – www.aviator.nl)

Before the advent of the Royal Navy's submarine-based deterrent in the late 1960s, the RAF's V-bomber fleet provided the most effective means of delivering nuclear weapons. Crews of Valiant, Victor and Vulcan bombers practiced for the unthinkable, but by the beginning of the 1970s, only the latter were still actively training for this possibility. The Valiant had been retired in 1965 due to wing spar fatigue problems and similar problems had forced the Victor B.2R strategic bombers to follow suit in 1968. When the Blue Steel air-launched nuclear missile was taken out of service in 1970, the Vulcan's strategic role ceased, although the type was retained to drop WE.177B free-fall nuclear bombs as a tactical (i.e. battlefield) measure. Thus, at the beginning of 1971, Vulcan squadron crews were still training in the low-level role, using the Pennines, the Lake District, Scotland and the Border Hills as "playgrounds" for these activities.

No.44 Squadron, based at RAF Waddington, just south of Lincoln, was one of the units engaged in such low-level training flights. On 7th January 1971, Flight Lieutenant Garth Alcock and his crew of four were tasked with a "high-low-high" training sortie that would take them at high level up the North-East coastline before turning north-west into the Northumberland low flying area and towards the Cheviot Hills at low level. Flights such as this were routine but low-flying skills deteriorated if not practiced and therefore the crews carried them out regularly. The huge delta-winged Vulcans were a common sight flying low along the valleys of northern England, southern Scotland and North Wales.

For the sortie in question, Garth Alcock was assigned Avro Vulcan B.2 XM610. His crew comprised the following: Flying Officer Peter Hoskins (co-pilot), Flight Lieutenant Jim Power (air electronics officer), Flight Lieutenant Jim Vinales (plotter navigator) and Flying Officer Roger Barker (radar navigator). Garth Alcock – known as "Bob", after his middle name, Robert, and his co-pilot sat up in the cockpit. Their three colleagues were seated to the rear of the cockpit and below, somewhat separate and with their own means of exit from the aircraft should the need arise.

Alcock and Hoskins guided XM610 up the Durham and Northumberland coast at high level, then turned and descended into the low-flying zone, heading for the northern Pennines. Just north of the Scottish border, near Kelso, the Vulcan was at 300 knots, its four Rolls-Royce Olympus engines at 75 per cent thrust. Flying at 500 feet through the Border Hills was a routine altitude for No.44 Squadron crews: they could even get down much lower in the nearby Yarrow Valley. Seeing the weather closing in ahead of them, Alcock elected to abandon the training flight and climb to a safe altitude. Low flying over hills and poor visibility did not mix.

Over the intercom, Bob Alcock informed his crew of his intentions, then increased power to 85 per cent, lifted the Vulcan's nose and prepared to monitor the ensuing climb. Seconds later, a loud explosion occurred aft, and the bomber slewed to port. Immediately checking his instrument panel, the pilot noticed the RPM for the No.1 Olympus engine dropping and the jet pipe temperature rising towards the limit. The fire warning light for the engine came on. Informing the crew of what was happening once more, Alcock shut the high-pressure cock for the engine and closed the throttle, pressing the fire suppressant button and closing the engine air switch. Jim Power, his air electronics officer, then informed him that he had alternator failure on the No.1 engine. He switched it off and isolated it for safety.

Vulcan aircraft were fitted with a rear-facing periscope, which allowed the crew to inspect the rear underside of the fuselage and engine areas. As he isolated No.1 engine's alternator, Jim Power peered through the periscope, informing Bob Alcock that he could see damage to the aircraft in the area of the problematic powerplant. With three engines still burning, the pilot checked the engine's fire warning system to ensure it was operating. As he did so, Alcock realised that the jet pipe temperature gauge for the No.2 Olympus engine was now also rising, then saw its fire warning light start to illuminate. Warning the crew, he pulled the ram air turbine handle, allowing it to fall into the aircraft's slipstream. As its name suggested, the turbine generated power by ram pressure due to the Vulcan's airspeed. Each of the aircraft's non-essential electrical loads were shed from the bus bars. In doing so, Alcock and Hoskins' cockpit instrument panel lit up like a proverbial Christmas tree. It was every pilot's nightmare. Warning lights illuminated across the board. The No.2 engine was shut down in the same manner as the first. With both engines on that side of the aircraft out of action, Alcock needed to put his left foot down hard on the rudder pedal to maintain level flight. Pushing the fire button for the No.2 engine, the fire warning light was extinguished after a few seconds.

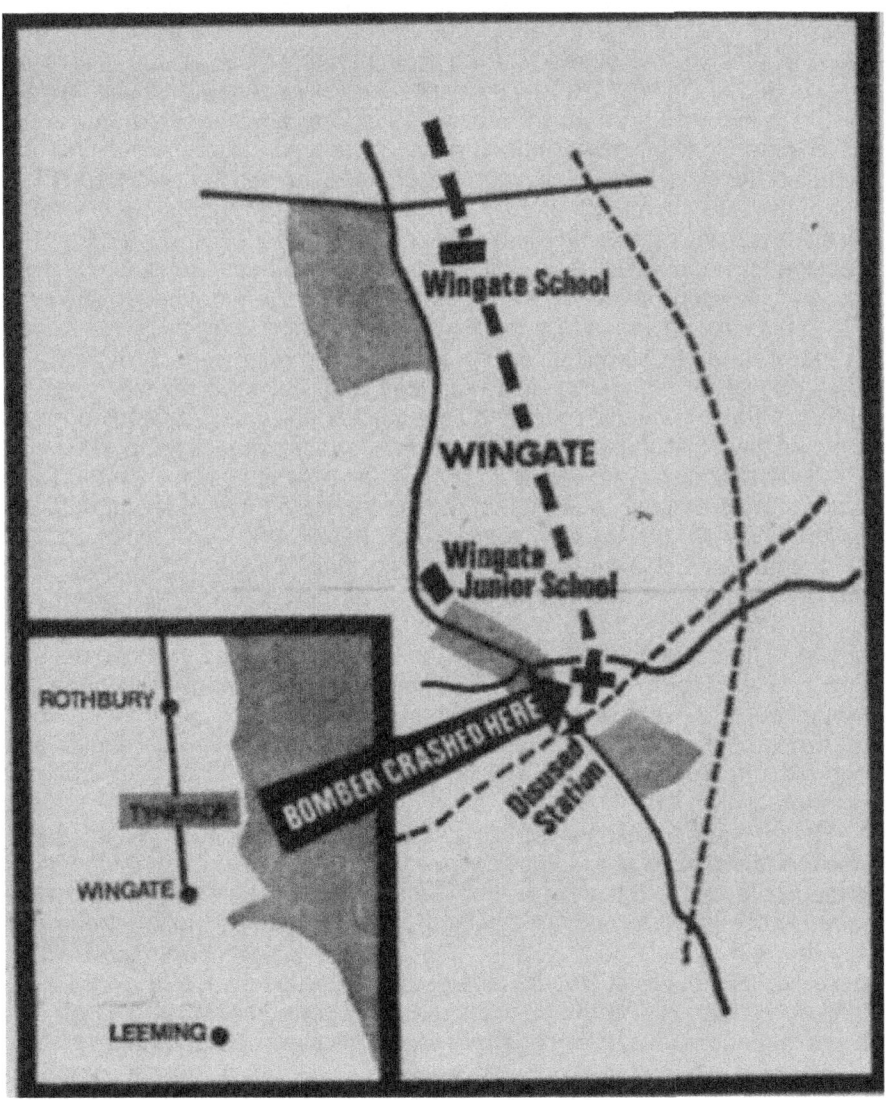

The final seconds of the Vulcan's flight are shown by the dotted line in this sketch that appeared in a contemporary newspaper report concerning the incident.

Alcock asked Power to start reading the emergency procedures from flight reference cards held onboard the aircraft for the event of engine failure and inflight fires. The latter looked again through the periscope, but nothing had changed. Tiring from the constant pressure on the left-hand rudder pedal, the pilot pushed the rudder trim switch to alleviate his distress and give him one less thing to worry about. There was one more thing to do.

Bob Alcock declared the situation to be an inflight emergency. Co-pilot Peter Hoskins opened the cross-feed cocks, transferring fuel from the port tanks to keep the aircraft's centre of gravity within acceptable limits.

Meanwhile, navigator Jim Vinales was calculating their exact position. After working that out, he passed the co-ordinates to Alcock so they could be transmitted along with the Mayday call. Jim Power was also busy using a cartridge system to fire up the Vulcan's auxiliary power unit so they could have more electrical power onboard the aircraft. He needed this to run the selected systems he was bringing back to life, as per the procedures laid out in the reference cards. Many of the bomber's flying controls, operated by electrical power, had been starved of juice when the ram air turbine was deployed. The air electronics officer had restarted these and was checking his cards when his attention was drawn to a red glow in the periscope.

To his utter shock and horror, Flight Lieutenant Power saw a fire raging in the area of No.1 engine. As he shouted a warning to Bob Alcock, the No.2 engine fire warning light illuminated and stayed lit for two minutes. Having already transmitted the Mayday message, it was repeated and then the pilot gave the order: *"Put on parachutes and prepare to bail out!"*

Power, Vinales and Barker donned their parachutes and awaited the order to jump. Alcock, seeing that they were flying through cloud, delayed giving the word. Exiting into clearer skies near Rothbury, a small town in Northumberland, the three airmen hooked their 'chutes to the static line, put on their oxygen masks and ensured their personal survival packs and life jackets were securely attached to their lanyards. Roger Barker was already crouched down by the exit door. Vinales pulled the handle that depressurised the cabin and one by one, as per emergency procedure, the trio announced over the intercom that they were ready to jump.

Around ten minutes had elapsed since the explosion in No.1 engine had occurred near Kelso. Bob Alcock gave the order: *"Static line manual override. Jump, jump!"*

Barker turned the door handle round to the emergency position and it opened, the aircraft's 200 knot airspeed causing a draught that blew right through the cabin. Sitting in a "ball" type position, his dinghy and survival gear clutched tight to prevent it being ripped when he hit the slipstream, he slid down the open door and fell into space. Falling away from the Vulcan, the static line jerked at Roger Barker's parachute pack, and he yanked the release handle. His 'chute successfully deployed. Jim Power was next in line to abandon the stricken bomber, swiftly followed by Jim Vinales.

All three crewmembers landed safely in fields near Rothbury. Once on the ground, they activated their personal emergency locator transmitters so that rescuers could find them. They had landed around 15 miles west of the RAF base at Acklington, home to a detachment of Whirlwind rescue helicopters. At least one of these was scrambled, their crew homing in on the beacons to effect pick-ups.

That left Bob Alcock and Peter Hoskins onboard what was increasingly becoming a mass of flames. The pilot had made up his mind to attempt an emergency landing at the nearest master diversion field, RAF Leeming, in North Yorkshire, with his co-pilot remaining at his side to assist. It was a noble but doomed effort.

A scene of devastation greeted firemen and police officers as they scoured debris lying in and around a huge crater caused by the Vulcan diving into a field close to Station Town, Wingate.

Low speed handling manoeuvres were increasingly difficult to carry out, so Alcock abandoned his attempts as XM610's airspeed dropped to just 185 knots. He needed to concentrate as the Vulcan approached Tyneside at 6,000 feet. Managing to set course slightly eastwards to avoid the largest built-up areas, the immediate danger of the aircraft crashing into Newcastle passed and the pilot soon saw Sunderland passing by on his port side. On the ground, thousands of people across North and South Tyneside had watched in horror and fascination as the huge delta-winged bomber, port wing by now firmly ablaze, staggered southwards. In addition, it could be seen shedding pieces of airframe and engines as it did so.

With Sunderland safely behind them, Alcock realised that it was futile to continue. XM610 wasn't going to make as far as Leeming, and maybe not even that far. Another built-up area lay directly ahead, a corridor of towns and villages stretching from Darlington to Saltburn. The fire in the port wing was getting worse. The pilot managed to slowly turn the aircraft south-eastwards, with the intention of sending it out over the North Sea.

Approaching the mining town of Easington, Alcock gave his final verbal order: *"Jettison canopy!"* Both he and Peter Hoskins reached for their respective seat levers and pulled them backwards. A loud bang signalled the departure of the cockpit canopy, which vanished in the slipstream. The pilot could now finally see the extent of the fire enveloping the rear of the aircraft's port wing. With its course set for open water, it was time to leave the stricken bomber behind. The noise of the exposed cockpit rendered all attempts at communication impossible, so Alcock simply raised a thumb. Grabbing his own seat pan handle, Hoskins straightened his back, braced himself for the ejection manoeuvre and yanked. Two further bangs and the seat shot up the rail at 60 feet per second. Bob Alcock had time for a brief check of his surroundings before carrying out his own ejection procedure.

Both men believed the Vulcan would simply fly out over the North Sea before the port wing fire caused the aircraft to either break up in mid-air or dive into the water. It is unclear whether they saw what happened next, but their proximity suggests that they may well have done. Instead of flying out to sea, XM610 turned to port, entering a downward spiral before heading westwards and finally south towards Wingate. Only seconds then remained before it dived into a field at Station Town. Local newspaper reporting now takes up the story on the ground, starting with *The Evening Chronicle's* 8th January 1971 edition:

"An RAF Vulcan bomber crashed in County Durham today after a dramatic life-or-death dash across Northumberland as its crew members baled out one by one.

And this afternoon, the people of the mining village of Wingate told of the terror in the town as the pilotless A-bomber plunged into a field behind the local Co-op shop. The plane's pilot and co-pilot had both ejected from the cockpit when the jet came screaming across the village with flames streaking from it, just 100 feet above houses and two schools.

Falling debris from the stricken plane showered the area up to a mile from the crash point. Several buildings were hit by pieces of metal, but no-one was reported hurt.

Mr. Arthur Nevens, of Wingate, said: 'I saw the aeroplane come across on fire. I was just sitting in the back kitchen when it came screaming over and the flames were belching out of it. I went out in the back yard, and I knew it was in trouble. There were flames about 20 feet long coming from the starboard engines. Then there was a great noise and a column of black smoke with flames leaping about 200 feet.'

Mr. Nevens said: 'It went right across the top of the secondary school, and I heard the children screaming. It was no more than 100 feet above the school.'

Mr. John Hall, caretaker at Wingate County Modern School, said: 'I was at the school when it came across. The kids were screaming their heads off. The plane came right across the top of the school, and it was absolutely on fire. I thought at first it was not going to clear the school. I was standing praying.'

Mr. Cyril Fleming, manager of the Station Town Co-op grocery store, said there was a 'frightening' roar as the plane went over the building before crashing 100 yards away. 'I have never witnessed anything so noisy and terrifying before in my life. I thought the world had come to an end,' he said. 'There was a big explosion and I heard glass breaking as the plane came down. Some people in the shop threw themselves on the floor, while some of the staff started crying because they were afraid the plane might drop on the school where their children attended,' he said. After the panic he went outside and saw 'a blazing inferno' in the field.

Mr. Eric Summerson, chief clerk at the store, saw the plane burst into flames. 'There was just flame and smoke and bits of burning aircraft flying all over the place,' he said.

One of the first people on the scene was Mr. William Harding, a fruiterer of Wingate, He was standing at the back door of his shop when he heard the plane flying low. Then he saw it. 'The port engine was on fire, and it seemed to climb and then suddenly nose-dived beyond a row of houses. There was a huge cloud of smoke and flames belched into the air. Just another 100 yards or so and this would have been a tragic day for Wingate,' he said.

Sixty-year-old William Tennant was walking home when he saw the burning plane in the sky, He said: 'It seemed to turn and then nose-dive not the field. Suddenly there was one hell of an inferno. Flames shot hundreds of feet into the air and shrapnel was sent flying all over the place. I waited for a few minutes and then went over to where the plane had landed. There was a crater about 25 feet deep. I have never seen anything like it in my life,' added Mr. Tennant, of Station Town.

One of the first policemen at the scene said: 'When we got here the heat was so intense that we couldn't approach the crater.'

Hundreds of police and firemen from all parts of the county were on the scene and as sightseers started to crowd into the field, policemen had to form a cordon to prevent them getting near the huge 'moon crater' which the plane had burrowed in the hillside.

Police started to hustle Pressmen and photographers from the scene after a special message had been received from the RAF that all information was classified, and no photographing was to be permitted."

CRASH JET'S SECRET PAPERS ARE MISSING

Despite the apparent clamp down on information from the crash scene, details of the Vulcan's flight leading up to it coming down at Wingate were also carried by the *Chronicle*:

"The drama started when the plane, one of Britain's atomic striking force from RAF Waddington, near Lincoln, was over North Northumberland. A spokesman at RAF Acklington said they received a 'Mayday' call at 10.37 am saying there was a fire aboard.

Three crew members baled out 15 miles west of Acklington while the pilot and co-pilot stayed aboard to try and wrestle the giant jet to the nearest big airbase – Leeming, in North Yorkshire.

A farm worker saw the three airmen eject from the bomber in lonely hill country. Mr. Alastair McCracken, of Lowbottle, near Rothbury, said: 'I saw the bomber coming over flying very low. One of its engines was burning furiously. Then I saw three men eject from the plane. They came down at distances quite far apart in the hills. One was faster than the others. Then a small plane came over and a helicopter hovered and picked up the airmen. I never saw any of them. The bomber was travelling fast and quickly disappeared.

Police set out to the Cheviot Hills near Rothbury and located the men who had parachuted to safety. And an Acklington helicopter left to take them to hospital. Meanwhile, other police areas were alerted as the plane continued its agonised flight south. Durham County police mounted a full-scale emergency operation as it entered their area.

It was 20 miles south of Sunderland when the last two crewmen decided they could not make the runway at Leeming and baled out. Before jumping, they turned the aircraft out to sea.

Mr. Harry Branch, a display advertising representative with the Evening Chronicle, and a keen aircraft spotter, was in Felling when he saw the Vulcan flying low in the distance. 'I could tell by the sound of the engine that it was in trouble,' he said. 'It just seemed as though it was gliding when it veered to the left and suddenly went diving down. As it went down, there was a big bang and a streak of flames and a pall of smoke in the distance.'

Mr. David Clattenburg, of Carrville, saw the bomber shoot very low over Carrville. 'The sound it made was like a ringing noise,' he said. 'Then black smoke began pouring out of the back, and shortly afterwards there was a roar and a burst of flame. It was just as if someone had opened a furnace door. Everybody in Carrville stood still.'

An AA patrolman in Co. Durham said he saw the aircraft directly overhead when it burst into flames. He saw someone bale out and the plane continued on a south-easterly course. It then plummeted earthwards with thick black smoke pouring in its wake.

Another eyewitness, Mr. Albert Ridley, of Washington, said that smoke and flames were pouring from the plane as it passed over him in the direction of Penshaw. 'It seemed to go out for a second, then suddenly got worse and the plane dropped. It kept going but dropped again and disappeared from sight. We expected to hear a crash, but there was just silence,' he said.

Mr. Anthony Richards, of Hastings Hill, Sunderland, said he and his workmates saw the plane with flames streaming from it. A figure jumped from it shortly before it crashed.

Trimdon newsagent Mr. Joseph Bennett saw one of the crewmen baling out. 'A customer rushed into my shop to say he had seen a plane on fire heading out towards the sea,' he said. 'I went outside and saw one parachutist, but he was a few miles away north-east of here, probably going toward Seaham.' And he told of a mystery aircraft in the area. 'Another aircraft of the same type – probably a Vulcan bomber – was circling around the parachutist,' he said.

Another man who said he saw other planes in the area was 65-year-old Mr. John Oliver, who was standing on a street corner in Shiney Row, chatting to two friends, when he spotted a 'bright light in the sky'. He said: 'At first, I did not know what it was. It was high up in the sky. Then, it came right overhead, and I saw it was a plane on fire. After it had passed, the flames suddenly went out. But seconds later, the plane burst into flames again and there was a cloud of black smoke.'

Mr. Oliver, of Shiney Row, said: 'Later I saw a number of planes overhead, probably searching for the lost plane.'

A motorist who was driving through Wellfield, near Wingate, said he looked up and saw a 'ball of flame' plunging down, missing a grammar school and landing in open ground. A piece of fuselage dropped in front of his car.

Farmer Mr. Jacob Proudlock said: 'The whole area is surrounded by houses. It's an act of God that it cleared it and landed in a field.' Mr. Proudlock, of Fairfield Farm, Wingate, said the tail of the plane was in flames when he saw it and 'suddenly the whole plane nose-dived to the ground.' Immediately beforehand, a man baled out. 'I don't think there was anyone else in the plane,' he said. He raced over to the field but was beaten back by the flames. The plane 'broke into a million pieces,' he said.

The plane hit a cow byre at Tilery Farm, Wingate, as it crashed, and more than 20 cows stampeded. Mrs. R. Glass, wife of the owner of the farm, said windows of their house were shattered as the plane crashed.

Mr. Glass had been working in the field 10 minutes earlier. He returned to his bungalow and was having a cup of coffee when he heard the plane overhead. He said: 'I though the roof was coming down. There was a terrible noise. The roof shuddered.' The farmhouse and bungalow are only about 100 yards from the crash spot.

The aircraft was seen by Bernard Park, a 29-year-old RAC patrolman at Middlesbrough Service Centre – 14 miles away. He said: 'As the aircraft came over, clouds of black smoke were pouring from it. Then I could see a glow coming up from the ground a long distance away,' he said.

The two officers who baled out over Co. Durham landed in the Peterlee area. One was picked up by ambulance men at Shotton Road end and the other near Toothill Colliery, in the same area. They were taken by ambulance to Durham County Hospital. The pilot was only slightly hurt, suffering from a cut lip and shock. The crewman was carried in on a stretcher and is believed to be suffering from a slight spinal injury. Casualty staff at the hospital were treating the men this afternoon.

The other three of the bomber's crew were taken by helicopter to People's Park, Ashington. All were able to walk to waiting ambulances, apparently unharmed, and transferred to Ashington Hospital. None of the three would make any comment.

A spokesman in London for the RAF said the bomber was on a routine training flight. Waddington is a strike command station. The Ministry of Defence refused to say whether the plane was armed. He said a board of inquiry is being convened. This is the usual procedure in such circumstances."

A fireman examines the huge "moonscape" caused by the Vulcan crashing into the field at Station Town.

Further details appeared in the following day's *Journal* newspaper:

"A bare second saved a County Durham town from being wiped out yesterday. An RAF Vulcan bomber, one wing on fire, screamed over the streets of Wingate before crashing in a ball of flame only 70 yards from a street of houses.

Just seconds earlier, the 28-year-old pilot, Flt-Lieut. G. R. Allcock, and his 23-year-old co-pilot baled out of the crippled bomber. Their desperate struggle to reach RAF Leeming had failed. Earlier the three other members of the crew parachuted to safety 15 miles west of RAF Acklington. Hundreds of people throughout the North-East had watched in horror as the crippled plane flew towards disaster.

Mrs. Dorothy Skinner, of Wingate, last night relived the final terrifying seconds as the plane skimmed over the roof tops of the town, narrowly missing the local secondary school. She said: 'I thought it was absolutely bound to hit us. Then the plane went overhead on one side as if banking and a second later bellied into the ground.'

The village postmaster, Mr. John Huntingdon, who watched the crash, said: 'It was just like an atom-blast.' Yet miraculously no-one was injured. Even two horses in the same field as the crash escaped unharmed."

One of the newspaper's inside pages carried even more information about the crash at Wingate:

"The 11,000 residents of Wingate, County Durham, were last night still recovering from the shock of a disaster that missed them by just 70 yards. A gaping 20-feet deep crater in the field behind Station Road showed how close tragedy had been when a pilotless Vulcan bomber skimmed over rooftops and plunged into the ground.

The crash happened after an epic struggle to get the blazing four-engined bomber to a crash landing on an RAF base had failed. The pilot and co-pilot baled out of the crippled plane seconds before it banked sharply over the roofs of Wingate, narrowly missing schools, shops and houses.

Residents in Station Road told last night of their narrow escape from sudden death. Miss Dorothy Skinner said: 'I looked out of my bedroom window when I heard a tremendous noise, more like a big wind than an aeroplane. It came just over the roof with flames streaming from one wing. I thought it was absolutely bound to hit us. The plane was over on one side as if it was banking and then just bellied into the ground behind the houses. Then there was a holocaust of flame, leaping 60 feet or more into the air.'

The village postmaster, Mr. John Huntingdon, said: 'The 11,000 people of Wingate were only a second away from death. Most of us were numb with the shock and only now is it hitting home how close we really were.' Mr. Huntingdon watched the bomber plummet to the ground from his back garden, only yards from the crash. 'It was just like a small atom bomb. The plane dropped vertically into the field and exploded in a sheet of flame.'

The headmaster of Wingate Modern School, Mr. William Moyes, said the children were playing in the yard when the bomber swooped just overhead. 'Thank God it missed the school. It would have been a terrible disaster. I saw it diving steeply in flames and after the impact it exploded.'

Experts were last night examining the countless pieces of debris, scattered over a wide area. A top-level inquiry will be held into the crash.

The drama began when the Vulcan, on a routine training flight from RAF Waddington, in Lincolnshire, put out a 'Mayday' call over North Northumberland saying there was a fire onboard. Three crewmembers – navigators Flying Officer R. Barker, aged 24, and Flt-Lieut. J. Vinales, aged 26, and electronics officer Flt-Lieut. J. Power, aged 34 – baled out 15 miles west of RAF Acklington. They were picked up by helicopter and taken to hospital in Ashington. Two were treated for bruises, then they were airlifted back to Acklington.

Meanwhile, the pilot and co-pilot, Flt-Lieut. G. R. Allcock, aged 28, and Flying Officer P. J. Hoskins, aged 23, both married men, battled with the crippled plane. Hundreds of people saw their flight across the North-East as they aimed the crippled bomber towards a crash landing at RAF Leeming in North Yorkshire.

As the blazing aircraft lost height, they baled out and landed near Shotton, about three miles from the point where the Vulcan finally plummeted into the ground. Flt-Lieut. Alcock and F/O Hoskins were taken to Durham County Hospital. One had a cut lip and the other, minor spinal injuries. After treatment they were transferred in an RAF ambulance to a military hospital near their home base.

RAF police cordoned off the crash area to prevent souvenir hunters disturbing vital bits of evidence. A Ministry of Defence spokesman said last night that a board of inquiry was being convened.

A herd of cows broke through the gates of their barn 50 yards from the crash when the blast ripped off its roof. They stampeded through three barbed-wire fences before they came to a halt. Last night, Mr. John Glass, who owns Tilery Farm, was left with the problem of finding shelter for the cattle. 'Seventeen of them were in calf so we can only wait to see what happens. I have another 15 calves and I have nowhere to put them for the night,' he said. 'All sorts of queer things have happened. Gates have for some unknown reason just disintegrated,' he added.

Two horses, both in foal, were in the field where the bomber crashed, but were found unhurt. The horses were calmed down by Mr. George Charlton of Wheatley Hill, who looks after them for their owner, Mr. Bert Bruce, of Station Road.

Mr. Bill Hume of Vigo, Birtley, was at work at an engineering factory on the Hetton Lyons Industrial Estate when the plane went overhead. Mr. Hume said: 'I ran outside and could see one of the plane's wings was on fire. I saw two objects fall out and parachutes opened. Seconds later the plane exploded as it hit the ground.'"

One of the RAF search and rescue Whirlwind helicopters can be seen in this photo, taken at the crash site. The proximity of buildings located in Station Town is all too apparent here – residents were extremely lucky to escape injury or death.

Crew from the Whirlwind helicopter pictured at the scene of the crash.

The words of two more local witnesses appeared in the *Lincolnshire Echo* on the evening of the crash:

"Mr. Jack Winn, a Wingate dairy worker, said visibility was poor, and he heard an explosion as the plane crashed about a mile away. Mrs. Margaret Malcolm, licensee of the Fir Tree Inn, Wingate, said she saw smoke coming from the aircraft. It must have missed the village of Station Town 'by only a few yards,' she said."

"Crash Jet's Secret Papers Are Missing", screamed the headline at the top of the *Evening Chronicle's* front page for 9th January 1971:

"Secret papers scattered over a wide area when the giant Vulcan jet bomber crashed at Wingate, County Durham, could be picked up by children playing. And the RAF and Durham police are anxious to trace the documents before they go missing, perhaps for good. The lost documents could be lying in fields after being scattered over a wide area.

'They may be found by children playing or people going for walks,' say police. 'We are anxious that anyone finding them should hand them to police.'

The documents are confidential, but a description has been issued. The first is in a green cover about nine inches by 12 inches and contains 12 pages. It carries the serial number BAM 02/30. Another document, which is five inches by 10 inches carries the number BAM 02/3, and the third document consisting of two pages six inches by eight inches in size has the number BIS 24/1. The fourth document is numbered BIS 24/9. It is in a small piece of black plastic with two windows. The document is in a blue folder, and the entire piece is in a blue-grey navigation bag,

The two airmen who baled out seconds before the Vulcan crashed are recovering today at Knockton Hall Hospital, near their base at RAF Waddington, Lincolnshire. They were taken to Durham County Hospital after being picked up near Shotton. But later they were transferred by ambulance. The pilot, Flt-Lieut. Garth Alcock, aged 28, from Sheffield, was treated for a cut lip. His co-pilot, Flying Officer Peter Hoskins, aged 23, from Basingstoke, has minor spinal injuries. The men, who are both married, were 'satisfactory' today.

The three other crewmembers who baled out 15 miles west of Acklington were treated at Ashington before being flown by helicopter back to Acklington.

Arrangements are going ahead today to set the date for an inquiry into the crash when the bomber crashed into the ground only 70 yards from Wingate – where the 11,000 residents are wondering how close many of them were to death."

The Chronicle's 13th January 1971 provided some news about the official RAF inquiry into the crash:

"The Board of Inquiry into the Vulcan bomber crash at Wingate, County Durham, on January 8, is likely to end later this month, Mr. Jack Dormond, M.P. for Easington, has been told by the Ministry of Defence.

But the findings are likely to be kept secret 'in the general interest of the public,' he was told by Mr. Anthony Lambton, Under-Secretary at the Ministry. In answer to a question about the crash, which narrowly missed a row of houses, Mr. Lambton said that the bomber was headed towards RAF Leeming, in Lincolnshire, because the length of the runway was important.

He said a long runway was needed in case the aircraft's controls were impaired. This was the case with the Vulcan."

Whilst the finding of the Board of Inquiry may have been kept secret at the time, over 50 years have passed since the crash and the cause of the fire is now known. A thorough investigation of the debris, plus questioning of the five crewmembers, revealed that metal fatigue had led to the failure of a high-pressure turbine blade in No.1 engine. Not only had the blade failed, but it had jammed in the turbine disc, rotating with the latter until the casing of the disc eventually ruptured. The turbine then broke up, sending debris at high speed into the engine casing and engine bay walls. This not only damaged the No.2 engine, but also sent fragments into the No.3 and No.4 engine fuel tanks. The ensuing fire was fed by fuel from the ruptured tanks.

Vulcan XM610 crashed into the sloping field situated directly in front of the houses in the background. The new houses were built on the site of the abattoir at the old Co-operative building in Station Town. The huge aircraft somehow managed to miss the abattoir and the line of buildings along Front Street, just off the right-hand edge of the image. This photograph was taken in February 2023, 52 years after the incident took place. (Author)

By the time Bob Alcock and Peter Hoskins finally ejected near the town of Easington, XM610 was in imminent danger of breaking up entirely. Pieces of the Vulcan's airframe had already fell away and the flames were rapidly advancing across the port wing. To prevent similar incidents happening in the future, all examples of the type received modifications, with titanium plates being fitted next to the high-pressure turbines in the engine bays, and over the bay roofs. This was to stop potential debris from exploding engines damaging adjacent ones or nearby fuel tanks.

A huge tragedy had been averted, but it was only by pure chance. If the Vulcan had come down seconds earlier or later, it would have hit a school, residential properties or shops, with horrendous loss of life on the ground. Not surprisingly, memories of the event remained strong for decades, and those who witnessed the event unfold cannot forget what happened – and dwell upon what might have been. *The Northern Echo*'s 20th May 2021 edition included a story which was titled *"The day an RAF Vulcan fell on a Durham village"*:

"'The pulse of a Durham pit village stopped beating yesterday as a doomed RAF Vulcan bomber streaked towards it,' reported The Northern Echo on January 9, 1971. 'Screaming children fled from the playground as the ball

of fire dive-bombed over their school. And seconds after the plane had steered a trail of terror over Wingate, relieved villagers were talking about a miracle which saved their homes – and their lives.'

Vulcan XM610 had been on a training flight over Northumberland when metal fatigue caused No.1 engine to explode near Kelso. The debris from the first explosion took out No.2 engine, and the broken fuel lines immediately caught fire.

Over Rothbury, the captain, Flt-Lt. Garth Robert Alcock, ordered the three crewmen in the rear of the plane to jump from around 600 feet. They landed safely. This left him and his co-pilot, Flying Officer Peter Hoskins, in the stricken aircraft. Their intention was to head for RAF Leeming, and they managed to get enough altitude to fly over Teesside and then Sunderland – but thousands of people heard and saw the plane. It was an orange ball with debris tumbling from it.

By now, Alcock had no control over the plane which appeared to have set itself on a course out to sea. Over Easington, he jettisoned the canopy over the cockpit, which enabled Hoskins to press his ejector seat button and fling himself clear. Then Alcock followed.

Their departures were witnessed by children and staff at Wingate County Junior School, and suddenly XM610 veered away from its harmless course to crash out at sea and came straight at Wingate.

'Many Wingate housewives were doing their weekend shopping when they heard the first screech of the approaching plane, abandoned by the pilot and co-pilot seconds earlier,' said the Echo. 'The empty plane hurtled towards the village. It appeared to be heading straight for the junior school where the children in the playground covered their ears but stood stock still, transfixed with terror (at nearby Wellfield Grammar School, the rugby coach ordered his charges on the field to 'run', prefixed by a colourful expletive). At the last second, though, it changed course and headed for a row of houses,

'Terrified women and children in Station Lane dashed for cover as the plane whistled overhead,' said the Echo. Mrs. Dorothy Skinner told the reporter: 'I couldn't see how it could miss the houses as it was coming down very low. At the last moment it lifted slightly, that's why everyone thought there was still someone inside – and then it just bellied into the field. There was a terrific whistling as it went over and then an explosion.'

Geographically, the plane crashed in Station Town, in a field behind the Co-op, creating a huge crater. Emergency services and RAF personnel were quickly on site, and recovered much of the debris, although the two remaining engines had penetrated an old mineshaft and had gone so deep, they had to be dug out later. It was an extraordinary occurrence. No one dead. No one harmed. Not even slightly, although a couple of windows were reported to have been broken in Wingate.

The four crew members were awarded the Queen's Commendation for Valuable Service while the pilot received the Air Force Cross for averting a major tragedy.

Fruiterer William Harding of Front Street told the Echo: '*I shudder to think what would have happened had the bomber crashed down any earlier. About two or three hundred people could have been killed.*'

It left Wingate peppered with debris – and with doubts, and plenty of 'what ifs'. The official version, of the plane heading harmlessly out to sea only for it to suddenly and unpredictably corkscrew into the ground nine miles inland, does not quite tally with all the eyewitness reports of it being on a trajectory aimed at Wingate only for it to flip upwards at the last moment and then – miraculously – flop into the field.

Gordon Morton brought this amazing story to our attention after our recent tales of nuclear-equipped Vulcan bombers being stationed at RAF Middleton St George in the early 1960s and appearing at airshows there. '*I was living in Wingate at the time, and my daughter was one of the pupils at the school,*' he says.

'*On the day I heard such a noise that I rushed out of the house to see the plane diving into a field, followed by the explosion. Jumping into my car, I went down to the bottom end of the village to see where it had gone in. It left such a hole that I could not believe an aircraft of that size had gone in there. Later, the people of Wingate were of the opinion that had the plane come down on the school, no medals would have gone to the crew. We could not understand why he did not fly down the coast away from any buildings and then cut inland to make for Leeming or Dishforth. Yes, as it happened there were no casualties, so a good outcome, but people are still a little resentful about what might have been.*'"

Paul Lewis, who at the time was a Leading Aircraftsman radar mechanic, had only arrived at RAF Waddington days before the crash. Assigned to XM610 before the aircraft departed on its final flight, he was one of the jet's "see off crew" and would later perform guard duty at the crash site itself. He recalled *"the field of mud and the enormously deep hole made by one of the Olympus engines which had penetrated a disused mine shaft."* In addition, he remembered seeing residents of the houses that backed onto the site leaning over their fences to hand bits of debris over. Despite being so close to death, they all wanted to help.

Tony Bean was a pupil at Moore Lane Junior School in January 1971. He recalled being in the playground as a "fireball" passed overhead. He remembered *"seeing parts of the fuselage falling away (trophies later to be coveted) and in the distance, the canopies of those bailing out of the aircraft opening up further to the north-east... The noise was deafening, and the ground shuddered as it dropped into the nearby farmland."*

Steve Mullen was another witness, one who watched the cripped RAF bomber heading south over Northumberland. He remembered seeing her port wing ablaze, a sight and sound he said he would never forget.

Vulcan bombers had a poor record for survivability during rear crew evacuations. The crash of XM610 was possibly one of only two incidents where full successful crew abandonments occurred. This was reinforced by a subsequent crash involving Bob Alcock, this time at Luqa in Malta. On 14th October 1975, he was flying XM645 (a No.9 Squadron aircraft) and whilst landing at Luqa, the aircraft touched down short of the runway there. On impact, the port main undercarriage leg was forced upwards through the wing, rupturing the fuel tanks. Alcock reacted by hauling the Vulcan upwards, trying to gain enough altitude so that his three colleagues in the rear of the crew section could bale out safely. However, the aircraft exploded in mid-air before they were able to jump. Alcock and his co-pilot managed to eject and survived, but a civilian on the ground was also killed when wreckage fell into the village of Zabbar.

Jim Vinale had a much better memory of the North-East 12 years later, when he was the navigation plotter onboard XL319 on its delivery flight to the North-East Aircraft Museum in January 1983, the year before Sunderland Airport was closed to make way for the Nissan Car Factory.

If XM610 had dropped out of the sky seconds beforehand or later, the story being told here could have been much different. The potential loss of life would have been huge. As the newspapers reported at the time, some 11,000 residents lived in and around Wingate and Station Town. Those whose houses backed onto the field where the crash occurred had been the luckiest of all. They had – literally – been seconds from disaster.

TURBI TURMOIL

Druine D.5 Turbi G-APBO was involved in a forced landing on the cliff tops near Seaham on 13th April 1975. The pilot survived but his aircraft was damaged. It sat dismantled in a hangar at Sunderland Airport before finally being repaired, rebuilt and repainted. (Aeroprints, CC BY-SA 3.0)

Renewed interest in recreational aviation during the 1960s and 1970s led to increased numbers of light aircraft types being based in the region. In addition to Cessnas and Pipers of various marques, all factory assembled machines, there was also a burgeoning home-build range of machines, kits that could be built in a garage or workshop with occasional inspection by qualified staff from the Popular Flying Association. One of these aircraft was badly damaged in a forced landing near Seaham on 13th April 1975.

Details of the incident appeared in *The Evening Chronicle's* 14th April 1975 edition:

"A quiet spin along the Durham coastline almost ended in disaster for Newcastle pilot John Rosser last night. But he managed to walk out uninjured from the wreckage of his single-engine plane which crash-landed on the cliffs at Seaham.

And today, looking ruefully at the remains, he said: 'Another 12 inches and I could have landed safely and flown out of here. Now it looks as if the plane is a write-off. John, who lives in Elswick Road, said things were going normally when the engine cut out.

'I wasn't very high but luckily I was near the cliffs and as I didn't have a lot of time I headed for the nearest land. There wasn't time to be frightened. I just pointed at the nearest grass field. Everything was going fine when the tail of the plane caught on a post, and I was swung round into a length of fencing. Just that 12 inches would have made all the difference.'

The plane, a Druine D5 Turbi, belongs to the Usworth Flying Group of which John is secretary. He added: 'We haven't had it all that long – just a few months and we pooled all our money to buy it. I'm very disappointed about this.'"

The Journal's 15th April 1975 edition carried more information about what had happened on the cliffs at Seaham:

"Pilot John Rosser landed only two feet from disaster when his light plane ploughed on to a Seaham clifftop. Last night he was thanking his lucky stars after escaping uninjured from the crash into a farmer's field. But with a bit more luck, his £2,500 plane would also have been spared.

John, a computer engineer, of Elswick Road, Newcastle, said last night: 'My engine suddenly cut out as I was flying over the sea. I had to make for the nearest piece of land as quickly as possible. Unfortunately, the tops of the cliffs have all been ploughed – if I'd landed there, the plane would probably have turned over and I could have broken my neck. So, I made for one green field. However, the plane wouldn't glide quite far enough. As I came in to land, the tail hit the fence, ripping the fuselage. If it had been two feet lower, the posts would have come up through my seat.'

He was flying a hand built Druine D5 Turbi, one of only three two-seater open planes in the country. Now the Usworth Flying Group, which owns the plane, fears it may be an insurance write-off.

John spent all yesterday bringing the plane back to the club's base at Sunderland airport. He added: It looks in rather a sorry state, with the tail and fuselage badly damaged. We had to take off the wings and tail to get the plane back. I really am very sad about this. A couple of feet more and I could have made a perfectly smooth landing in the field. But it just wasn't possible.'

With nearly 15 years of flying experience, John takes out one of the club's three planes nearly every weekend. One of his favourite flips is following the coastline low over Seaham."

A poor newspaper photograph of the Druine D.5 Turbi after it was force-landed on the cliff tops near Seaham in April 1975.

Despite the damage reported in the newspaper articles and the potential for being an insurance write-off, Druine G-APBO was in fact repaired and returned to airworthiness. It was subsequently sold to new owners and can be seen in UK skies today, especially at fly-ins and airshows that feature older homebuilt types of aircraft.

Another post-rebuild shot of G-APBO, showing the open cockpit arrangement and tubular framed undercarriage. The pilot, quite rightly, believed that the latter would not be strong enough to withstand a forced landing in a ploughed field. (Wiltshire Spotter, CC BY-SA 2.0)

THE FALLEN MUSKETEER

Beech A23 Musketeer G-AVYF is pictured here at the Popular Flying Association Rally at Leicester Airport on 4th May 1981 – the same day that it crash-landed in a field near Sunderland. (Ken Haynes)

The early evening of Saturday, 4th July 1981 saw a twin-engined aircraft make a forced landing in a field close to houses near Sunderland. All four onboard survived unharmed, although the situation could have been much worse but for the skill of the pilot and help from an unexpected source. The aircraft was returning from the annual Popular Flying Association fly-in held at Leicester Airport when the incident happened. The Newcastle *Sunday Sun* newspaper's 5th July 1981 edition contained the following story which provided details of what had transpired towards the end of the return flight:

"A North pilot and his three passengers escaped last night when their light aircraft crash landed into a field. Ken Cochrane was blinded by leaking oil splashing on his windscreen, but he managed to bring the stricken craft down less than 100 yards from nearby houses.

He was helped by an instructor from the nearby Sunderland Flying School, who saw his desperate situation and guided the 'blind' pilot down by radio. Tom Watson, of East Boldon, was flying with a pupil 1,000 feet about the Beachcraft [sic] Musketeer when he saw smoke pouring from its rear. Learner pilot Roy Howarth carried on flying their aircraft as Tom contacted Ken by radio and told him of his position.

Ken, of Silksworth Lane, Sunderland, brought his aircraft down safely in a field at Ferryboat Lane, near Hylton Castle Estate, Sunderland, only seconds after his engine cut out.

He and his fellow passengers Maurice Clyde, of Dawdon, James Welch, of Washington, and Jack Harkess, of Ponteland, all escaped serious injury. Mr. Clyde and Mr. Harkess were taken to Sunderland General Hospital but were released after treatment.

'They all had a very lucky escape,' said Insp. Keith Rowland of Northumbria Police. 'The plane came down only about 100 yards from the houses and about the same distance from the main A19 road. He also stopped where he came down and didn't leave a trail through the grass. Considering the situation, it is amazing that no one was really hurt.'

Michael Cowans, aged 14, saw the crash landing from his garden nearby. Michael, of Ferryboat Lane, said: 'I was watching out of my bedroom window when I saw the plane come overhead. It was really close, and I heard the engine cut out. I dashed outside and saw it come down in the field.' His friend Paul Baker, aged 14, of Cullercoats Road, Sunderland, said: 'The plane just missed the chimneys.'

Bystanders were warned to keep well away as the plane still had 20 gallons of high-octane fuel in its wing tanks. Sub-Officer Bill Charlton of Washington fire station said: 'The engine was still warm when we got here. If a spark had ignited all that fuel, we could have had a disaster on our hands.'

Last night Ken, who has crash-landed three times in the last 10 years. Was not available for comment but flying instructor Tom told of the drama. He said: 'We were about five miles south of Sunderland Airport when I realised he was in trouble. He could not see out of his windscreen because it was covered in oil. I talked to him over the radio, guiding him to the right or left. At first, we thought we could make it back to the airport, but the engine cut and he had to bring it down in the field. He is a very competent pilot and as he got closer, he could see out of the side windows to land.'

A spokesman for Sunderland Airport said: 'Mr. Cochrane followed all the correct procedures and brought the aircraft down safely. Through his skill, no one was in any danger.'"

Beech Musketeer G-AVYF is pictured here where it came to rest in a field near Hylton Castle Estate, Sunderland, after experiencing engine problems.

Beech A23-24 Musketeer Super III G-AVYF had been built back in 1968. It was owned by the Wearside Flying Group at the time of the crash. Despite the damage sustained in the July 1981 forced landing, the aircraft was eventually restored to airworthiness. However, it was a short-lived reprieve for the Beech. It was cancelled from the UK Civil Aircraft Register in 1986.

AN EXERCISE IN DISASTER: PART TWO

SEPECAT Jaguar GR.1 XX972/DF belonged to No.31 Squadron at RAF Bruggen, West Germany. It is pictured here at Luqa Airport, Malta, on 19th May 1978, three years before it was lost over County Durham in circumstances that were not fully understood at the time. (John Visanich)

The Cold War between East and West was always a time of uncertainty. In preparation for the worst occurring, the RAF, together with other NATO air arms, practiced low flying virtually every weekday, 12 months a year, apart from public holidays. Those living in the upland regions of Britain became only too accustomed to military aircraft, whether they were fighter or strike types, transports or helicopters, flying almost at what seemed like treetop level along hill and mountain valleys in North Wales, the Lakes, the Pennines and right across Scotland. The numbers of machines performing such missions often increased five-fold or more when exercises were being held in British skies. However, the flights did not come without a hefty price tag attached. Several aircraft failed to return from their training sorties, their crews safely ejecting, sustaining injuries in the process or unfortunately dying when they failed to leave their machines for whatever reason.

Exercise "OSEX 4" took place in early August 1981. Featuring aircraft drawn from British, American and Danish air force units, training missions including simulated attacks on targets located inside the Otterburn Training Range in north-western Northumberland. Otterburn had an "Impact Area", a patch of hillside to the north of the range where several retired airframes were laid out next to a mock "airstrip", together with a few vehicles for good measure. Close inspection on the ground showed these for what they were – bullet-ridden wrecks – but from the cockpit of a military jet flying at 300 or 400 knots, they provided a realistic target.

RAF units based in West Germany were frequent attendees at these exercises. The Germans had few large areas of sparsely inhabited ground for which to use as low-flying training grounds and some opposition existed regarding those that did exist. Britain's large expanses of upland territory provided much more attractive operating locations.

No.31 Squadron based at RAF Bruggen was one of the West Germany-based units that took part in "OSEX 4". Equipped with SEPECAT Jaguar strike-attack aircraft (an Anglo-French collaboration), the unit had detached some of its jets to Lossiemouth, located on the Moray Firth in Scotland, to participate in the exercise. On the morning of 6th August 1981, Jaguar XX972 (carrying the tail code "DF", the "D" signifying No.31 Squadron and "F" the individual aircraft) was one of a four-ship formation that took off from the Scottish airbase for a mission over the Otterburn Ranges.

The four Jaguars, with the unit's commanding officer, Squadron Leader Roger Matthews, flying XX972/DF as the formation's No.4 aircraft, took off from Lossiemouth shortly before 0900 hours. They followed the coast south until reaching a point just off Hartlepool, where a turn inland was made, the jets flying westwards to turn again, this time northwards for the so-called "Hexham Gap" and the run-in to Otterburn. At 0926 hours, the formation ran into low cloud and heavy rain, the pilots flying on instruments as visual flight rules no longer applied. XX972 was lost just a few minutes later, the aircraft coming down just to the west of the town of Barnard Castle. News of the incident was published by the *Aberdeen Evening Express* in their 6th August 1981 edition, the same evening as the crash:

"The pilot of a fighter jet which took off from Lossiemouth today was killed when his plane crashed in the English countryside, missing three farmhouses by 30 yards.

The aircraft was from No.31 Squadron, RAF Bruggen in West Germany. It was based at Lossiemouth for a week's low-level training exercise involving British, American and Danish aircraft over the north of England. The dead pilot has not yet been named. The Jaguar crashed on open ground half a mile west of Barnard Castle in County Durham – only an hour after take-off.

A spokesman at RAF Lossiemouth said: 'Weather conditions were very poor. The aircraft was one of a formation of four which were on transit to the Otterburn Ranges. They were not flying at low level at the time. They were at a height of 1,500 feet and were in clouds. They decided to break formation and pull out to rendezvous over the sea. It was at this stage that one of the aircraft went missing.'

The pilot only arrived at RAF Lossiemouth yesterday although the Bruggen Jaguars have been operating on a detachment from the Moray station all week. An RAF Board of Inquiry has been set up to investigate the accident."

The *Aberdeen Press & Journal* carried more information the following day:

"Sqn. Ldr. Matthews, who came from Avon, near Bristol, had been living in married quarters in Germany and had arrived at Lossiemouth only on Wednesday. He was due to return to Germany today.

A spokesman at RAF Lossiemouth said weather conditions over the North of England at the time of the crash, shortly before 10 am, had been very poor. 'The aircraft was one of a formation of four Jaguars which were on transit to the Otterburn Ranges,' added the spokesman. 'They were not flying at low level at the time. They were at a height of 1,500 feet and were in clouds. They decided to break formation and pull out to rendezvous over the sea. It was at this stage that one of the aircraft went missing.'

An RAF board of inquiry will probe the cause of the accident – the sixth involving a Jaguar this year."

More local coverage was contained in *The Newcastle Journal*'s 7th August 1981 edition:

"*A top-level inquiry began last night into the cause of an RAF fighter crash in Co. Durham which killed the pilot. Sqdn. Ldr. Roger Matthews, aged 33, was flying on a low-level training exercise when his Jaguar aircraft exploded in mid-air and plunged into fields near Barnard Castle. The plane missed a farmhouse by only 100 yards and the crash happened less than two miles from the town. The impact left a gaping crater and wreckage was strewn over 20 fields, one piece killing a bullock. One eyewitness said the aircraft 'smashed up into millions of pieces, the size of a handbag.'*

Sqdn. Ldr. Matthews, who is married and whose father lives in Avon, died instantly. He belonged to RAF Squadron 31, based at RAF Bruggen in West Germany, but operating out of Lossiemouth in Scotland during the last day of an exercise codenamed OSEX 4, involving British, American and Danish aircraft. The exercise involved 200 sorties a day against targets on ranges in Cumbria and the North-East. RAF and USAF aircraft acted as 'enemy forces'. The minimum height for operations was set at 250 feet.

An RAF spokesman said: 'It could be some weeks before the cause of the crash is known. A board of inquiry is automatically set up after any incident like this and will sift all evidence, wreckage and visit the site during its investigations, before drawing up a report.'

The shock wave from the crash was felt in Barnard Castle town centre and the explosion was heard three miles away. Mr. Harry Gill, of Smart Gill Farm, who was in his farmyard when the plane crashed 100 yards away, added: 'I heard the plane coming in low but thought nothing of it. We are used to them skimming our rooftops. But then I heard a big bang, and I knew straight away what had happened. The first thing I actually saw was a big ball of flame. I could feel the heat from where I stood. Then, small pieces of debris came fluttering down through the air.'

Immediately after the crash, his son, Graham, raised the alarm and then walked down the trail of wreckage left by the disintegrated aircraft. 'There was only one large piece left. The rest was in millions of bits no bigger than a handbag,' he said.

Farmer Tony Howson was in a field 500 yards from the point of impact. 'I thought the plane was going to hit the house at first. It was too close to be comfortable. A vibration of the explosion shook the house and brought part of a barn wall down,' he added.

Farmer Mr. John Dowson, of Startforth Grange, timed the crash at exactly 9.32 am. For that is when the plane cut power to his house, stopping an electric clock."

Pilot stayed at jet's controls

No attempt to eject

AN RAF fighter pilot clung to the controls of his Jaguar jet as it plunged into a field in County Durham last week, narrowly missing a busy town.

By FRASER DAVE

was multiple injuries, and death

Sqn. Leader Matthews he was flying at the same height."

Flt. Lieut. Kenneth McKenzie, aged 26, also stationed at RAF Brüggen told the deputy coroner

The Newcastle Journal' ran a story with this headline on 13th August 1981.

The newspaper also published a second story in the same edition that looked at the sad history of military pilots who had died during training flights:

"Even in peacetime the life of an RAF pilot can be a short one. In the last two-and-a-half years, 33 pilots have been killed in 69 plane and helicopter crashes on routine flights.

But the riskiest of all are the hair-raising, 400 mph swerves in and out of the Durham Dales, Northumberland hills and Lake District valleys, practicing flying below the level of enemy radar in £7M Jaguar strike aircraft. Here, split seconds stand between the pilots and death as any number of things can go wrong.

As RAF investigators, who have called in civilian help, began their probe in County Durham yesterday, engine failure, instrument malfunction, a bird being sucked into a jet engine, or simple pilot error were all put forward by experts as possible causes.

It is likely to be a year before the RAF announces its findings and the scattered fragments of the crashed plane may even be pieced together at Farnborough air base to try to find the cause. Whatever went wrong, it happened so quickly that the pilot had no time to flash a message to the other pilots flying in formation. They only knew something was wrong when they tried to radio him minutes later.

Twenty-seven RAF planes crashed in 1978, taking 14 lives. 26 crashed last year with 13 dead and another 17 have gone down this year, with six fatalities."

An inquest and an RAF Board of Inquiry were opened. *The Newcastle Journal's* 13th August 1981 edition carried news of the former:

"An RAF fighter pilot clung to the controls of his Jaguar jet as it plunged into a field in County Durham last week, narrowly missing a busy town.

Squadron Leader Roger Matthews, aged 33, made no attempt to eject before his single seater strike aircraft crashed and disintegrated less than two miles from Barnard Castle during a low-level flying exercise over the North-East.

At the opening of an inquest into his death, deputy South Durham coroner Mr. David Mason heard yesterday that the injuries to Squadron Leader Matthews' hands had been typical of the sort caused by holding aircraft controls on impact. 'I believe he was trying to fly the aircraft at the time of impact and was conscious and did not try to eject,' said RAF pathologist Group Capt. Anthony Balfour. The cause of death, he added, was multiple injuries, and death would have been instantaneous.

Flt. Lieut. Bernard Mills, stationed at RAF Bruggen in West Germany, said that on the morning of the plane crash he took off in formation with Sqn. Leader Matthews and two other pilots from Lossiemouth in Scotland. The four aircraft flew down to Montrose and then over the North-East coast before turning inland near Teesside and taking a course over Bishop Auckland towards Barnard Castle.

'Throughout the flight I had been in both visual and radio contact with the other three aircraft until 9.26 am,' he said. 'We entered cloud within the next 30 seconds and that caused us to lose contact. I was flying at 1,500 feet and when I last saw Sqn. Leader Matthews he was flying at the same height.'

Flt. Lieut. Kenneth McKenzie, aged 26, also stationed at RAF Bruggen, told the deputy coroner he was attached to the board of inquiry which was investigating the crash. He said he had examined the aircraft's tail plane found among the wreckage and there were the identification letters 'DF' on both sides of it. A certificate signed by Sqn. Leader Matthews showed that it had been the aircraft he had taken out on the morning of the crash, he added. Serial numbers on other parts of the wreckage also helped identify the aircraft as that flown by Sqn. Leader Matthews, he said.

Adjourning the inquest until October 28, Mr. Mason said the hearing had clearly established the identity of the deceased and his cause of death."

The *Teesside Aviation News* aircraft enthusiast's newsletter for October 1981 contained details which had been published by the *Evening Despatch* on 13th August:

"At 0926 the aircraft ran into low cloud and heavy rain, losing VMC [Visual Meteorological Conditions]. The crash happened minutes later as the aircraft descended from FL10 [10,000 feet] for a bombing run. The aircraft were part of a joint NATO exercise, involving USAF F-4s, A-10s and OV-10s, WGAF F-4s, RDAF F-104s and aircraft from other RAF units, including TWU Hawks."

Among the plaques at the Barnard Castle Aviation Memorial Garden is this one, dedicated to Squadron Leader Roger Matthews, who was killed when his Jaguar crashed near the town on 6th August 1981. (Author)

Eventually, the Board of Inquiry set out its findings, which appeared in Ministry of Defence Military Aircraft Accident Summary "MAS 20/82" dated 9th December 1982. This was a detailed breakdown of the events leading up to the crash itself and its suspected cause. As the pilot had died in the incident, the reason could only be surmised:

"Jaguar XX972 was one of several Jaguars detached from their base in West Germany to an airfield in Scotland to take part in an exercise. On 6 August it was flying as No.4 of a 4 aircraft formation at low level when deteriorating weather forced the aircraft to climb. The leader's radio became unserviceable just before the decision to climb was made and, although the No.2 assumed control of the formation, some confusion occurred and the formation split into 4 individual aircraft. During the climb in cloud, No.4 made 2 routine radio calls enquiring about the height his element leader was passing. It was decided that all 4 aircraft would reverse their course and fly back to where the weather was clear. An order to this effect was transmitted but no acknowledgement was received from No.4. The formation was unable to contact No.4 again; XX972 had crashed at high speed, virtually wings level, in a nose-up attitude. The pilot did not eject and was killed.

There was no evidence among the wreckage of a technical failure which could have caused the accident. Although a positive cause of this accident could not be determined, the most likely was thought to be disorientation. The radar picture of the 4 Jaguars showed that XX972 was climbing at a slower speed than his element leader; when the 4 aircraft were ordered to turnabout, XX972 entered a very tight turn. Flight simulator tests revealed that, in order to maintain a turn as tight as that seen on radar, a considerable rate of descent would have developed. It is possible that the pilot was flying on his Head Up instruments, where the Rate of Climb and Descent Indicator has a maximum reading of 2,500 ft/min; he may, therefore, have been unaware of the high rate of descent (up to 6,000 ft/min) developed by XX972. Had he suffered an instrument failure at the same time, the situation would have been exacerbated; by the time the pilot became aware of the proximity of the ground, it would have been too late."

The Military Aircraft Accident Summary went onto describe what payments had been made to the farmer and the local utility company to compensate for their losses:

"An interim payment of £1,500 has been paid to a farmer in respect of a bullock that was killed and for damage to fields and hedges. A sum of £843.25p has been paid to the North Eastern Electricity Board for damage to power lines."

TRAGEDY AT KIP HILL

Less than three weeks before it was destroyed by fire in a fatal crash near Stanley, County Durham, Bell 206 JetRanger G-PATW is pictured at Ascot Racecourse on 20th June 1990. Carrying "Whelan Construction Development" titles, it was owned and operated by Pat Whelan, the company's owner. (Bill Teasdale)

In the years 1989 and 1990, two prominent North-East businessmen would die in helicopter crashes in the region within eight months of each other. In the first incident, 62-year-old Eddie Ferguson, owner of Fergusons of Blyth, a well-known local transport company, and his son died in December 1989 when his Hughes 500 plunged into a field in Cumbria and burst into flames. In July 1990, a second prominent company owner, Pat Whelan, owner of a successful building firm responsible for numerous projects throughout the North East of England, died in a helicopter crash near Stanley, one which also claimed the life of his wife.

News of this tragedy was published by Newcastle's *Evening Chronicle* on 13th July 1990. The accident had occurred earlier that morning:

"A Newcastle company boss and his wife died today when their helicopter crashed on take-off. The copter was engulfed in flames as it hit a telegraph wire – killing Pat Whelan and his wife Margaret. The 10.45 am crash happened at Kip Hill, just north of Stanley in Co. Durham. Mr. Whelan's private helicopter had just left the ground.

Five fire engines raced to the scene, but eyewitnesses said there was no chance of anyone surviving the blaze. And company director Joe Grieves, of builders P. Whelan Limited, or New Bridge Street, Newcastle, confirmed that his boss, believed to be in his late 40s, and his wife had died.

The helicopter came down in a field close to the South Causey Hotel, part of the South Causey Equestrian Centre, near Stanley. Mr. Whelan, who lived at Low Fell, Gateshead, was the builder behind the £6m-plus Manors cinema at Manors, Newcastle.

He and his wife had two children, and his daughter is believed to work at the hotel. It is understood Mr. Whelan, a former director of Gateshead Football Club, only gained his pilot's licence a short time ago after training at Tees-side Airport. He has also designed, developed and built the £8.5m development in Sunderland for supermarket chain Sainsburys. In 1985 he sponsored the complex's indoor winter dressage series.

His company, based in New Bridge Street, Newcastle, was started in 1971 and his wife Margaret was a director. His first two projects were to build the Moat House Hotel, Wallsend, and the Regent Centre, Newcastle. During the 1970s he concentrated on housebuilding in the North-East but by the beginning of the 1980s the amount of work in the region fell.

His first major contract outside the area was with a 'major food plc' in East Kilbride, Scotland. He also worked at the Longbenton Industrial Estate, Newcastle, and built the Waters and Robson plant in Morpeth, Northumberland. In November last year he also won a contract to develop the bus/retail station in Carlisle."

The Chronicle report went onto describe eyewitness accounts of the crash:

"Horrified eyewitnesses today described how the helicopter suddenly turned into a ball of fire. Frank Osborne, managing director of Auckland Trailers in Tanfield Lea, was standing outside his factory when he heard the helicopter come down. He drove to the crash site and was one of the first people on the scene.

Mr. Osborne, 46, said: 'I saw a big pall of smoke, which went up from the helicopter. It was completely devastated – completely wrecked. There was no way – it's impossible – anyone could survive. The tailplane of the helicopter was approximately 30 or 40 yards from the helicopter. Mr. Osborne, who runs a company in Stanelaw Way, added: 'I was outside the factory when I heard what sounded like machine-gun fire. I heard one bang and two quick bursts. I saw smoke go up. I jumped in the car and went there.' He said the copter was a regular user of the site. 'I was there three or four times a week. There is a helicopter pad there.' He added that Mr. Whelan was a part owner of the South Causey Hotel. 'He had been there and was apparently leaving with his wife when he hit an overhead cable.'

Mr. Osborne knew Mr. Whelan through their work with a charitable organisation for the building industry. 'I came away when the fire brigade arrived. It was too macabre for me.'

Shocked riding school groom Ann Crow also witnessed the crash. 'It was flying quite low when the tail piece caught the wire. It dropped and burst into flames. It was awful – everyone is really shocked,' said 18-year-old Ann.

Gillian Kaye, the landlady of the Blue Bell, Kip Hill, near Stanley, was in the bedroom when she heard a loud bang, and the lights went out. 'I knew what had happened straight away,' she said. 'I saw palls of black smoke. My children were outside, but I quickly got them in again. I think everybody in the area must have been there within 20 or 30 seconds. I heard the helicopter take off. It used to go above us two or three times a day. It had taken off from the South Causey Equestrian Centre. We'd been expecting something like this. It always used to fly quite low. I've said every time I have to take my children in because it flies so low.'

A farmer was making hay in the field just yards from where the helicopter crashed. It is believed that he is unhurt and went to the Equestrian Centre."

Numerous homes temporarily lost their electricity supply due to the crash, as confirmed by newspaper reporting of the incident at Kip Hill:

"Electricity engineers are this afternoon trying to reconnect homes after the 20,000-volt wire was brought down in the crash. But it was feared some people in Stanley would have to be hooked up to a generator because it was thought it could take several hours to reconnect them to the supply. A Northern Electric spokesman said: 'We have workmen down there at the moment working on the 34 homes which do not have any power. We hope to have electricity as soon as possible.'

A press photograph taken at the scene shows the tail boom and tail rotor stabiliser, which had landed some 50 metres short of the main impact site.

The same article also stated that staff from the Civil Aviation Authority's Air Accidents Investigation Branch were due to visit the site in order to establish the cause of the crash. Superintendent Ned Lawson of Durham Constabulary had confirmed that *"the tail fin snapped off the helicopter."*

In the following day's *Journal*, there were further details about the farm worker who had been in the same field in which the crash occurred:

"The main section of the Bell 206 JetRanger helicopter was sent spinning and erupted in flames just yards from a man driving a tractor. People who saw the crash said the couple stood no chance of surviving. Wreckage from the five-seater aircraft was spread across a wide area of the hay field. An air accident investigation team from the Department of Transport has started inquiries.

The tractor driver, who has not been named by police, is understood to be Mr. Philip Moiser, the son-in-law of a business associate of Mr. Whelan's. He was unhurt but shocked. He did not wish to discuss the accident last night. The field where the crash happened is only about 100 yards from the nearest house.

The tragedy, the second helicopter crash involving a businessman from the region in recent months, happened at about 10.35 am. Five fire crews were at the scene in minutes, but were unable to do anything to save the couple.

The South Causey Hotel was built by Mr. Whelan's firm and had only recently opened, forming part of a complex which also includes the South Causey Equestrian Centre and Shafto's bar and restaurant. It is believed Mr. Whelan was a partner in the venture.

Mr. Danny Hogarth, 52, saw the accident from the garden of his home in nearby James Street, Kirkhill, Stanley, and said the couple had no chance of surviving the crash and fire that followed. 'I saw the helicopter take off from near the equestrian centre. It appeared to be backfiring and didn't seem to have much power. Its tail caught an overhead cable and came off. It spiralled into the ground and burst into flames. They didn't stand a chance.'"

Superintendent Ned Lawson, the Durham Constabulary officer who had suggested that the machine had struck an electricity cable, provided more details about what was believed to have happened that morning: *"We think the occupants of the helicopter were acquainted with the tractor driver, and may have been distracted."*

The Air Accidents Investigation Branch carried out a detailed search of the crash site, together with a thorough examination of both the wreckage and its surroundings. Eyewitnesses, including the tractor driver, were also questioned to shed light on what had occurred that day. The findings were subsequent published and made for interesting reading. Pat Whelan and his wife were intending to fly down to Oxford that day. Weather at the site at the time of take-off (0940 hours) was reported as "ceiling and visibility okay", with an easterly wind of around 10 knots – which was therefore not considered to be a factor in the ensuing crash. However, the South Causey Hotel's immediate surroundings were relevant to the investigation. Part of the report read as follows:

"Directly in front of the hotel, which faces south-east, is a 110m wide field which slopes upwards fairly sharply from the hotel and, halfway up the

slope, a triple set of 20,000-volt power cables runs directly across the field, supported by 'telegraph' poles situated at each side of the field. The pole on the north side of the field was obscured by trees and that on the south was silhouetted against distant buildings. The three 8mm thick copper cables had oxidised to a green colour which blended into the green field behind. Near the top of the slope, a tractor was being driven by a man known to the pilot and his wife."

Another image of the impact site, showing the burning remains of the JetRanger.

As for the actual crash itself, the following couple of paragraphs provided a summary of the events that occurred, based on a combination of witness accounts and evidence on the ground at the impact site:

"The helicopter had been parked side-on to the hotel and, as it took off, it turned south-eastwards and climbed away from the hotel towards the field, crossing over a (different) set of cables at the bottom of the field. It was then seen to fly towards the rising ground in the general direction of the tractor on a heading of approximately 170°. About 150m into the field, it struck the cables. There was a bright flash followed by a loud report and the helicopter began to pitch severely whilst climbing slightly and moving onwards up the slope. A second or two later, its tail rotor assembly fell to the ground and the helicopter began to rotate anticlockwise whilst continuing to travel towards the tractor. It passed directly over the tractor, leaving a length of cable straddling the bonnet, and fell to the ground 10m beyond it, some 400m from its take off point, where it burst into flames.

Although witness evidence as to the final manoeuvre varies greatly, evidence provided by the ground marks and structural deformation of the helicopter show that it struck the ground hard, in a nose high attitude, banked slightly to the left on a heading of approximately 280° and with negligible forward speed but with some left drift. The main rotor struck the ground and separated from the rotor mast and the helicopter rolled violently to the left and pitched nose down, striking the ground hard on the left forward side of the fuselage and rolling inverted. A severe fire developed which destroyed most of the cabin structure and the main gearbox casing.

Considerable amounts of Perspex debris were found in a region extending from beneath the cables forward for a distance of approximately 40m up the slope in the direction of travel, beyond which were found fragments of tail rotor shaft, drive shaft cover, the OAT [outside air temperature] gauge, and more fragments of Perspex from the cockpit. The aft section of tail boom together with the tail rotor vertical stabiliser was lying approximately 100m forward of the line of cables, some 50m before the main wreckage impact point."

However, this wasn't the full extent of the debris field, and information that related to cables striking and being caught by the helicopter's structure had a part to play in the Branch's determination into the cause of the crash:

"The skids had broken up in the impact and were lying in, or nearby, the main wreckage. The remains of the forward left skid tube had a cable still wrapped around it and the right forward skid displayed clear evidence that cables had become wrapped around that also. A separate cable was wrapped several times around the lower section of the main rotor mast in the region of the swash plate. Detailed examination of the Perspex debris from the early part of the wreckage trail revealed score marks consistent with cable scrapes, and the bezel of the OAT gauge was lightly dented and had a greenish deposit on the surface of the dent. Both the size of the dent and the nature of the green deposit were entirely consistent with the dimensions and surface corrosion observed on the power cables. The gauge is located on the upper windscreen with the face and bezel on the inside of the windscreen panel, and the position of the dent on the gauge indicated that the windscreen had been broken by a tightly stretched cable running over it."

The arrangement of the nearby power cables and their supporting poles was examined, and their dimensions measured. It was calculated that the lowest cables were approximately eight-and-a-half metres above ground level at the poles, but due to sag, just six to seven metres at mid-span. All three power cables had been broken by G-PATW when it was airborne, each of them possessing a breaking load of around 2,800lbs of force. The cable that had been wrapped several times around the rotor mast area had become trapped by the swash plate and pitch control mechanism, crushing the cable itself. The lower pitch control rods were destroyed so it was not possible to determine whether control of the main rotors had been lost.

As for the Air Accidents Investigation Branch's conclusion, this was set out in two final paragraphs:

"The pattern of cable damage was consistent with the aircraft picking up the lower pair of cables on the skids, and the third (centre) cable riding up over the nose. The relative geometry between the helicopter skids, nose section, and the cables indicated that the aircraft was flying approximately horizontally in a nose-down attitude, consistent with it having been in level accelerating flight at the time it struck the cables. The lower cables were *held in place between the skid tubes, the forward skid supports, and the footsteps, and the upper cable lodged in the region of the bottom of the main rotor mast. The cables evidently provided a balanced decelerating force which tended to maintain the aircraft in a level attitude until the cables started to break.*

The fact that the aircraft had broken (not cut) all three cables and thereafter continued to fly in a semi-climbing flightpath indicates that the aircraft had considerable kinetic energy at the time the wires were struck, and that the engine was delivering adequate power."

Since no defects or pre-accident equipment malfunction was discovered, it was assumed that the helicopter had struck the cables whilst under power and in forward flight. Although not directly mentioned as a cause, mention of one "telegraph" pole being obscured by trees and the cables themselves blending into the background due to oxidisation may well have contributed to the pilot flying into an obstruction that he was unfamiliar with, had not seen or had simply forgotten was there.

The loss of Pat Whelan and his wife robbed the region of a successful and well-liked businessman and developer. Martin Bellinger, the president of the Tyne and Wear Chamber of Commerce, spoke for many at the time:

"This comes as a great shock. Pat Whelan was a much-respected man in the area. There are many developments with Pat's name on them. He was a prominent figure and will be greatly missed."

BACK TO SCHOOL WITH A BUMP

Evans VP-1 Volksplane PH-VPI is pictured here on display at Lelystad in the Netherlands. A similar homebuilt example, one on the British civil aircraft register and operated from a private airstrip near Chester-Le-Street, crashed into a school in September 1990. The extremely simple nature of the aircraft's design can easily be made out here. (AlfvanBeem, CC0)

Light aircraft come in different shapes and a variety of sizes. Although the most numerous seem to be factory-built examples from the large Cessna and Piper companies, home-built machines started to become popular in the 1970s, various types being constructed from plans. The Popular Flying Association sponsored such enterprises, providing advice on home-builds, regulating assembly and test-flying through its network of regional branch organisations and qualified local inspectors. Everything was geared toward safety of materials and construction, plus flying the completed machines. Nowadays, homebuilders can obtain "kits" that contain the necessary parts to put together a complete airframe, with only a compatible engine needing to be sourced and installed.

    As far as Britain was concerned, one of the first popular home-built type of recreational aircraft was the Evans VP-1 Volksplane. Originally designed in America back in 1966, it was conceived as an all-wood, single-seat open cockpit machine with ease of construction in mind. The VP-1 was designed to use a modified 1,200cc Volkswagen air-cooled car engine, as fitted in the extremely successful Beetle. Ease of assembly, however, meant that the Volksplane was rather crude in aerodynamic terms, one that required more engine power than others of the same size and weight.

Despite its somewhat crude nature and lack of visual aesthetics, the VP-1 became extremely popular and over 6,000 sets of plans were sold. Would-be British builders snapped them up in droves. One of many Volksplanes constructed in this country was G-PFAZ, originally built between 1978 and 1982 by Brian Kylo of Consett. Rather than the designer's intended powerplant, it had a 1,600cc Volkswagen engine fitted.

Mr. Kylo sold the aircraft in early 1990 to Denis Ridley and Robert Ryle. Ridley owned an agricultural engineering business at Cornsay Colliery, west of Durham, whilst Ryle ran High Flatts Farm near Chester-le-Street, just behind the Plough Inn on Pelton Lane. The farm had its own grass airstrip, located just to the south-west of Pelton village itself, and although aircraft movements were normally restricted to weekends, apparently some concern existed among residents regarding the potential for a crash at the nearby school complex. The airstrip ran south-east to north-west, roughly parallel to the road leading up to the village, its last 400 yards being uphill. The schools were situated just off to the right of a direct line from the Runway 12 threshold, around 400 yards or so further uphill. In September 1990, the fears of those residents suddenly came true.

"Home-made light aircraft crashes into infants' school" ran the headline in *The Newcastle Journal* on 17th September 1990. It was only fortunate that the accident had occurred at a weekend when the Pelton schools had been closed, although as the *Journal's* story confirmed, some residents were near the aircraft when it crashed:

"A home-made aircraft crashed into a school, somersaulted and landed upside down in a road yesterday. Two youths with a baby in a pushchair ran for cover as debris showered around them.

The Evans VP-1 broke in two, the engine was thrown out and landed in a gutter, and kerosene was spewed over the area around Pelton Infants' School, Pelton, Chester-Le-Street, County Durham. The aircraft's undercarriage became embedded in the school roof, scattering ridge tiles.

Pilot Denis Ridley, 46, of Cornsay Colliery, near Esh Winning, County Durham, was freed by villagers and motorists and carried to safety, his face covered with blood. He was taken to Dryburn Hospital, Durham City, with a cut in his throat, and an arm injury. He was allowed home after treatment. Mr. Ridley had just taken off from a field at High Fields Farm, Pelton, about 800 yards from the school. The field is used as a landing site by farmer Robert Ryle.

Eyewitnesses gave dramatic accounts of the crash, which happened at 2 pm. Glenn Cameron, 38, of South View, Pelton, just across the road from the school, said: 'I heard up and saw the plane. I thought 'it is never going to clear that', and it didn't. It hit the roof and flipped over, landing on its back in the road. I ran over and the pilot was shouting, 'My leg, my leg.' We lifted the weights off him. I grabbed him and pulled him out. He had blood over his face, as if he had a broken nose, but he didn't look too bad. There were quite a few people gathering and we pulled the plane off the road and put it on the pavement.'

Scott McDade, 15, of Perkinsville, had been pushing his niece, Lee Dixon, not yet one-year-old, in a pushchair in front of the school. He said: 'I heard a big bang and ran with the pushchair to get it safely out of the way. Wood was flying all over the place and splattering around us. I was just concerned about getting the bairn out of the way. Then we went to help. Petrol was pouring out of the engine and running down the road.' With Scott was his friend Ian Robson, 17, of Burnmoor.

Mrs. Joan Gordon, whose eight-year-old daughter Anna attends the adjacent junior school, said: 'It is terrible. It doesn't bear thinking about. A day later and it could have been a disaster.'

Pelton councillor Mrs. Peggy Potter said: 'The field is used by aircraft, mostly on Sundays, but also other days of the week. It has been going on for a few months and I have been afraid one of the planes would hit the school. People are now coming to me and saying I must do something about it. I will bring it up at the council meeting tomorrow and see what we can do. There is a junior school, infants' school and nursery school all on the same site. The planes fly very low over the schools' playing field at times.'

A Durham Police spokesman said the Northumbria Police helicopter had been called in to look for scattered debris. The Air Accident Investigation Unit had been informed. The wreckage was put on a trailer and taken back to High Flatts Farm.

Farmer Mr. Ryle, 38, said he did not know Mr. Ridley very well and believed he had flown in to see one of the men on the farm. He said the aircraft was home-made. Mr. Ryle said: 'The field is only used by aeroplanes at the weekend. It has been used safely for years, by myself and my father before me. I'm the one who uses it most, but I am 100 pc for safety and if the council banned its use, I would not fight the move.'"

A photo taken at the scene of the crash shows the wreck of Evans VP-1 G-PFAZ lying in the road at Pelton village on 16th September 1990.

More details about the incident were published by the Newcastle *Evening Chronicle* in its 17th September 1990 edition:

"A pilot had a miracle escape when his home-made aircraft crashed upside down in a road after colliding with a school. Air crash investigators began an inquiry today into the accident which saw the Evans VP1 destroyed after hitting the roof of a school building in Co Durham before somersaulting and coming to rest on the nearby road.

The crash has sparked calls from villagers in Pelton, near Chester-le-Street, for the closure of the airstrip at a nearby farm which was used by the plane.

Passers-by, some of whom had just managed to avoid being hit by debris, rushed to help pilot Denis Ridley from the cockpit. The 46-year-old businessman was taken to Durham's Dryburn Hospital and treated for the cut in his throat, and an arm injury. He was later allowed home to Cornsay Colliery, Co Durham, from where he runs an agricultural plant engineering business. Mr. Ridley was well enough to return to work.

The crash broke the Sunday afternoon calm in Pelton shortly after 2pm, less than a minute after the light aircraft had taken off from the private airstrip in a field at High Flatts Farm, between Pelton and Chester-le-Street. It appears that the plane failed to gain height and it collided with the roof at Pelton Infants' School, throwing the engine into nearby guttering and cracking the plane in two.

Eyewitnesses, some of whom ran for cover from flying debris, reported that the plane literally flipped over. Ridge tiles were scattered round, and repairs were needed at the school today, although classes resumed as normal."

Denis Ridley was an experienced light aircraft pilot, with 534 flying hours on all types at the time of the crash in September 1990. However, he only had three hours on the VP-1, so may well have been unaccustomed to the relative lack of power the 1,600cc Volkswagen engine could deliver.

On the day in question, the pilot elected to take off from the High Flatts Farm airstrip using Runway 30, i.e., in the north-westerly direction, which would take him over the eastern outskirts of Pelton village. Runway 30/12 – the only one at the farm – was 600 yards in length, with a downslope for the first 200. After that point, the ground sloped upwards for the remaining 400 yards, beyond which lay a continually rising slope before reaching the first buildings in Pelton. Immediately west of the airstrip and the climb out was the road from Chester-le-Street to Pelton, which had electric cables running along its other side.

As far as the condition of the Evans VP-1 was concerned, it was said to be in full working order and both its fuel and oil tanks were topped up prior to take off. This meant that the aircraft was close to its maximum permitted take-off weight of 341kg. A light breeze of between two and ten knots was coming in from the west. After running the modified Volkswagen engine up properly, the pilot satisfied himself that it was performing normally, and he prepared to take off. The Air Accidents Investigation Branch's report for the subsequent incident included the following details:

"The aircraft was taxied to the 30 threshold and a normal full power take-off was commenced. The aircraft became airborne after a ground run of about

250 yards at a speed of 50 mph, which the pilot states is 5 mph lower than usual. It initially climbed to about 20 feet above ground level when the pilot felt that he needed to lower the nose to gain airspeed. However, the aircraft failed to accelerate and by this time there was insufficient distance in which to land back on the strip. Being aware of the close proximity of buildings immediately to his left and right, he reports that he realised that he could not turn the aircraft but thought that he would clear the buildings ahead. In the event he did not, and the main landing gear struck the top ridge tiles on the roof of a school building which was fortunately unoccupied at the time. The force of the impact detached the main landing gear, pitched the aircraft nose down and it crashed onto a road beyond the building. There was no fire and the pilot, who had suffered minor injuries, was released from the wreckage by local people who had witnessed the accident. He had been wearing full restraint harness which held throughout the impact. There was minor damage to tiles on the roof of the school building.

In a detailed report of the circumstances, the accident pilot considers that a contributory cause was the marginal performance of the engine. Due to the severity of the damage, this could not be determined by subsequent examination."

High Flatts Farm would be in the news again 12 years later, when a hangar fire badly damaged or destroyed several privately-owned aircraft housed within. One of them was Cessna FR.172F G-BBXH, which the author remembers performing a parachute jump from at Peterlee (Shotton) Airfield back in November 1995.

NOT ON THE MAP

Taken two days after the crash involved a Teesside Airport-based Piper Cherokee, a single severed supporting cable can be just made out dangling from the top of the Muggleswick radio mast. (Trevor Littlewood, Creative Commons licence)

At 1554 hours on the afternoon of 7th April 1992, G-AYIO, a Piper PA-28 Cherokee based at Teesside Airport, crashed into one of the Muggleswick Radio Station mast's supporting cables. The mast, some 1,702 feet above sea level on Horseshoe Hill, just north of the road to Rookhope, a couple of miles north-east of Stanhope, was in an area covered with low cloud and poor visibility. Eyewitnesses saw the aircraft flying just a couple of hundred feet above the ground near Castleside, a village located between Consett and the mast. It was just below cloud and heading north-westwards in the direction of Hexham. The Newcastle *Journal* newspaper's 9th April 1992 edition reported the crash, as it had taken some time to locate the wreck of the four-seater machine and the body of its pilot, the only occupant:

"A pilot who died when his light aircraft crashed into the side of a hill hit the steel supports of a radio mast. Arthur Whitley, 52, of Norton, near Stockton died when his Piper Cherokee crashed on the moors near Consett, County Durham. It snapped a steel stabilising cable on British Telecom's 230-foot Muggleswick Radio Station mast.

The wreckage of the plane was discovered 1,500 feet up on Horseshoe Hill, three miles south of the Derwent Reservoir. A spokesman for RAF Pitreavie in Fife, which co-ordinated the search for the plane, said that it had crashed into the side of a hill.

The spokesman said: 'From what we are able to reconstruct, he had gone into a left-hand turn, getting gradually lower and lower, and at one point the hill was higher than he was, and he went straight into it.'

A BT spokeswoman confirmed that one of the steel cables supporting the now obsolete mast had been cut. The cable, 1.5 inches in diameter, cannot be repaired until after the team from the Air Accidents Investigation Branch of the Department of Transport had looked over the damage. 'The plane clipped and snapped one of the 12 cables supporting the mast but this has not disrupted our service. The mast does not carry any warning lights, which are not required by the Civil Aviation Authority rules because it is in a remote area and not on any flightpath,' she added.

Police, mountain rescue teams and three helicopters scoured 40 square miles in Derwentside, hampered by low cloud and heavy rain after the plane disappeared from radar screens at Newcastle Airport. Mr Whitley is believed to have been a member of Teesside Aero Club, flying from Teesside Airport to Carlisle when the accident happened. Last night, a spokesman from the Department of Transport air accidents unit said the investigation into the cause of the crash could take months.

A team has already visited the site of the crash and they may decide to transport the wreckage to the headquarters at Farnborough for further tests. 'We will be interviewing eyewitnesses and the local air traffic control and looking at wind and weather conditions,' the spokesman added. An inquest opens at Bishop Auckland today."

The Newcastle *Evening Chronicle*, in their 3rd September 1992 edition, confirmed more personal information regarding the pilot and details of his flying experience:

"College lecturer Arthur Whitley died when his light aircraft crashed into the steel supports of a radio mast not shown on the chart he used to plot his route. Mr. Whitley, 52, who had limited flying experience, had taken off at Teesside Airport for Carlisle where he was to pick up an instructor, an inquest at Bishop Auckland heard.

On the flight he became disorientated in low cloud and his Piper Cherokee crashed into the supports of the Muggleswick radio mast on the moors near Consett, Co Durham.

Mr. Whitley, of Norton, Stockton, had gone to Teesside Airport on April 7 for further instruction in instrument meteorological rating, needed by pilots to fly through cloud. He had held a pilot's licence for 18 months and had logged 74 hours flying time.

Air accident inquiry branch investigator David Miller said the approved chart Mr. Whitley used to prepare his flight via Hexham did not show the 230-foot high Muggleswick mast. Such charts, he said, only showed masts 300 feet high or more.

He said Mr. Whitley was handed over to Newcastle air traffic control when he was 11 miles north-west [sic] of Newcastle. He reported cloud closing in and asked to adjust his altitude. The controller told him to use his discretion. Then Mr. Whitley radioed control to say he was trying to see Hexham and that the ground was just visible. The controller asked him if he wanted to turn back to Teesside.

Search and rescue teams were sent out when it was realised he must have crashed. Said Mr. Miller: 'The pilot got himself into a situation in cloud he was not practiced in.' Verdict: Accident."

The crash site in February 2023. The summit of Horseshoe Hill is a somewhat flat, featureless expanse of peat hag and heather-covered moorland. (Author)

Arthur Whitley had begun his flight training in July 1989 and had amassed 48 flying hours by February 1991. He received his Private Pilots' Licence in April of that year, and in the year to March 1992 notched up a further 26 hours of general handling experience and training to receive an Instrument Meteorological Conditions (IMC) rating, which would allow him to fly using instruments only, in conditions of lower visibility. By that time Mr. Whitley had 17 hours simulated instrument flying but had yet to qualify for his IMC rating. He was therefore ill-equipped to handle a situation where the rating applied in terms of operating under deteriorating weather conditions.

The Air Accidents Investigation Branch report dealing with the loss of Cherokee G-AYIO provided details of the nature of the fatal flight:

"On 7 April 1992 the pilot had booked an IMC dual training flight for 1430 hrs. He arrived at Teesside Aero Club at approximately 1330 hrs to prepare for his flight. He had to wait for his instructor, however, who was airborne with another student. When his instructor landed, the pilot was asked if he would prefer to ferry a PA-28 to Carlisle to collect the instructor who was to fly another aircraft to Carlisle for maintenance. The IMC training that had been booked, would take place on the dual return flight from Carlisle to Teesside. The pilot chose to fly the usual club cross-country route, that he had flown several times before, which goes from Teesside direct to Hexham, keeping clear of the high ground of the Pennines, then turning along the South Tyne valley to Carlisle."

Although the instructor would not be present on the flight across to Carlisle, he discussed with the pilot the route the latter would take, plus the winds and weather to be encountered on the way. Mr. Whitley had obtained en-route weather information from Teesside Airport and had been informed that some hill fog had been reported between there and Hexham. He was told to remain in visual meteorological conditions (visual flight rules, i.e., always keeping the ground in sight), but to return to Teesside Airport if the weather prevented him from doing so. Without an IMC rating, he could not continue flying through marginal visibility conditions on instruments only.

The instructor had a deadline to arrive at Carlisle Airport with the aircraft he was ferrying across for maintenance, so departed Teesside at around 1515 hours and took a direct track for his destination. En route, and flying at an altitude of 3,000 feet, which was above all of the hilltops between him and Carlisle, he noticed that the area was free of cloud but that the cloud base to the north was considerably lower.

Arthur Whitley took off from Teesside in G-AYIO at 1532 hours, bound for Carlisle, his initial track taking him towards Hexham. He climbed to his pre-planned cruising altitude of 2,000 feet, which again should have kept him clear of any high ground en route. Some 11 nautical miles north-west of his departure point, Teesside air traffic control assigned the aircraft a transponder code and handed him over to Newcastle Approach Control at 1539 hours. Just 15 minutes later, the pilot would be killed when he flew into a radio mast's support cable. The Air Accidents Investigation Branch's report provides information relating to that final quarter of an hour:

"At 1540 hrs the pilot made contact with Newcastle Approach Control who told him to 'Maintain VFR, report at Hexham'. At 1545 hrs, several witnesses in the village of Castleside, 3 nm south-west of Consett, saw the aircraft flying just below cloud, at a height estimated to be between 200 feet and 300 feet above ground, north-west towards Hexham.

Three minutes later, at 1548 hrs, in the vicinity of Derwent Reservoir, 5 nm west of Consett, the pilot transmitted to Newcastle Approach 'Requesting further descent, weather closing in... Request descent to one thousand feet.' Newcastle Approach replied, 'Descend at your discretion, the Tyne Regional (QNH) is nine nine two'. At 1553 hrs the pilot transmitted that he was trying to see Hexham and requested a QDM [steer] for Carlisle. The approach controller, seeing the aircraft on radar south of Hexham, flying in the opposite direction, replied that the 'QDM for Hexham is about three six zero'.

Some 30 seconds later, the controller asked the pilot if he had contact with the ground. The pilot replied 'Yes, just visible but deteriorating'. At this point the controller suggested to the pilot 'Perhaps you ought to think about returning back to Teesside?' Immediately the pilot requested a QDM for Teesside, which was passed by the controller.

At 1553 hrs and 50 seconds, during the readback of the information, the transmission terminated. At 1605 hrs, with no further radiotelephony contact, the Newcastle controller contacted a police helicopter in the area and requested a search for the missing aircraft which he believed had crashed 18 nm south-west of Newcastle. The London Air Traffic Control Centre was also informed of the missing aircraft, and they alerted their Distress and Diversion cell."

The Rescue Co-ordination Centre at RAF Pitreavie, Fife, ordered rescue teams located at RAF Leeming, Leuchars and Stafford to head for the last known radar position. However, by the time they reached County Durham, the weather had deteriorated still further. Cloud and hill fog shrouded the whole area, reducing visibility on the ground down to just 25 metres. This hampered the teams' attempts to locate the Piper Cherokee. Almost six hours after it had crashed, the wreckage of G-AYIO was discovered some 250 metres west of the Muggleswick Radio Station mast, atop Horseshoe Hill, located just a few miles north-west of Stanhope. The aircraft had been destroyed and the pilot had sustained fatal injuries. The accident report provided details of the crash site:

"Wreckage and site examination showed that the aircraft had collided with the support cables of a radio mast, Muggleswick Radio Station Tower. The tower is 1,702 feet above mean sea level on undulating moorland and stands 230 feet above ground level. It is supported by twelve guy cables, in four orthogonal sets of three cables, with each set anchored in the ground approximately 100 feet from the base of the tower. Each cable is of multi-strand braided steel of 7/8 inch overall diameter."

A diagram of the mast is reproduced on the following page. As for damage to the aircraft itself, the report described this in detail:

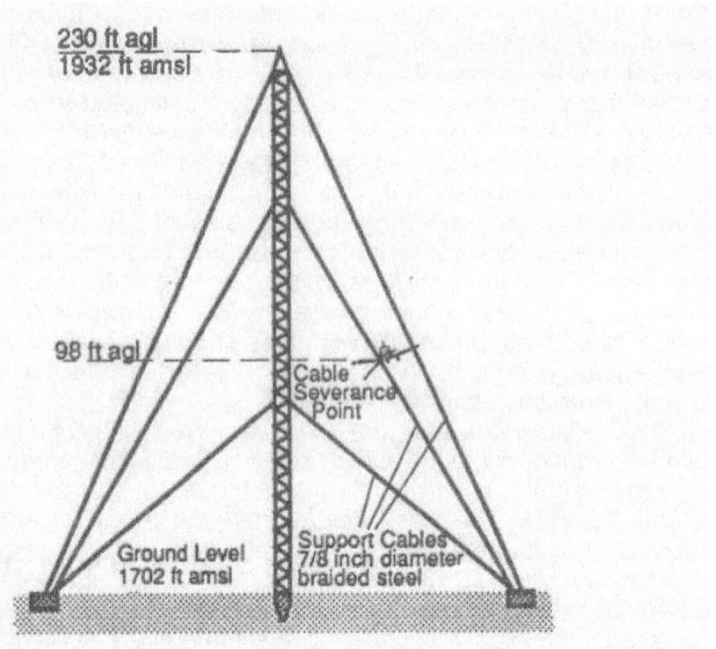

An Air Accidents Investigation Branch diagram of the Muggleswick Radio Station mast, showing the point at which Cherokee G-AYIO severed one of the support cables. (Open Government Licence v3.0.)

"Three regions of the aircraft sustained cable strikes. This had caused detachment of the glass reinforced plastic top of the left wing, the left aileron and the outboard four feet of the left wing; minor damage to the propeller, disruption of the right side of the forward fuselage; and gross damage at the right wing root that almost detached the right wing.

Inaccessibility of the cables prevented full identification of the details and sequencing of the strikes, but it was clear that the major impact had been near the centre of the mid cable in the westerly set, from the propeller, the right side of the forward fuselage and the right wing root, causing severance of the cable.

Geometric considerations suggested that the left wing had probably collided with the upper cable in the westerly set. The evidence suggested that at initial impact the aircraft had been erect, banked to the right and tracking between 290-340° True and had been approximately 100 feet above ground level (i.e., at 1,800 feet amsl). The pitch angle and the direction of the flight path in the vertical plane could not be determined, but the subsequent travel of the aircraft suggested that it had probably been level or climbing and had been flying at a relatively high speed."

It was determined that G-AYIO had struck the ground 230 metres west of the point of major cable impact, this being 150 feet below the impact point itself. The ground surface was made of wet peat covered with heather.

Piper PA-28-140 Cherokee C G-AYIO is pictured here at the 1982 Popular Flying Association rally, held at Cranfield aerodrome. Less than ten years later, it would fly into a support cable on top of a remote hillside above Stanhope in County Durham. (Photo courtesy of Ken Haynes)

The impact had caused severe damage to the engine and forward fuselage area, including the whole forward cabin section. In addition, there had been gross longitudinal crushing of the wing leading edges and buckling of the rear fuselage. No fire had started after impact. No evidence could be found to suggest equipment, airframe or engine malfunction.

The pilot's body was found to be restrained by the lap strap. However, the diagonal upper torso restraint, which could be clipped to a spigot on the lap strap via a keyhole-type fitting, was unattached and there was no evidence to suggest it had been at the point of impact. Examination of the wreckage showed that the deceleration forces involved in the crash meant that it was not survivable and that even if the pilot had been wearing his upper torso restraint, it would not have altered the outcome. The accident report gave detailed information on the movements made by the aircraft in the final minutes of its flight, based on radar data:

"Computerised radar information, obtained from the radar transmitter situated on Great Dun Fell [20 miles south-west of the crash site], and supplied by the Scottish Air Traffic Control Centre, was used to plot the aircraft's ground track. The information was not available during the initial emergency phase. The information is accurate to within one eighth of a nautical mile and one tenth of a degree. The radar head rotates eight times a minute, producing a return approximately every eight seconds.

The radar plot confirmed the aircraft's route as having overflown Castleside on a heading of 290°. The aircraft then skirted the north of Derwent Reservoir before turning left onto a heading of 130°. Radar returns were then lost but reappeared in the vicinity of Horseshoe Hill. The final six plots then showed the aircraft turning rapidly right onto a heading of 290°. The penultimate radar return coincided with the Muggleswick radio mast position and the final return coincided with the crash site. An RT transcript of Newcastle Approach Control frequency was used in conjunction with the radar information to determine the correlation of events."

An image taken at the crash site on Horseshoe Hill showing the wreckage of Piper PA-28 Cherokee G-AYIO in relation to the Muggleswick Radio Station mast. (Open Government Licence v3.0.)

The official accident report also confirmed investigator David Miller's statement regarding the omission of the radio mast's location from aviation charts. The pilot had used a current 1:250,000 Topographical Air Chart of North-East England to plan his route from Teesside to Carlisle. Land sited obstacles less than 300 feet above local ground level were not shown, and were not required to be shown, on that chart.

Despite the damage to the mast, the radio tower was not removed until some years later. Two new aerials were erected in the vicinity although not quite in the same exact spot as the one that claimed the life of a Teesside-based pilot back in April 1992.

THE STAINMORE TORNADO

No.43 Squadron ("The Fighting Cocks") Panavia Tornado F.3 ZE203/DE is pictured here flying at low level near Loch Tummel in Perthshire, Scotland. An identical jet from the same unit was lost in a crash near Stainmore in October 1993. (Author)

Low flying in military aircraft is a skill that has to be constantly practiced in order to maintain currency. Flying at 300 to 400 knots, just 100 feet off the ground, in a twisting mountain valley, can't simply be trained for one day, forgotten about for several years and then possibly performed in a real-world situation. Flying at such low altitudes was deemed necessary for aircrew to survive in operations against the former Soviet Union, keeping them below radar coverage until it was too late to react with ground-to-air missiles, anti-aircraft guns or aircraft.

On 21st October 1993, four Panavia Tornado F.3 interceptors belonging to No.43 Squadron at RAF Leuchars were detailed to carry out a training sortie at low level over southern Scotland and northern England. Part of the mission involved the four crews defending a pair of Tornado GR.1 strike aircraft from a flight of four more Tornado F.3s from another station, which were acting as aggressors.

In the cockpit of ZE858, Flight Lieutenant Stuart Walker was piloting the aircraft with Flight Lieutenant Liam Taylor as his navigator. 40 minutes into the flight from Leuchars, the Tornado suffered a serious problem in one of its engines. During a turning manoeuvre, the pilot experienced a massive loss of power from the affected engine. Going through their checklist cards, the crew quickly identified that it was suffering from a fuel leak. Walker elected to divert to the nearest suitable diversion airfield, climbing as he did so. He selected engine reheat on both the jet's powerplants during the ascent, an action which quickly led to the leaking fuel igniting. A fire then developed around the starboard jet pipes, which soon spread to the port ones. With his fire warning lights illuminating for one and then both of his engines, Walker quickly engaged the aircraft's onboard fire extinguishers, but these had no effect. The crew had no alternative but to abandon the stricken Tornado, which they did by ejecting. Both men landed safely, although they were taken to a hospital in Hexham to be checked for possible spinal injuries caused by the ejection sequences.

Tornado F.3 ZE858 crashed into open moorland next to the A66, close to the Stainmore Service Station, located on the Durham-Cumbria border between Bowes and Brough. A thorough clean-up operation was carried out by the RAF and the large crater caused by the impact was filled in and then landscaped, but small parts of the aircraft's structure were still visible around the site many years later. The exact location is only marked by a small piece of disturbed ground. It lies around a quarter of a mile south of the busy trans-Pennine A66 road.

News of the crash was carried by the Newcastle *Journal* newspaper in their 22nd October 1993 edition:

"An RAF Tornado crashed and exploded in a ball of flame during a training sortie over the North yesterday. The fighter came down on open ground on the Durham-Cumbria border, near Brough, at about 4 pm yesterday after its two-man crew ejected safely.

Eyewitnesses reported seeing flames from the downed aircraft light up the early evening sky for miles around. An RAF Board of Inquiry has been set up to investigate the cause of the crash, which comes only four months after two civilians were killed when their helicopter collided with a Tornado – also in Cumbria.

Last night low flying campaigners expressed concern at the latest incident, although it is unclear what height the Tornado was flying at. Coun John Whiteman, deputy leader of Northumberland County Council, said: 'There has to be a safer way of training our pilots. Brough is a built-up area and although I'm pleased there have been no fatalities this time, questions have got to be asked.'

The Tornado pilot and navigator from RAF Leuchars, who have not been named, are not badly injured and were flown by rescue helicopter to Hexham General Hospital. Airmen who eject often suffer back injuries and the hospital has a spinal injuries unit.

A mountain rescue team from RAF Leeming sealed off the crash site near the Stainmore service station to wait for the arrival of investigators. Flt Lt Pete Waugh, of the Edinburgh-based Rescue Co-ordination Centre, said: 'At this stage, we have no information as to what caused the accident.'"

The following day, the same newspaper carried further details of what had happened close to a very busy cross-country road:

"RAF accident inspection experts yesterday sifted through the wreckage of a Tornado F.3 fighter that crashed on a County Durham hillside. Although the hi-tech fighter planes do not carry so-called black box flight recorders, investigators still hoped to turn up vital clues on the accident.

A Ministry of Defence spokesman said: 'We have the best flight recorders in the form of the pilot and navigator who ejected safely.' The swing-wing jet crashed three miles west of Bowes and just a few yards from the A66 Trans-Pennine Road late on Thursday. The pilot and navigator came down nearby by parachute.

The villagers recently complained to their MP, Derek Foster, about low-flying aircraft and Mr. Forster tackled Defence Secretary Malcolm Rifkind. Some people have asked for the flight recorders in RAF aircraft to be checked regularly to see how low they had been flying. Mr. Rifkind said it was not practical to monitor them. 'They are designed for use after accidents, rather than for routine examination and to remove them would be a substantial engineering task,' he said.

But a Ministry of Defence spokesman in London said yesterday there were no flight recorders on Tornadoes. 'Flight recorders, which are bright red so they can be found, not black, are carried in our passenger aircraft because they are a civilian requirement,' he said. 'They are not fitted to fighters which are cramped for space. The accident inspection people are at the site and when they are finished, the wreckage will be removed, sometime over the weekend. Any claims by landowners will be processed. Our activities when removing wreckage sometimes cause damage because of the heavy equipment used. A board of inquiry will come up with the reason for the crash. But we have the two most important witnesses. They were alive and able to give evidence. We are not naming them because it is not our policy to do so unless they are killed.'"

Following an examination of the wreckage of ZE858, the cause of the fuel leak was traced to a faulty V-clamp, which had allowed two parts of a fuel feed pipe to become separated. The clamp itself was similar to a jubilee clip, one with a V-shaped compression ring that was designed to pull two flanged joints together. However, as far as the loss of the Tornado F.3 was concerned, this was attributed to the pilot selecting reheat in the climb. It was believed that the crew may well have been able to reach their nearest diversion airfield (RAF Leeming, in North Yorkshire) if this action had not been carried out – providing the jet did not exhaust its fuel supplies first.

Both pilot and navigator lived to tell the tale. However, Flight Lieutenant Stuart Walker would be killed in a second accident less than a year later off Cyprus. On 8th July 1994, he was piloting another Tornado, ZH558, when it crashed into the sea on the return flight to RAF Akrotiri following a gunnery exercise. Both he and his navigator failed to eject from the aircraft. His body was returned to Leuchars for burial. He was 32 years of age at the time of his death.

ONE LEG ONLY

Bede BD-4 G-BOPD is pictured here landing at the Druridge Bay Fly-In held near Hadston, Northumberland, on 15th August 2015. (Author)

Several accidents involving light aircraft have occurred at airfields located in County Durham since the year 2000. One such incident featured a very unusual type of aircraft, the Bede BD-4. Only a few examples of this type have ever been included on the UK Civil Aircraft Register. For many years, G-BOPD has been a regular sight at fly-ins across the North-East and over in Cumbria. It was built back in 1974 and had been owned by the pilot involved in the incident described here since May 1988.

In July 2022, the aircraft was badly damaged during a landing accident at Fishburn aerodrome, just north of Sedgefield. On the 10th of that month, G-BOPD's 68-year-old pilot took off from Yearby aerodrome, south-east of Middlesbrough, intending to fly up to Fishburn. On touchdown at the grass airfield, the left-hand landing gear leg broke off and the Bede's propeller struck the ground. The machine slewed around to the left, ending up in a farmer's field next to the runway. There was damage to the left wing, left cockpit door and engine cowling in addition to the propeller.

The Air Accidents Investigation Branch received details of the incident from the pilot and after further enquiries, published their report:

"After a normal landing the left landing gear leg detached. The leg fracture surface revealed beachmarks which were consistent with a failure due to metal fatigue. The pilot estimated that the aircraft landing gear had probably made over 2,000 landings, which the manufacturer said was probably the highest number of landings of this aircraft type.

The pilot had owned the BD-4 high-wing tail wheel aircraft since 1984 and had logged 1,444 hours with it. The aircraft was operated on a Permit to Fly and had accumulated 1,686 hours since manufacture in 1974. After a normal landing the pilot applied the brakes and the left landing gear leg detached. The propeller struck the ground and the aircraft veered to the left, coming to rest in a field of crops on the left side of the grass runway.

A photograph of the landing gear leg fracture surface revealed beachmarks which were consistent with a failure due to metal fatigue. The pilot contacted the aircraft manufacturer who informed him that they had not seen a fatigue failure in these landing gear legs before. The pilot estimated that he had probably made over 2,000 landings on it, which the manufacturer said was probably the highest number of landings of this aircraft type. The manufacturer no longer makes this landing gear leg type as it has been redesigned."

The aftermath of the landing accident at Fishburn in July 2022. (Open Government Licence v3.0.)

The pilot had nearly 1,600 flying hours in total, of which 1,444 were logged on his Bede BD-4. He was unhurt in the accident. Given the damage to the airframe and the fact that the manufacturer no longer made that landing gear leg any more, it may be a while before G-BOPD is seen in the skies of County Durham again.

THE BARNARD CASTLE AVIATION MEMORIALS

The main memorial stone located at the Barnard Castle Aviation Memorial Garden is dedicated to all of the aircrew who lost their lives in crashes in Teesdale and the Western Pennines. (Author)

Prior to 2015, a memorial commemorating aircrew who had lost their lives in aircraft crashes in Teesdale and over the Western Pennines had been situated on land owned by the Deerbolt Young Offenders Institution. The original site had been earmarked for housing development and therefore the memorial needed to be moved to another location. In January 2015, planning permission was sought to relocate it to the Galgate Memorial Garden in Barnard Castle.

The Barnard Castle Aviation Memorial Garden contains several plaques. (Author)

One of two memorials that flank the main stone is this one, commemorating the airmen killed when Meteor NF.11 WD778 was lost on Dufton Fell on 24th March 1954. (Author)

The memorials themselves stem from a project dreamt up by two former employees at Deerbolt, Tony Galley and John Yarker. Galley had been given the job of arranging a summer event to link the Young Offenders' Institution with Barnard Castle and the wider area of Teesdale. He knew that Yarker, an aviation archaeologist in his spare time, had participated in licenced "digs" at aircraft crash sites in Teesdale. The idea to create a memorial to the fallen airmen arose from a conversation the two had about the numbers of crashes that occurred and the death toll that resulted. The Teesdale Aviation Day was therefore established, first held in July 1995. It grew into an annual event, one that included personnel from RAF Leeming and the Durham Region of the Royal Air Force Association. Each event featured military-themed attractions, music and even flypasts courtesy of the Battle of Britain Memorial Flight. As with many events across Britain, Covid prevented the 2020 Aviation Day from taking place, but a modest commemoration was performed on 27th September 2022.

The memorial site at Deerbolt was created by the same team, including plaques commemorating the loss of individual aircraft over Teesdale and the Pennines, plus the 86 aircrew in total who had been killed in crashes in the area. Relocated to Galgate in Barnard Castle, it is now very visible to visitors arriving in the town from the direction of Darlington, and less than a few minutes' walk from the main shops.

Memorial stones specifically mention the loss of Blackburn Botha L6416 and Gloster Meteor NF.11 WD778. The former belonged to No.2 Air Observer School based at Millom, Cumbria, and crashed at Stainmore on 22nd August 1941, killing all four crewmembers onboard. Meteor WD778 was from No.228 Operational Conversion Unit at Leeming, North Yorkshire and crashed on Dufton Fell (then in Westmorland) on the evening of 24th March 1954. Both the pilot and the navigator/radar operator were killed. Details of these incidents will feature in a subsequent volume of this series.

ACKNOWLEDGEMENTS AND SOURCES

Ken Haynes, Stuart Reid, Bill Teasdale, Ad Vercruijsse and John Visanich were all kind enough to allow me to reproduce their images in this book. I also used the National Archives' impressive stash of wartime records whilst searching for documents relating to various incidents. The files consulted are listed below with their respective "AIR" reference numbers. I also used several Facebook pages to find further details regarding certain events. The British Newspaper Archive proved to be an invaluable resource of on-the-spot reporting, allowing me to locate relevant articles and reports.

AIR 27/263	No.21 Squadron Operations Record Book
AIR 27/441	No.43 Squadron Operations Record Book
AIR 27/480	No.49 Squadron Operations Record Book
AIR 27/624	No.72 Squadron Operations Record Book
AIR 27/1365	No.220 Squadron Operations Record Book
AIR 27/1428	No.232 Squadron Operations Record Book
AIR 27/1610	No.279 Squadron Operations Record Book
AIR 27/1825	No.420 Squadron Operations Record Book
AIR 27/2093	No.607 Squadron Operations Record Book
AIR 50/18	No.41 Squadron Combat Reports
AIR 81/4359	Loss Report Blenheim R3914
AIR 81/8521	Loss Report Hurricane Z7052

Aberdeen Evening Express
Aberdeen Press & Journal
Air Accidents Investigation Branch bulletins
Air North magazine
Banffshire Advertiser
Belfast Telegraph
British Newspaper Archive
Buckinghamshire Advertiser & Free Press
Coventry Evening Telegraph
The Daily News (London)
Evening Despatch
Hartlepool Northern Daily Mail
Jarrow Express
London Gazette
The Malvernian
Manchester Evening Chronicle
Manchester Guardian
Ministry of Defence Aircraft Accident Summaries
Morpeth Herald
Newcastle Evening Chronicle
Newcastle Guardian & Tyne Mercury
Newcastle Journal

Newcastle Sunday Sun
Northern Echo
Northern Whig (Northern Ireland)
North East Land, Sea & Air Museum, Sunderland
Otago Times (New Zealand)
The Shields News
Sunderland Daily Echo
Teesdale Mercury
Teesside Aviation News
The Times
Westmorland Gazette
Yorkshire Air News
Yorkshire Evening Post
Yorkshire Observer
Yorkshire Post & Leeds Intelligencer

ABOUT THE AUTHOR

Graeme has been interested in aviation since he was four years old, being given Airfix model kits by his mother to "keep him quiet". He progressed to exhausting his local library's supply of aircraft-related titles and went onto seeking out more titles from second-hand bookshops around the country. A spell as the editor of a regional aviation enthusiast's newsletter followed in his early 20s before he travelled to North-East Siberia to witness at first-hand Aeroflot operations in that far-flung part of the world. Graeme wrote his first book about his experiences in Siberia back in 1992, publishing it in early 2021. He has followed this up with titles regarding the history of RAF Morpeth in Northumberland and RNAS Anthorn in Cumbria.

Another of his interests is Unidentified Aerial Phenomenon (what used to be known as UFOs) and he drew upon his knowledge of World War Two aviation to write a critically acclaimed history of the Foo-Fighters of World War Two. He has followed this up with two further volumes describing aerial encounters with strange objects in the late 1940s and early 1950s, with another book to be released shortly dealing with 1953/54 sightings. All of Graeme's books are available from Amazon, either as direct purchases or via their Kindle Unlimited subscription service.

When he is not writing, Graeme occasionally appears on Internet-based talk shows dealing with the subject of UAP or can be found walking on the hills in Weardale, where he now lives following retirement from the National Health Service. He is now a full-time writer.

ALSO BY THE AUTHOR

The books shown on the following pages are obtainable from Amazon, in either eBook, softback and hardback formats. They can be read for free with a Kindle Unlimited subscription.

RAF MORPETH: A FORGOTTEN AIRFIELD IN NORTHUMBERLAND

GRAEME RENDALL

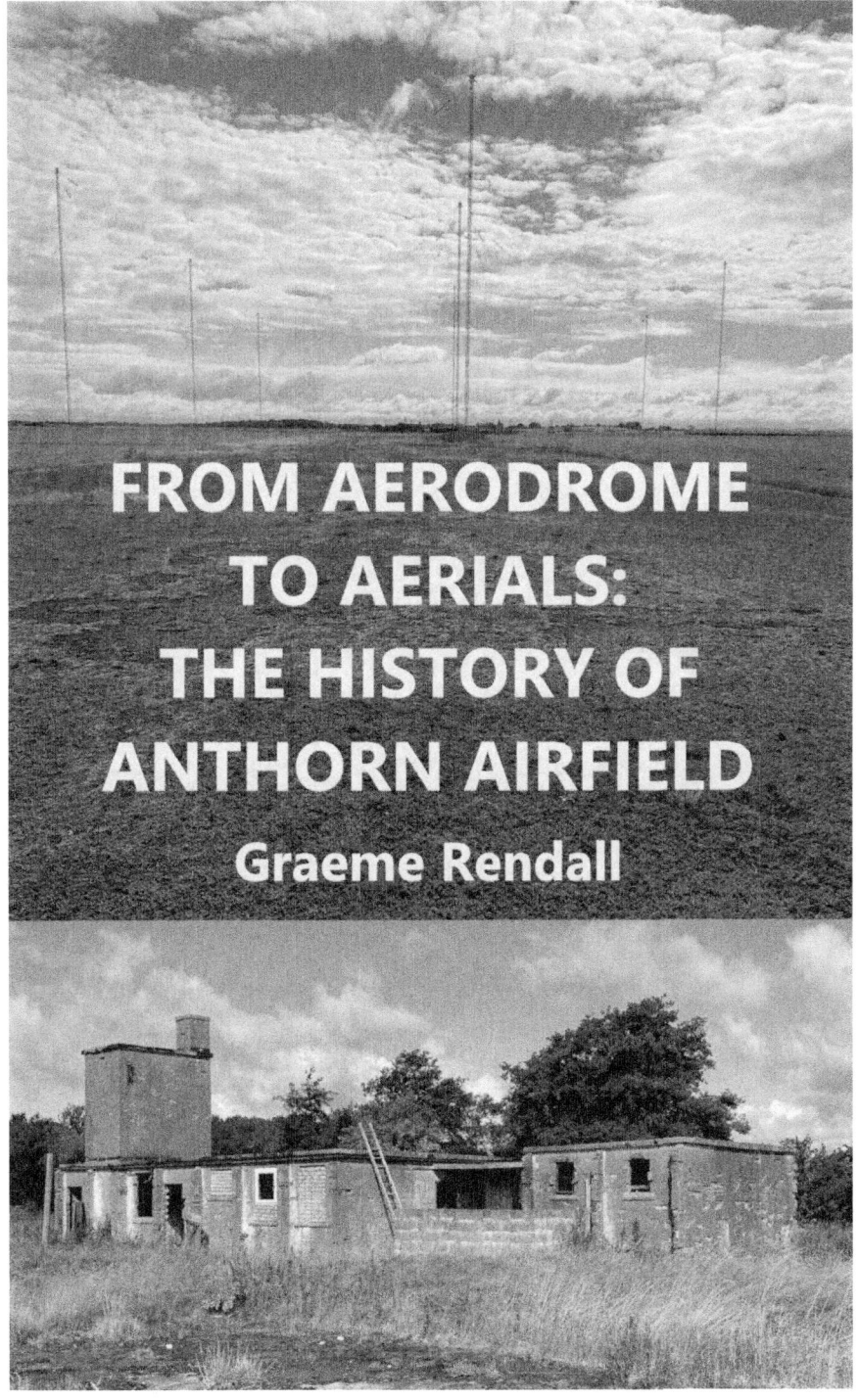

NORTHUMBERLAND AVIATION STORIES: VOLUMES 1-3
Graeme Rendall

TO THE ENDS OF THE EARTH
A SNAPSHOT OF AVIATION IN NORTH-EASTERN SIBERIA, SUMMER 1992
GRAEME RENDALL

UFOs BEFORE ROSWELL:
EUROPEAN FOO-FIGHTERS
1940-1945

GRAEME RENDALL
FOREWORD BY SEAN CAHILL

Printed in Great Britain
by Amazon